345 Creative Candy Recipes

(345 Creative Candy Recipes - Volume 1)

Susan Perrin

Copyright: Published in the United States by Susan Perrin/ © SUSAN PERRIN

Published on October, 12 2020

All rights reserved. No part of this publication may be reproduced, stored in retrieval system, copied in any form or by any means, electronic, mechanical, photocopying, recording or otherwise transmitted without written permission from the publisher. Please do not participate in or encourage piracy of this material in any way. You must not circulate this book in any format. SUSAN PERRIN does not control or direct users' actions and is not responsible for the information or content shared, harm and/or actions of the book readers.

In accordance with the U.S. Copyright Act of 1976, the scanning, uploading and electronic sharing of any part of this book without the permission of the publisher constitute unlawful piracy and theft of the author's intellectual property. If you would like to use material from the book (other than just simply for reviewing the book), prior permission must be obtained by contacting the author at author@bisquerecipes.com

Thank you for your support of the author's rights.

Content

345 AWESOME CANDY RECIPES............. 8

1. 1881 Chocolate Caramels Recipe 8
2. AZTEC Chocolate Bark Recipe 8
3. Almond Butter Crunch Recipe 9
4. Almond Coated Dark Chocolate Peanut Butter Balls Recipe 9
5. Almond Ganache Cups Recipe 9
6. Almond Joy Bars Recipe 10
7. Almond Joy Candy Recipe 10
8. Almond Roca Recipe 11
9. Almond Fudge Recipe 11
10. Amaretto Fudge Recipe Recipe 11
11. Amaretto Truffles Recipe 12
12. Amish Country Peanut Butter Fudge Recipe 12
13. Angel Food Christmas Candy 13
14. Apple Cider Creme Caramels Recipe 13
15. Applets Recipe 14
16. BAILEYS SNOWBALL TRUFFLES Recipe 14
17. Baileys Fudge Recipe 14
18. Baileys Irish Creme Fudge Recipe............. 15
19. Bavarian Mints Recipe 15
20. Benne Sesame Brittle Recipe 16
21. Blue Ribbon Pralines Recipe 16
22. Blueberry Cheesecake Fudge Recipe 16
23. Brown Sugar Fudge Recipe 17
24. Brown Sugar Fudge Old Recipe 17
25. BuckEye Balls Recipe 17
26. Buckeye Candies Recipe................................ 18
27. Buckeye Peanut Butter Candy Recipe 18
28. Buttermilk Candy Recipe 19
29. Butterscotch Chews Recipe 19
30. Butterscotch Fudge Recipe............................ 20
31. Buttery Cashew Brittle Recipe 20
32. CANDY CANE WHITE FUDGE Recipe 20
33. CHRISTMAS CARAMEL CHEWS Recipe 21
34. COPY CAT York Peppermint Patties Recipe 21
35. CROCK POT CANDY Recipe 21
36. California White Chocolate Fudge Recipe 22
37. Candied Nuts Recipe 22
38. Candy Cane Fudge Recipe 23
39. Candy Corn Recipe 23
40. Candy Easter Eggs Recipe 24
41. Candy Strawberries Recipe 24
42. Candy Train A Candy Craft Recipe............ 24
43. Candy Box Caramels Recipe........................ 25
44. Caramel Apple Smores Recipe 25
45. Caramel Candy Pretzel Rods Two Ways Recipe.. 26
46. Caramel Kisses Recipe................................ 26
47. Caramel Peanut Butter Fudge Recipe 26
48. Caramelized Party Mix Recipe 27
49. Cashew Brittle Recipe.................................. 27
50. Cashew Truffles Recipe 28
51. Cereal Bars Recipe.. 28
52. Champagne Truffles Recipe 28
53. Chattanooga Chew Chews Recipe.............. 29
54. Chewy Chocolate Nut Candies Recipe....... 29
55. Chipotle Fudge Recipe 30
56. Chocolate Billionaires Recipe 30
57. Chocolate Orange Sesame Truffles Recipe 30
58. Chocolate Bourbon Truffles Recipe 31
59. Chocolate Butter Toffee Recipe 31
60. Chocolate Buttercream Cherry Candies Recipe.. 32
61. Chocolate Cappuccino Candy Recipe........ 32
62. Chocolate Caramel Walnut Fudge Recipe. 33
63. Chocolate Cherry Sweets Recipe 33
64. Chocolate Chip Cookie Brittle Recipe....... 33
65. Chocolate Coated Macaroon Balls Recipe 34
66. Chocolate Covered Cherries Recipe........... 34
67. Chocolate Covered Easter Eggs Recipe 35
68. Chocolate Cream Cheese Fudge Recipe..... 35
69. Chocolate Dipped Caramallows Recipe 35
70. Chocolate Filled Strawberries Recipe......... 36
71. Chocolate Marshmallow Cashew Fudge Recipe.. 37
72. Chocolate Mint Candy Recipe..................... 37
73. Chocolate Mint Fudge Recipe..................... 38
74. Chocolate Orange Truffles Recipe 38
75. Chocolate Peanut Butter Cake Eggs Recipe 38
76. Chocolate Peanut Butter Fudge Recipe...... 39
77. Chocolate Peanut Sweeties Recipe 39
78. Chocolate Raspberry Truffles Recipe 39

79. Chocolate Truffles Recipe 40
80. Chocolate Peanut Butter Truffles Recipe . 40
81. Chocolate Coconut Candiesmounds Like Recipe 41
82. Chocolate Coconut Truffles Recipe 41
83. Chocolate Dipped Peanut Butter Balls Recipe 42
84. Christmas Cracker Candy Recipe 42
85. Christmas Gift Chocolate Fudge Recipe... 43
86. Christmas Rum Balls Recipe 43
87. Christmas Strawberries Recipe................. 43
88. Cobblestone Candy Recipe...................... 44
89. Coconut Bon Bons Recipe 44
90. Coconut Bon Bons My Way Recipe 44
91. Coconut Candy Recipe............................. 45
92. Coconut Creams Recipe 45
93. Coconut Curry Macadamia Nuts Recipe .. 45
94. Coconut Fudge Recipe 46
95. Coconut Kisses Recipe 46
96. Coconut Patties Recipe 46
97. Copycat Pay Day Candy Bars Recipe 47
98. Cornflake Chewies Recipe 48
99. Cotlets Recipe 48
100. County Fair Cream Candy Recipe 48
101. Cranberry Candy Recipe 49
102. Cream Cheese Fudge Recipe.................... 49
103. Cream Cheese Pumpkin Truffles Recipe .. 50
104. Cream And Butter Toffee Recipe 50
105. Creole Candy Recipe................................ 50
106. Crock Pot Candy Recipe........................... 51
107. Crock Pot Chocolate Fritos Candy Recipe 51
108. Crockpot Peanut Clusters Recipe............... 51
109. Crockpot White Chocolate Candy Recipe 52
110. DATES WITH SESAME SEEDS Recipe52
111. Darianas Easy Chocolate Truffles Recipe 52
112. Dark Chocolate ButterCrunch Recipe....... 53
113. Dark Chocolate Cococans Recipe 54
114. Deep Fried Candy Bars Recipe.................. 54
115. Delicious Copycat Almond Joy Bars Recipe 54
116. Delicious Homemade Creme Filled Chocolate Candy Recipe 55
117. Diabetic Chocolate Candy Recipe 55
118. Dipped Chocolate Graham Sticks Recipe .. 56
119. Double Nut English Toffee Recipe Recipe 56

120. Dr Pepper Fudge Recipe........................... 57
121. Dressed Up Chocolate Bark Recipe........... 57
122. Drunk Gummie Bears Recipe 58
123. Dulce De Leche For Non Cheaters Recipe 58
124. Dulce De Leche Under Pressure Recipe ... 59
125. EASTER COOKIES Recipe 59
126. Easiest Fudge In The World Recipe 59
127. Easter Baskets Recipe 59
128. Easy Apricot Balls Recipe 60
129. Easy Breezy Fudge Recipe......................... 60
130. Easy Chocolate Cashew Clusters Recipe... 60
131. Easy Chocolate Dipped Coconut Creams Recipe 61
132. Easy Chocolate Mint Truffles Recipe 61
133. Easy Chocolate Truffles Recipe 61
134. Easy Fudge Yummy Recipe....................... 62
135. Easy Ham Bake Recipe 62
136. Easy Microwave Pralines Recipe 63
137. Easy Peanut Butter Fudge........................ 63
138. Easy Tiger Butter Candy Recipe 63
139. Easy Peasey Rocky Road Fudge Recipe ... 64
140. Eggnog Fudge Recipe............................... 64
141. Egyptian Stuffed Colorful Sweet Peppers Filfil Rumi Mahsi Maaa Lon Recipe 64
142. Elegant Marshmallows Recipe 65
143. Elizabethan Orange Cakes Recipe............ 66
144. English Toffee Recipe 66
145. Extravagant Old Fashioned Fudge Dated 1942 Recipe... 66
146. Fabulous 5 Minute Prep Fudge Recipe 67
147. Famous Chocolate Bourbon Balls Recipe. 67
148. Fancy Coffee Cup Truffles Recipe 67
149. Fannie Mae Caramels Recipe................... 68
150. Fantasy Fudge Recipe.............................. 68
151. Five Minute Fudge Recipe 69
152. Foolproof Microwave Fudge Recipe 69
153. French Caramels Recipe........................... 69
154. Frito Munch Candy Recipe....................... 70
155. Frosted Walnuts Recipe........................... 70
156. Frozen Peppermint Patties Recipe 71
157. Fruit Leather Recipe................................ 71
158. Fruit And Nut Chocolate Chunk Candy Recipe 72
159. Fudge Recipe... 72
160. Fudge For ONE Recipe 74
161. Fun Taffy Pull Recipe............................... 74

162. Ganache Recipe 75
163. Glacé Orange Slices Dipped In Dark Chocolate Recipe 76
164. Goobers Recipe 76
165. Grand Marnier Truffles Recipe 77
166. Grand Marnier And Chocolate Truffles Recipe 77
167. Grandma's Strawberry Candies Recipe 77
168. HAYSTACKS Recipe 78
169. HOT Hot Chocolate Espresso Beans Recipe 78
170. Halloween Candy Bark 78
171. Harvest Moon Lollipops Recipe 79
172. Hazelnut Fantasy Fudge Recipe 79
173. Hazelnut Truffles Recipe 80
174. Home Made "mozart Kugel" Recipe 80
175. Homemade Caramels Recipe 80
176. Homemade Cinnamon Praline Pecans Recipe 81
177. Homemade Gum Drops Recipe 81
178. Homemade Marshmallows Recipe 82
179. Homemade Mini Peanut Butter Cups Recipe 82
180. Homemade Tootsie Rolls Recipe 83
181. Homemade Twix Bars Recipe Recipe 83
182. Honey Caramels With Pistachios Recipe ..84
183. Honey Maple Mac Nuts Recipe 84
184. Incredible Brown Sugar Or Penuche Fudge Recipe 85
185. Irish Potato Candy Recipe 85
186. Jamaican Marshmallows Recipe 85
187. Just Like A Payday Bar Recipe 86
188. Kahlua Truffles Recipe 87
189. Key Lime "truffles" Recipe 87
190. Krafts Chocolate Peanut Butter Snowballs Recipe 87
191. Lemon Fudge Recipe 88
192. Lemonade Jellies Recipe 88
193. Light Cranberry Fudge Recipe 88
194. Low Sugar Nutty Fudge Recipe 89
195. Low Carb Fudge Toffee Recipe 89
196. MARSHMALLOW FLOWERS Recipe ...90
197. MICROWAVE PEANUT BUTTER FUDGE Recipe 90
198. MICROWAVE RAINBOW PRETZELS Recipe 90
199. MILKY WAY FUDGE Microwave Recipe 91
200. Macadamia Cashew Crunch Recipe 91
201. Mackinac Island Fudge Recipe 92
202. Maine Potato Candy 92
203. Make Your Own Gummi Bears Recipe.....92
204. Mamas Peanut Butter Fudge Recipe 93
205. Marbled Orange Fudge Recipe 93
206. Marbled Peanut Clusters Recipe 93
207. Marshmallow Goodies Recipe 94
208. Marshmallow Peanut Butter Fudge Recipe 94
209. Marshmallows Recipe 94
210. Marshmallows With Variations Recipe......95
211. Marzipan Caramel Apples With Sesame N Almonds Recipe 96
212. Mayan Truffles Recipe 96
213. Microwave Peanut Brittle Recipe 96
214. Microwave Pralines Recipe 97
215. Microwave Toffee Recipe 97
216. Mint Cookie Candies.................................98
217. Mint Meltaways Recipe 98
218. Missouri Colonels Recipe 98
219. Mocha Macadamia Candy Recipe 99
220. Mochi With Nutella Strawberry Filling Recipe 99
221. Molasses Taffy A Family Affair Recipe ..100
222. Moms Remarkable Fudge Recipe 100
223. Moms Secret Fudge Recipe Recipe 101
224. My Grandmas Peanut Butter Fudge Recipe 101
225. Never Fail Fudge Recipe 102
226. No Bake Cashew Brittle Bars Recipe...... 102
227. No Cook Fudge Recipe 102
228. Nut Goodie Candy Bars Recipe............... 103
229. Nut Goody Candy Bars Recipe................ 103
230. Nutty Buddies Recipe 104
231. Old Fashioned Date Confection Recipe 104
232. Old Fashioned Sponge Toffee Recipe.... 105
233. Orange Creamsicle Fudge Recipe 105
234. Pa & Ma's Peanut Butter Fudge Recipe . 105
235. Pa & Ma's Wonderful Holiday Fudge Recipe 106
236. Pasteli Greek Sesame Seed Candy Recipe 106
237. Pasteli Recipe.................................107
238. Pates De Fruits Fruit Jewels Recipe 107
239. Payday Candy Bar Squares Recipe........... 108

240. Peach Jelly Chews Recipe 108
241. Peanut Brittle From Microwave Recipe .. 108
242. Peanut Butter Balls 1 Recipe 109
243. Peanut Butter Bonbons Recipe 109
244. Peanut Butter Chocolate Balls Recipe 109
245. Peanut Butter Easter Eggs Recipe 110
246. Peanut Butter Fudge Recipe 110
247. Peanut Butter Meltaways Recipe 110
248. Peanut Chew Ee Recipe 111
249. Peanut Crunchies Recipe 111
250. Peanut Sesame Candy Recipe 111
251. Pecan Caramel Candies 112
252. Pecan Roll Recipe 112
253. Peppermint Balls Recipe 112
254. Peppermint Patties Recipe 113
255. Peppermint Taffy Recipe 113
256. Pink Popcorn Candy Recipe 114
257. Pistachio Fudge Recipe 114
258. Polka Dot Fudge Recipe 115
259. Popcorn Balls Recipe 115
260. Positively Yummy Pumpkin Fudge Recipe 115
261. Potato Candies Or Bonbons Recipe 116
262. Potato Candy Recipe 116
263. Pumpkin Caramels Recipe 116
264. Pumpkin Flan With Chile Spiced Brittle Recipe 117
265. Pumpkin Fudge Recipe 119
266. Pumpkin Pie Fudge Recipe 119
267. Punkin Pie Fudge Recipe 119
268. Queen Anne Salted Peanut Caramel Nougat Rolls Recipe 120
269. Quick And Easy Fudge Recipe 121
270. ROCK CANDY Recipe 121
271. Rachael Rays Fabulous Five Minute Fudge Wreath Recipe 121
272. Raspberry Fudge Truffles Recipe 122
273. Raspberry Mousse Tartelettes Recipe Recipe 122
274. Red Pepper Fudge Recipe 123
275. Red Velvet Fudge Recipe 124
276. Rice Krispies Treats Recipe 124
277. Rocky Road Recipe 125
278. Rolo Pretzel Turtles Recipe 125
279. Rum Balls Recipe 125
280. SWEET BHOR Recipe 125
281. Salt Caramel Recipe 126

282. Salted Chocolate Caramels Recipe 126
283. Saltine Candy Recipe 127
284. Salty Sweet Treat Recipe 127
285. Scottish Whisky Tablet Recipe 128
286. Seeds And Nuts Brittle Recipe 128
287. Sees Candy Recipe 129
288. Sees Fudge The Best Recipe 129
289. Sees Fudge Candy The Quote Original Recipe Recipe 130
290. Semi Sweet And White Chocolate Peanut Butter Cups Recipe 130
291. Semolina Halva Recipe 130
292. Simple Hard Candy Recipe 131
293. Simple Strawberry Pte De Fruit Real Fruit Jelly Candy Recipe 131
294. Snicker Bar Candy Recipe 132
295. Snickers Candy Recipe 132
296. Sour Cream Orange Fudge Recipe 133
297. Sour Cream Walnuts Recipe 134
298. Southern Peanut Brittle Recipe 134
299. Spiced Almond Brittle Recipe 134
300. Spiced Nuts Recipe 135
301. Spiced Pumpkin Fudge Recipe 135
302. Spiced Pumpkin Fudge Recipe 135
303. Spicy Caramel Coated Apples Recipe 136
304. Spicy Fudge Recipe 136
305. St Patricks Day Layered Mint Chocolate Fudge Recipe 136
306. Stained Glass Fudge Recipe 137
307. Steamed Cassava Sweets Khanoom Monsompalang Recipe 137
308. Strawberry Candies Recipe 138
309. Strawberry Sparkling Wine And Chilli White Chocolate Truffles Recipe 138
310. Sugar Free Coconut Balls Recipe 138
311. Sugar Nuts Recipe 139
312. Sugar Free Chocolate Fudge Recipe 139
313. Sugared Nuts Delight Recipe 139
314. Super Easy Homemade Marshmallow Recipe 140
315. Superfood Peanut Butter N' Cookies Fudge Recipe 140
316. Sweet Cocoa Flax Truffles Recipe 141
317. Terrific Toffee Recipe 141
318. Texas Style Microwave Pralines Recipe .. 142
319. The Best Christmas Fudge Recipe 142
320. The Best Chunky Candy Ever Recipe 142

321. The Snow Candy Recipe 143
322. Toffee Almond Crunch Recipe 143
323. Toffee Apples Recipe 144
324. Traditional Buttermilk Pralines Recipe 144
325. Turkish Delight Recipe 144
326. Tutti Frutti Fudge Recipe 145
327. Vegan Caramels Recipe 146
328. Vinegar Candy Recipe 146
329. Vinegar Taffy Dated 1932 Recipe 147
330. Vinegar Taffy Recipe 147
331. Vitafiber Tootsie Rolls No Sugar Added Recipe 147
332. Whipped Fudge Recipe 148
333. White Choc Fudge Different Recipe 148
334. White Chocolate Marshmallow Drops Recipe 149
335. White Garbage Snack Recipe 149
336. White Popcorn Balls Recipe 150
337. White Trash Candy Recipe 150
338. YOU GOTTA BE KIDDING ME FUDGE Recipe 150
339. Yogurt Pretzels Recipe 151
340. Braunschweiger Recipe Recipe 151
341. Coconut Fudge Recipe 151
342. Coffee Walnut Recipe 152
343. Easy Chocolate Fudge Recipe 152
344. White Chocolate Truffles Recipe 152
345. ~ Rock Candy ~ Recipe 153

INDEX 154

CONCLUSION 157

345 Awesome Candy Recipes

***

1. 1881 Chocolate Caramels Recipe

Serving: 50 | Prep: | Cook: 20mins | Ready in:

Ingredients

- 3 tablespoons unsalted butter, plus more for greasing the baking dish
- 4 1/2 ounces bittersweet chocolate, chopped (about 1 cup)
- 1 cup whole milk
- 1 cup molasses
- 1 cup sugar
- 1 teaspoon vanilla extract
- Softened butter, for cutting the caramels.

Direction

- Butter an 8-by-8-inch baking dish. Clip a candy thermometer to the side of a medium, heavy saucepan. Combine the butter, chocolate, milk, molasses and sugar in the pan and cook over medium heat, stirring constantly, until the mixture reaches 248 degrees on the thermometer. Do this slowly, scraping the bottom of the pan with a silicon spatula (or a wooden spoon) so the mixture doesn't stick and burn.
- Wearing an oven mitt, remove the pan from the heat and add the vanilla to the hot mixture. Give it a quick stir, then pour the mixture into the buttered baking dish.
- As soon as the caramel is cool enough to handle, transfer it to a cutting board and use a buttered chef's knife (or scissors) to cut the caramel into ¾-inch-wide strips, and then crosswise into ¾-inch pieces.
- When the caramels are completely cool, wrap them individually in wax paper, or layer in parchment paper in an airtight container. Store in a cool, dry place for up to 1 month. Makes about 100 pieces.

2. AZTEC Chocolate Bark Recipe

Serving: 6 | Prep: | Cook: 4mins | Ready in:

Ingredients

- * 1/2 cup of hulled, unsalted pumpkin seeds
- * 1/4 teaspoon of cayenne pepper, plus a dash extra
- * 3/4 teaspoon of cinnamon, plus a dash extra
- * 3/4 teaspoon of ancho chili powder, plus a dash extra
- * 12 oz. of bitter or semi-sweet chocolate
- .

Direction

- 1 Place the pumpkin seeds in a skillet over medium-low heat. Toast the pumpkin seeds for about 5 minutes, they'll pop and jump a bit as they release their oils and moisture. Allow to cool.
- 2 Melt the chocolate according to the manufacturer's directions. (Or Microwave) Once melted add the cinnamon, cayenne pepper, Ancho chili powder, and most of the pumpkin seeds saving some to decorate the top with.
- 3 Spread onto a flat baking pan lined with a Silpat or wax paper. Sprinkle over and press into the chocolate the last few pumpkin seeds and sprinkle on a dash more of the spices for color and taste. Place in the freezer for 5 minutes or until hardened. Break into pieces

and serve or store in the fridge in an airtight container. Best consumed in one or two days

3. Almond Butter Crunch Recipe

Serving: 1 | Prep: | Cook: 15mins | Ready in:

Ingredients

- 1 c. sugar
- 1 c. unsalted butter, no substitutes
- 2 TB water
- 1 TB light corn syrup
- 3/4 c. chopped toasted almonds
- 1/2 c. chocolate chips

Direction

- Butter a 9"x9" pan. Heat sugar, butter, water and corn syrup to boiling in a heavy 2 quart pan over medium heat, stirring constantly to 290 degrees on a candy thermometer. Remove from heat, stir in almonds. Spread evenly in the 9"x9" pan. Sprinkle with chocolate chips evenly over hot candy. Cover 1-2 minutes until chocolate is softened, then carefully spread over the candy. Sprinkle with additional almonds if desired. Let stand at room temperature until chocolate is firm (about 3 hours). Loosen from pan and break into pieces. Cover and refrigerate.

4. Almond Coated Dark Chocolate Peanut Butter Balls Recipe

Serving: 48 | Prep: | Cook: 10mins | Ready in:

Ingredients

- 1 pound smooth peanut butter
- 1 stick softened butter
- 1 pound powdered sugar
- 3-1/2 cups Rice Krispies
- 1/4 teaspoon salt
- 1 teaspoon vanilla extract
- 1 pound dark chocolate melted
- 2 cups chopped almonds

Direction

- Mix all ingredients except chocolate and almonds together until well blended.
- Roll into balls then dip in chocolate then roll in nuts and place on cookie sheet in refrigerator until hardened.

5. Almond Ganache Cups Recipe

Serving: 60 | Prep: | Cook: 10mins | Ready in:

Ingredients

- 8 ounces (226 grams) bittersweet or semisweet chocolate, coarsely chopped
- 3/4 cup (180 ml) heavy whipping cream
- 1 tablespoon alcohol (brandy, Grand Marnier, rum or bourbon) or 1 teaspoon pure vanilla extract (optional)
- 2/3 cup (100 grams) almonds, toasted and finely ground plus 60 whole almonds to be used for garnish

Direction

- Preheat oven to 350 degrees F (177 degrees C). Bake the almonds for 10 - 15 minutes or until the nuts are fragrant. Remove from oven. Let cool. Remove 60 almonds to be used as garnish and then place the remaining cooled almonds in a food processor and process until finely ground. Set aside.
- Coarsely chopped the chocolate and place in a heatproof bowl.
- In a small saucepan bring the cream to a boil. Immediately, remove from heat and pour over the chopped chocolate. Gently stir the mixture until smooth and then add the alcohol (or vanilla extract) and finely ground almonds. Cover with plastic wrap and refrigerate the

mixture until thick but not solid (about 30 minutes).
- Transfer the mixture to a pastry bag fitted with a large plain tip and pipe the ganache into small candy cups until they are 3/4 full. Place a toasted almond on top of each cup. Chill the ganache cups until they are firm (about 1 hour).
- Store in an airtight container in the refrigerator for several weeks or they can be frozen for a few months. Best served at room temperature.
- Makes about 60 1-inch (2.54 cm) ganache cups.

6. Almond Joy Bars Recipe

Serving: 26 | Prep: | Cook: 3mins | Ready in:

Ingredients

- 4 c (8 1/2-oz) shredded coconut
- 1/4 c light corn syrup
- 1 pk (11 1/2-oz) milk chocolate pieces
- 1/4 c vegetable shortening
- 26 Whole natural almonds (1-oz)

Direction

- Line two large cookie sheets with waxed paper. Set large wire cooling rack on paper; set aside.
- Place coconut in large bowl; set aside.
- Place corn syrup in a 1-cup glass measure. Microwave on high (100%) 1 minute or until syrup boils. Immediately pour over coconut. Work warm syrup into coconut using the back of a wooden spoon until coconut is thoroughly coated.
- This takes a little time, and yes, there is enough syrup.
- Using 1 level measuring tablespoon of coconut, shape into a ball by squeezing coconut firmly in palm of one hand, then rolling between both palms. (HINT: Measure out all of the coconut then roll into balls.) Place 2 inches apart on wire racks. Let dry 10 minutes. Reroll coconut balls so there are no loose ends of coconut sticking up.
- Place milk chocolate and shortening in a 4-cup glass measure or 1 1/2 quart microwave-safe bowl. Microwave on high 1 to 2 minutes or until mixture can be stirred smooth and is glossy; stirring once or twice.
- Working quickly, spoon 1 level measuring tablespoon of the chocolate over each coconut ball, making sure chocolate coats and letting excess chocolate drip down onto waxed paper. While chocolate coating is still soft, lightly press whole almond on top of each. Let stand to set or place in refrigerator. Store in a single layer in airtight container.
- Keeps best if refrigerated. Makes 26.

7. Almond Joy Candy Recipe

Serving: 26 | Prep: | Cook: 3mins | Ready in:

Ingredients

- 4 c (8 1/2-oz) Mound coconut
- 1/4 c light corn syrup
- 1 pk (11 1/2-oz) milk chocolate chips
- 1/4 c vegetable shortening
- 26 whole almonds, toasted

Direction

- Line two large cookie sheets with waxed paper.
- Set a large wire cooling rack on the paper; set aside.
- Place the coconut in a large bowl; set aside.
- Place corn syrup in a 1-cup glass measuring cup.
- Microwave on high (100%) 1 minute or until syrup boils.
- Immediately pour over coconut.
- Work warm syrup into coconut using the back of a wooden spoon until coconut is thoroughly coated.

- This takes a little time, and yes, there is enough syrup.
- Using 1 level tablespoon of coconut, shape into a ball by squeezing coconut firmly in palm of one hand, then rolling between both palms.
- HINT: Measure out all of the coconut then roll into balls.
- Place 2 inches apart on wire racks.
- Let dry 10 minutes.
- Reroll coconut balls so there are no loose ends of coconut sticking up.
- Place milk chocolate and shortening in a 4-cup glass measuring cup or 1 1/2 quart microwave-safe bowl.
- Microwave on high 1 to 2 minutes or until mixture can be stirred smooth and is glossy; stirring once or twice.
- Working quickly, spoon 1 level tablespoon of the chocolate over each coconut ball, making sure chocolate coats and letting excess chocolate drip down onto waxed paper.
- While chocolate coating is still soft, lightly press 1 almond on top of each.
- Let stand to set or place in refrigerator.
- Store in a single layer in air-tight container.
- Keeps best if refrigerated. Makes 26.

8. Almond Roca Recipe

Serving: 6 | Prep: | Cook: 20mins | Ready in:

Ingredients

- 1 T. corn syrup
- 1 1/4 c. white sugar
- 1 c. butter
- 1/4 c. water
- 1 1/4 c. toasted slivered almonds*
- 1 (6-oz.) pkg. chocolate chips

Direction

- In large saucepan, gently boil syrup, sugar, butter & water until hard crack stage on candy thermometer (300°) do not stir!
- This step takes at least ten minutes.
- I mean don't stir after you have initially stirred up to make sure it is well combined and dissolved and started to boil.
- Remove from heat, add almonds and mix well.
- Spread on ungreased cookie sheet and sprinkle with chocolate chips.
- As they melt, spread chips evenly over the candy.
- Cool in fridge or freezer.
- Break into bite size pieces and hide.
- *You can toast the almonds in a fry pan over medium heat until slightly brown.

9. Almond Fudge Recipe

Serving: 20 | Prep: | Cook: 15mins | Ready in:

Ingredients

- 1 cup almonds
- ½ cup milk
- ¾ cup sugar
- 1 cup clarified butter

Direction

- Soak the almonds overnight.
- Grind the almonds to a paste using milk.
- Heat the butter in a heavy bottomed vessel, add the almond paste and sugar.
- Keep mixing this mixture on low heat till it starts leaving the sides of the vessel.
- Remove from heat and spread on a greased tray and allow it to cool.
- After it cools, you can cut it out into desired shapes.

10. Amaretto Fudge Recipe Recipe

Serving: 32 | Prep: | Cook: 20mins | Ready in:

Ingredients

- 2 c sugar
- 1/3 c milk
- 1/3 c half-and-half
- 2 tb light corn syrup
- 2 tb almond-flavored liqueur
- 2 tb margarine or butter
- 1/2 c Chopped almonds, toasted

Direction

- Butter loaf pan, 9 X 5 X 3 inches.
- Cook sugar, milk, half-and-half, corn syrup and almond-flavored liqueur in 3-quart saucepan over medium heat, stirring constantly, until sugar is dissolved.
- Cook, stirring occasionally, to 234 degrees on candy thermometer or until small amount of mixture dropped into very cold water forms a soft ball that flattens when removed from water; remove from heat.
- Add margarine.
- Cool mixture to 120 degrees without stirring.
- (Bottom of saucepan will be lukewarm.
-) Beat vigorously and continuously 5 to 10 minutes or until candy is thick and no longer glossy.
- (Mixture will hold its shape when dropped from a spoon.
-) Quickly stir in almonds.
- Spread in pan; cool.
- Cut into 1-inch squares.

11. Amaretto Truffles Recipe

Serving: 30 | Prep: | Cook: 10mins | Ready in:

Ingredients

- 1/4 cup heavy cream
- 2 tablespoons Amaretto
- 6 ounces sweet chocolate
- 4 tablespoons sweet butter softened
- Powdered unsweetened cocoa

Direction

- Boil cream in a small heavy pan until reduced to 2 tablespoons.
- Remove from heat then stir in amaretto and chocolate.
- Return to low heat and stir until chocolate melts.
- Whisk in softened butter.
- When mixture is smooth pour into a shallow bowl and refrigerate about 40 minutes.
- Scoop chocolate up with a teaspoon and shape into 1" balls.
- Roll balls in unsweetened cocoa.
- Store truffles covered in the refrigerator.
- Let truffles stand at room temperature for 30 minutes before serving.

12. Amish Country Peanut Butter Fudge Recipe

Serving: 1 | Prep: | Cook: 5mins | Ready in:

Ingredients

- 1 2/3 cups peanut butter chips
- 3/4 cup evaporated milk
- 2 1/4 cups Granulated sugar
- 1/4 cup unsalted butter
- 7 ounces marshmallow cream
- 1 teaspoon vanilla

Direction

- Butter a loaf pan.
- Place peanut butter chips into a medium bowl.
- In a heavy 3-quart saucepan, combine sugar, marshmallow crème, evap. Milk and butter. Cook over med. Heat, stirring constantly, until mixture boils; boil and stir 5 mins.
- Remove from heat; stir in vanilla.
- Immediately stir mixture into peanut butter chips until chips are completely melted; quickly pour into prepared pan. Cool completely.

- Remove from pan; place on cutting board. Cut into 1" squares. Store tightly covered. Makes about 2 pounds of candy.

13. Angel Food Christmas Candy

Serving: 1 | Prep: | Cook: 30mins | Ready in:

Ingredients

- 1 cup sugar
- 1 cup dark corn syrup
- 1 tablespoon white vinegar
- 1 tablespoon baking soda
- 1 pound milk chocolate candy coating, melted

Direction

- In a heavy saucepan, combine the sugar, corn syrup and vinegar. Cook over medium heat, stirring constantly, until sugar dissolves. Cook without stirring until the temperature reaches 300° (hard-crack stage) on a candy thermometer. Do not overcook.
- Remove from the heat and quickly stir in baking soda. Pour into a buttered 13x9-in. pan. Do not spread candy; mixture will not fill pan.
- When cool, break into bite-size pieces. Dip into melted chocolate; place on waxed paper until the chocolate is firm. Store candy tightly covered.
- Note: We recommend that you test your candy thermometer before each use by bringing water to a boil; the thermometer should read 212°. Adjust your recipe temperature up or down based on your test.
- Nutrition Facts
- 2 ounces: 337 calories, 11g fat (10g saturated fat), 0 cholesterol, 356mg sodium, 63g carbohydrate (61g sugars, 1g fiber), 1g protein.

14. Apple Cider Creme Caramels Recipe

Serving: 64 | Prep: | Cook: | Ready in:

Ingredients

- 2 1/2 cups fresh apple cider (I used Filsinger's: http://www.filsingersorganic.com/prdd_ap_cidersweet.php)
- 2 (1 cm wide) slices fresh gingerroot
- 2/3 cup full-fat coconut milk (pick the highest fat concentration you can find, I used Thai Kitchen)
- 2 tsp apple pie spice
- 1/2 tsp sea salt
- 1/3 cup heavy cream
- 1/4 cup water
- 1 cup sugar
- 1/2 cup dark brown sugar
- 1/3 cup corn syrup
- 2 tbsp maple syrup
- 1/2 cup unsalted, cultured butter, cubed (you can use regular unsalted if that's what you have)

Direction

- Combine apple cider and ginger slices in a pot and boil until the liquid has been reduced to 1/3 cup. Remove ginger, discarding (or eat it if you want...) and set aside to cool.
- Line a 9" square pan with well-greased parchment paper, leaving 2" overhang on all sides, and set aside.
- In a cup or bowl, combine coconut milk, spice, salt and reduced cider and set aside.
- In a large, heavy bottomed pot, mix heavy cream, water, sugars, corn syrup and maple syrup.
- Place over medium heat and cook, gently swirling the pan occasionally, until the sugar dissolves.
- Insert a candy thermometer and continue to cook, stirring occasionally and brushing down sides of the pot with water, until the syrup reaches 235F.

- Remove from the heat, and slowly whisk in the spiced cream mixture.
- Return to low heat and add the cubed butter. Cook, stirring constantly, until the mixture is homogenous.
- Re-insert the candy thermometer and increase the heat to medium.
- Cook, stirring almost constantly, until the temperature measures 252F.
- Pour the caramel immediately into the lined pan, and cool at room temperature at least 4 hours. Place in the refrigerator a further 2 hours, until firm.
- Unmould and cut into 64 squares, wrapping each in heavy duty wax paper (I used wax paper on the inside and foil on the outside so they'd stay closed.
- Store in an airtight container up to 2 weeks, or in the fridge for 1 month.

15. Applets Recipe

Serving: 24 | Prep: | Cook: 20mins | Ready in:

Ingredients

- 2 envelopes unflavored gelatin
- 1 1/4 cup applesauce, divided
- 2 cups sugar
- Pinch of salt
- 1 cup finely chopped walnuts
- 2 tsp. vanilla
- powdered sugar

Direction

- Soak gelatine in 1/2 cup applesauce for 10 minutes.
- In a heavy saucepan, bring remaining applesauce, sugar and salt to a boil; add gelatine mixture and boil for 15 minutes, stirring constantly. Remove from heat and add nuts and vanilla.
- Pour into a greased 11x7" baking dish. Cover and let set for 48 hours before cutting into squares and rolling in powdered sugar.

16. BAILEYS SNOWBALL TRUFFLES Recipe

Serving: 60 | Prep: | Cook: 30mins | Ready in:

Ingredients

- 1 1/4 LLB white chocolate
- 3/4 CUP heavy cream
- 1/4 CUP BAILETS irish cream
- 1/4 CUP unsalted butter SOFTENED
- sliced almonds, CRUSHED
- CONFECTIONERS sugar

Direction

- COARSELY CHOP CHOCOLATE, SET ASIDE.
- COMBINE CREAM BAILEYS IN SAUCEPAN AND BRING TO A BOIL.
- REMOVE FROM HEAT AND STIR IN CHOCOLATE UNTIL MELTED.
- STIR IN BUTTER UNTOL MELTED.
- CHILL THE CHOCOLATE MIXTURE.
- SPOON OUT CHOCOLATE MIXTURE.
- SHAPE INTO 1 INCH BALLS.
- ROLL YOUR BALLS INTO CRUSHED ALMONDS.
- DUST YOUR BALLS WITH SUGAR.
- KEEP YOUR BALLS REFRIGERATED UNTIL READY TO SERVE.
- EAT YOUR BALLS.

17. Baileys Fudge Recipe

Serving: 12 | Prep: | Cook: 10mins | Ready in:

Ingredients

- Here is the recipe for Bailey's fudge; and trust me, it's to die for.
- Bailey's Truffle Fudge
- 3 cups semisweet chocolate chips
- 1 cup white chocolate chips
- 3 cups powdered sugar
- 1/4 cup butter
- 1 cup Bailey's irish cream
- 1 1/2 cups nuts, chopped -- optional
- Truffle Topping:
- 1 cup semisweet chocolate chips
- 1/2 cup white chocolate chips
- 4 tbsp Bailey's irish cream
- 2 tbsp butter -- cut in pieces

Direction

- Melt chocolates with butter until chocolates are soft enough to stir smooth.
- Do not overheat. Add chocolate/butter mixture to powdered sugar and Baileys.
- Stir until smooth, add nuts and mix well. Place fudge in an 8" X 8" pan, oiled. Lay a sheet of plastic wrap on top and gently press to smooth fudge.
- Truffle Topping:
- Melt chocolates until soft. Remove from heat. With a fork, beat in butter and Baileys until smooth. Spread topping over fudge with knife. If a very smooth top is desired, place plastic wrap over top as in above. Refrigerate until firm; 1-2 hours. Can be frozen.
- Using all semi-sweet chips (instead of white chocolate) will yield a deeper, darker fudge.

18. Baileys Irish Creme Fudge Recipe

Serving: 1 | Prep: | Cook: 11mins | Ready in:

Ingredients

- 4 1/2 Cups sugar
- 1 12 oz can of evaporated milk
- 1/2 lb butter
- 2 12 oz pkgs of milk chocolate chips
- 1 12 oz pkg semisweet chocolate chips
- 2 7 oz jars marshmallow cream
- 2 tsp vanilla
- 2/3 Cup bailey irish cream
- 2 Cups chopped nuts

Direction

- Follow directions EXACTLY.
- Set chocolate chips, marshmallow cream, vanilla, Bailey's and nuts in a VERY large bowl. Set aside for later.
- Bring butter, sugar and milk to a boil and then cook slowly for exactly
- 11 minutes (don't ask why - just works), stirring CONSTANTLY.
- Pour milk mixtures over the other ingredients and stir slowly to blend.
- DO NOT USE MIXER
- Pour into a buttered 9x13 inch pan and chill very well. Cut cold.
- I also lined the pan with foil and removed from pan to cut.

19. Bavarian Mints Recipe

Serving: 16 | Prep: | Cook: 25mins | Ready in:

Ingredients

- 3 cups milk chocolate chips
- 1 (1 ounce) square unsweetened chocolate, chopped
- 1 tablespoon butter
- 1 (14 ounce) can sweetened condensed milk
- 1 teaspoon peppermint extract
- 1 teaspoon vanilla extract
- Add to Recipe Box

Direction

- Butter an 8x8 inch dish.
- In a medium saucepan over low heat, combine milk chocolate chips, unsweetened chocolate

and butter. Heat until melted and smooth, stirring occasionally. Remove from heat and stir in condensed milk, peppermint extract and vanilla extract.
- Beat with an electric mixer at a low speed for 1 minute, then at a high speed for 1 minute. Chill mixture for 15 minutes, beating by hand every 5 minutes. Beat again with electric mixer two minutes more. Pour into prepared pan and chill until firm. Cut into 1/2 inch squares.

20. Benne Sesame Brittle Recipe

Serving: 2 | Prep: | Cook: 5mins | Ready in:

Ingredients

- 2 cups sugar
- 3/4 teaspoon vanilla extract
- 1/2 teaspoon lemon extract
- 2 cups poached benne seeds or sesame seeds

Direction

- In a saucepan, melt sugar, stirring constantly.
- When sugar is melted, remove from heat and add benne seeds stirring quickly.
- Pour into lightly buttered pan(s) or onto marble slab to cool.
- Mark 1-inch squares while still warm.

21. Blue Ribbon Pralines Recipe

Serving: 10 | Prep: | Cook: 10mins | Ready in:

Ingredients

- 1 4-serving-size pkg. cook-and-serve butterscotch pudding mix
- 1 cup granulated sugar
- 1/2 cup packed brown sugar
- .
- 1/2 cup evaporated milk
- 1 Tbsp. butter
- 1-1/2 cups toasted pecan halves
- Opional: For chocolate... add 1/2 cup good semi-sweet chocolate when you add nuts.

Direction

- Line cookie sheet with waxed paper; set aside.
- In 2-quart saucepan, combine pudding mix, granulated sugar, brown sugar, evaporated milk, and butter. Cook and stir over medium heat until mixture boils (about 12 minutes). Clip a candy thermometer to side of pan. Reduce heat to medium-low; continue boiling at a moderate, steady rate, stirring frequently, until thermometer registers 234 degrees F, soft-ball stage (8 to 10 minutes). Remove saucepan from heat. Remove candy thermometer.
- Stir in pecans. Beat with a wooden spoon until candy just begins to thicken but is still glossy (about 3 minutes). Working quickly, drop by teaspoonfuls onto prepared cookie sheet. (If candy sets up too much, add a few drops of hot water and stir until smooth again.) Let stand until firm. Makes about 30 pieces.

22. Blueberry Cheesecake Fudge Recipe

Serving: 12 | Prep: | Cook: 20mins | Ready in:

Ingredients

- 2 three ounce packages of cream cheese, cubed and at room temperature
- 2 1/2 cups of granulated sugar
- 2/3 cup of evaporated milk
- 3 cups of mini marshmallows
- 8 ounces of dried blueberries
- 1 12 ounce bag of white chocolate chips
- 1/4 cup of butter
- 2 teaspoons of pure vanilla extract

Direction

- Place parchment paper or "release" aluminum in a 9 inch pan.
- In a large saucepan, combine the butter, sugar, milk, and marshmallows and bring to a rolling boil over medium heat.
- Stir constantly!
- Boil for five minutes (Or until candy thermometer reaches 234 degrees). Keep stirring!
- Remove from heat and stir in the cream cheese and chips until smooth and melted.
- Add blueberries and vanilla and stir well.
- Pour into your pan and cool at room temperature.
- Cut into squares when firm enough to cut and serve.
- *You sprinkle the top with white or yellow cake crumbs before the fudge sets.

23. Brown Sugar Fudge Recipe

Serving: 12 | Prep: | Cook: 20mins | Ready in:

Ingredients

- 2 cups brown sugar
- 1 cup whipping cream

Direction

- Combine brown sugar and whipping cream in a heavy saucepan. Boil until a candy thermometer reads 240 F (stirring constantly).
- Take off the heat and plunge pan into cold water, to an inch of the top of the pan. Beat with portable beaters until mixture thickens. Pour into a buttered pan. Cool and cut into squares.

24. Brown Sugar Fudge Old Recipe

Serving: 8 | Prep: | Cook: 15mins | Ready in:

Ingredients

- brown sugar Candy
- * 2 cups brown sugar
- * 1/2 cup milk or cream
- * butter (size of a walnut)
- * 1 cup chopped walnuts
- * 1 tes. vanilla

Direction

- Boil until it forms a soft lump when dropped into cold water, remove from fire. Beat until it begins to thicken, then add 1 cup chopped walnuts and vanilla. Pour into buttered dish.

25. BuckEye Balls Recipe

Serving: 20 | Prep: | Cook: 15mins | Ready in:

Ingredients

- 1 lb powered sugar
- 3 c. rice crispies cereal
- 2 cups creamy peanut butter (cruncy works too)
- 1 stick softened butter not melted
- 12-16 oz semi sweet chocolate chips
- 1/2 block paraffin wax
- wax paper
- tooth picks

Direction

- In large mixing bowl add softened butter, powdered sugar and peanut butter first mix well.
- Add rice krispies and fold into the mix.
- Use your hands to roll into tablespoon balls or a little bigger.
- Set balls on to wax paper.
- Once done put in freezer for about an hour 2 harden so they won't fall apart.
- After that melt chocolate in a sauce pan on low heat.
- Shave the wax into it until all is melted

- Use a toothpick to dip the peanut rice krispies balls into chocolate, place back on wax paper dry pretty quickly.
- Then enjoy your little chocolate peanut butter ball treats. Buckeye balls...

26. Buckeye Candies Recipe

Serving: 72 | Prep: | Cook: 2mins | Ready in:

Ingredients

- 2 cups creamy peanut butter, (not all-natural)
- 1/4 cup (1/2 stick) butter or margarine, softened
- 3 3/4 cups (16-oz. box) powdered sugar
- 2 cups (12-oz. pkg.) NESTLÉ® TOLL HOUSE® Semi-sweet chocolate Morsels
- 2 tablespoons vegetable shortening

Direction

- LINE baking sheets with wax paper.
- BEAT peanut butter and butter in large mixer bowl until creamy. Beat in powdered sugar until mixture holds together and is moistened. Shape into 1-inch balls; place on prepared baking sheets. Freeze for 1 hour.
- MELT morsels and shortening in medium, uncovered, microwave-safe bowl on HIGH (100%) power for 1 minute; STIR. Morsels may retain some of their shape. If necessary, microwave at additional 10- to 15-second intervals, stirring just until melted.
- DIP peanut butter centers into melted chocolate using a toothpick, leaving a small portion of the center uncovered. Shake off excess chocolate and scrape bottom of candy on side of bowl. Return to baking sheets; refrigerate until chocolate is set. Store in covered container in refrigerator.

27. Buckeye Peanut Butter Candy Recipe

Serving: 40 | Prep: | Cook: 30mins | Ready in:

Ingredients

- 2 cups peanut Butter, smooth (for best results, don't use natural, organic for this)
- 2 sticks of butter, softened
- 22 oz powdered sugar
- 1 - 12 oz bag semisweet chocolate chips (you make want to have another bag on hand just in case - my family tends to like them double dipped in chocolate for a thicker chocolate crust)

Direction

- Mix well all 3 ingredients until evenly incorporated. Line a baking sheet or tray with waxed paper to place the peanut butter balls.
- Make balls the size of walnuts or smaller. If mixture is too wet to roll into balls, you can add more powdered sugar, though this will make the balls denser and not as creamy in texture. I put them on a tray and in freezer for an hour or so until they are firm and ready to roll. You can use a melon-baller to make the job of rolling easier.
- Place rolled balls on tray and refrigerate overnight or in freezer for a few hours. This will make them easier for dipping.
- Melt chocolate chips in double boiler. Dip the balls in melted chocolate and place on lined cookie sheet. I use toothpicks to dip the balls in chocolate. Cover about 3/4 of the ball in chocolate. YOU WANT SOME OF THE PEANUT BUTTER FILLING TO SHOW. This makes them look like the buckeye nuts.
- Place back in refrigerator or freezer until chocolate sets.
- Enjoy!

28. Buttermilk Candy Recipe

Serving: 4 | Prep: | Cook: 15mins | Ready in:

Ingredients

- Makes 8 inch squares.
- 3 cups sugar
- 1 cup buttermilk or sour cream
- 1 teaspoon butter
- 1/2 cup white Karo
- 1 teaspoon soda
- 1/2 cup chopped nuts

Direction

- Mix first your ingredients in large (like Dutch oven) pan and bring to good rolling boil. Remove from fire and add soda. Replace on fire and cook slowly to soft boil stage. Beat while hot. When creamy, add nuts and pour in BUTTERED pan.
- Cut when set.
- To make pralines, add 2 cups whole nuts and drop on waxed paper

29. Butterscotch Chews Recipe

Serving: 24 | Prep: | Cook: 30mins | Ready in:

Ingredients

- 1 cup granulated sugar
- 1/2 cup brown sugar
- 1 tsp vinegar
- 1/2 cup light corn syrup
- 1/4 cup water
- 1/4 tsp salt
- 1/2 cup butter
- 1/2 tsp vanilla
- 1 pound chocolate or chocolate chips (optional)

Direction

- Prepare an 8x8 pan by lining it with aluminum foil and spraying the foil with non-stick cooking spray.
- 2. Combine the sugars, vinegar, corn syrup, water, and salt in a medium saucepan over medium-high heat. Stir while the sugars dissolve, then insert a candy thermometer. Cook the candy without stirring until it reaches 245 on the thermometer.
- 3. Once the candy reaches 245, add the butter and continue to cook, stirring frequently, until it reaches 255 degrees.
- 4. Remove the pan from the heat immediately and add the vanilla, stirring until it is well-incorporated. Pour the candy into the prepared pan and allow it to set, preferably overnight at room temperature. If you need to speed up the process, the candy can be refrigerated until it is set, about 4 hours.
- 5. Once the candy is set, pull it out of the pan using the foil as handles, and place it face-down on a cutting board. Peel the foil off the back of the candy block, and use a large sharp knife to cut the candy into small one-inch squares. At this point, you can choose to dip your chews in chocolate or leave them plain. If you don't dip them, I recommend wrapping each piece in cellophane or waxed paper so that they don't become sticky.
- 6. To dip them in chocolate, place the chocolate in a large microwave-safe bowl. Microwave the chocolate in one-minute intervals until melted, stirring after each minute to prevent overheating. Cover a baking sheet or large plate with aluminum foil and set aside.
- 7. Using dipping tools or two forks, dip a square into the chocolate until it is full immersed. Bring it up out of the chocolate and drag the bottom against the lip of the bowl to remove excess chocolate. Place the dipped candy on the prepared baking sheet and repeat with remaining butterscotch chews and chocolate.
- 8. Refrigerate the chews to set the chocolate for 20 minutes. They will be very hard out of the refrigerator, so let them sit at room

temperature for 10 minutes before serving. Store plain, wrapped chews in an airtight container at room temperature, and store chocolate-dipped chews in the refrigerator for up to a week.

30. Butterscotch Fudge Recipe

Serving: 16 | Prep: | Cook: 10mins | Ready in:

Ingredients

- 1c firmly packed dark brown sugar
- 1(7.5oz.)jar marshmallow Fluff
- 2/3c evaporated milk
- 6Tbs unsalted butter
- 1/2tsp salt
- 1(12oz)bag white chocolate chips
- 2c chopped almonds,pecans or walnuts
- 1tsp vanilla extract

Direction

- Line an 8" square baking pan with heavy duty foil, leaving a 1" overhang on 2 sides.
- In a heavy medium saucepan, combine brown sugar, marshmallow fluff, milk, butter and salt and bring to a boil over med-high heat. Reduce heat to medium and simmer, stirring constantly with wooden spoon, for 5 mins. Remove pan from heat, add white chocolate chips and stir till melted. Blend in nuts and vanilla.
- Scrape fudge into prepared pan. Refrigerate till firm, 2-3 hours.
- Remove fudge from pan, using foil to lift it out. Then cut into 16 cubes, serve. Or chill in an airtight container for up to a week.

31. Buttery Cashew Brittle Recipe

Serving: 5 | Prep: | Cook: 40mins | Ready in:

Ingredients

- 2 sticks salted butter (no substitutions)
- 1 cup sugar
- 1 Tablespoon light corn syrup
- 1 1/2 cup cashews (whole, halves or pieces - salted or unsalted)

Direction

- Line a baking sheet with a lightly buttered piece of waxed paper, set aside. In a heavy medium sized saucepan, heat the butter, sugar and corn syrup on medium low heat. Stir occasionally and heat until temperature reaches 290 degrees on a candy thermometer (about 30 minutes). Take pan off heat and stir in cashews. Pour mixture out onto the waxed paper lined pan, and spread the candy out across the pan. Let it cool in the pan for 10 minutes, then in the fridge for 5 more minutes before peeling off the waxed paper. Break into bite sized pieces and store in an airtight container.

32. CANDY CANE WHITE FUDGE Recipe

Serving: 24 | Prep: | Cook: 5mins | Ready in:

Ingredients

- 12 oz white chocolate, coarsely chopped
- 14 oz can sweetened condensed milk
- 1/4 C coarsely chopped peppermint candies

Direction

- Butter an 8-inch square baking pan; line bottom and sides with foil allowing foil to extend over sides of pan by about 1".
- Butter foil.
- Over medium-high heat in top of double-boiler or heatproof bowl set over pot of hot water combine white chocolate and condensed milk.

- Cook, stirring frequently, until melted and smooth, 5 minutes. Pour mixture into pan; sprinkle candy over top.
- Using knife lightly swirl candy into chocolate mixture. Refrigerate until firm, about 6 hours or overnight. Cut into 1" squares, diamond shapes or rectangles.
- Store in refrigerator.

33. CHRISTMAS CARAMEL CHEWS Recipe

Serving: 6 | Prep: | Cook: 25mins | Ready in:

Ingredients

- 3 sticks butter
- 2 c. oatmeal
- 2 c. flour
- 1 tsp. baking soda
- 1 1/2 c. brown sugar
- 1 12 oz. bag semi-sweet chocolate morsels
- 64 caramels
- 10 tbsp. milk
- 1/2 tsp. salt

Direction

- Crumb first 6 ingredients together. Spread in 9x13 inch pan, reserving 1/3 of mixture for top. Bake 10 minutes at 350 degrees. Sprinkle bag of semi-sweet chocolate morsels over baked oatmeal mixture. Melt caramels and milk and pour over the top. Sprinkle remaining crumbs over this and bake 15 minutes more at 350 degrees.

34. COPY CAT York Peppermint Patties Recipe

Serving: 30 | Prep: | Cook: 60mins | Ready in:

Ingredients

- York Peppermint Patties
- 1 (14-ounce) can Eagle Brand sweetened condensed milk
- 1 tablespoon peppermint extract
- green or red food coloring, optional
- 6 cups confectioners' sugar
- Additional confectioners' sugar
- 1 - 16 oz. bag semi-sweet chocolate chips

Direction

- In large mixer bowl, combine Eagle Brand, extract and food coloring if desired.
- Add 6 cups sugar; beat on low speed until smooth and well blended.
- Turn mixture onto surface sprinkled with confectioners' sugar.
- Knead lightly to form smooth ball.
- Shape into 1-inch balls.
- Place 2 inches apart on wax paper-lined baking sheets.
- Flatten each ball into a 1 ½-inch patty. Let dry 1 hour or longer; turn over and let dry at least 1 hour.
- Melt the chocolate chips in a microwave set on high for 2 minutes. Stir halfway through the heating time. Melt thoroughly, but do not over heat.
- Melting the chocolate chips can also be done using a double-boiler over low heat.
- With fork, dip each patty into warm chocolate (draw fork lightly across rim of pan to remove excess coating).
- Invert onto wax paper-lined baking sheets; let stand until firm.
- Store covered at room temperature or in refrigerator.

35. CROCK POT CANDY Recipe

Serving: 8 | Prep: | Cook: | Ready in:

Ingredients

- INGREDIENTS:
- 1 jar (16oz.) dry roasted peanuts, unsalted
- 1 jar (16oz.) dry roasted peanuts, salted (I personally use all salted)
- 1 pkg. (12oz.) semi-sweet chocolate chips
- 1 bar (4oz.) German chocolate, broken into pieces
- 3 lbs (or 2 planks) white bark, broken into pieces

Direction

- Put ingredients into a 4 or 5 quart crock pot in the order listed above. Cover and cook 3 hours on low. DO NOT REMOVE LID. Turn off and cool "slightly". Mix thoroughly and drop by teaspoon onto waxed paper, or Teflon pan. Let cool thoroughly. Makes approx. 170 pieces.
- Toasted pecans, walnuts, almonds, etc. would also be good. I use 3lbs of chocolate bark also. Try anything, you really can't hurt this recipe, much.

36. California White Chocolate Fudge Recipe

Serving: 24 | Prep: | Cook: 14mins | Ready in:

Ingredients

- 1 1/2 cups sugar
- 3/4 - cup sour cream
- 1/2 - cup butter12- ounces white chocolate, coarsely chopped
- 1- (7 ounce) jar of kraft marshmallow creme
- 3/4- cup chopped walnuts
- 3/4- cup chopped dried apricots

Direction

- In a heavy saucepan 3-4 quart size, bring sugar, sour cream and butter to a full rolling boil over medium heat, stirring constantly.
- Continue boiling 7 minutes or until candy thermometer reaches 234 degrees stirring constantly.
- Stir in remaining ingredients until well blended.
- Pour into a greased 9 inch square pan cool until set.
- Cut into squares and enjoy.
- Makes about 2 1/2 pounds of candy.
- Try it with macadamia nuts. I made it like that it was truly heavenly.

37. Candied Nuts Recipe

Serving: 1 | Prep: | Cook: 8mins | Ready in:

Ingredients

- 3 3/4 Cups walnuts (1 pound bag)
- Bake in 375 Degree oven for 5 minutes, stirring once or twice. Cool while syrup cooks.
- Syrup:
- 1 1/2 Cup sugar 1 1/2 tsp cinnamon
- 3/4 Cup water 3/4 tsp salt

Direction

- Butter sides of heavy pan. Cook syrup & stir until sugar dissolves and mixture boils. Cook without stirring to 236 degrees, using candy thermometer. Remove from heat. Add 2 1/4 tsp. vanilla & nuts. Beat by hand 1 minute or until nuts are coated. Spread out on buttered pan. Break into pieces when cool.
- These were so addicting and so yummy. They tasted like you bought them somewhere!! We paid $16.00 for a cone full at the NASCAR race and fairs! These are so much better! You can use any nuts.

38. Candy Cane Fudge Recipe

Serving: 48 | Prep: | Cook: 5mins | Ready in:

Ingredients

- * 2/3 cup evaporated milk
- * 1 2/3 cups granulated sugar
- * 2 tablespoons butter
- * 1/2 teaspoon salt
- * 2 cups miniature marshmallows
- * 1 1/2 cups white chocolate chips
- * 2 teaspoons mint (peppermint) extract
- *1/4 teaspoon vanilla extract
- * 1/4 teaspoon red food coloring

Direction

- Combine the Fudge Ingredients:
- In a medium saucepan over medium-high heat, combine the sugar, salt, evaporated milk, and butter, and stir until the sugar melts.
- Bring the mixture to a boil and boil, stirring constantly, for five minutes.
- After five minutes, remove from the heat and stir in the marshmallows, white chocolate chips, and mint extract.
- Pour fudge into an 8x8 pan that has been lined with aluminum foil or sprayed with non-stick cooking spray.
- Sprinkle drops of red food coloring over the top, and cut through gently with knife, creating red swirls.
- Rotate pan and repeat, creating a "marbled-effect"
- Do not over-stir, otherwise the candy will turn pink.
- Place in the refrigerator to set the fudge for at least one hour.
- Cut in small pieces and enjoy!

39. Candy Corn Recipe

Serving: 10 | Prep: | Cook: 15mins | Ready in:

Ingredients

- 1 cup sugar
- 2/3 cup white corn syrup
- 1/3 cup butter
- 1 tsp. vanilla
- 2 1/2 cups powdered sugar, lightly packed
- 1/4 tsp. salt
- 1/3 cup powdered milk
- food coloring
- disposable gloves

Direction

- Heat sugar, corn syrup and butter in saucepan. Stir constantly until it comes to a boil. Reduce heat and simmer for 5 minutes, stirring occasionally. Remove from heat and add vanilla.
- In a large bowl, combine powdered sugar, salt and powdered milk. Add the hot mixture and stir until smooth.
- Grab two additional bowls and divide the mixture into three equal parts. Stir a couple drops of yellow food coloring into one batch and mix thoroughly. Combine red and yellow to make orange for another batch. Leave the third batch white.
- Let the dough stand until cool and firm.
- Put on the gloves, which will protect your hands from staining as well as keeping your candy free of fingerprints.
- Grab a wad of each color of dough and roll into a rope 1/4 inch to 1/2 inch in diameter. Carefully push the three rolls together, using a rolling pin to slightly flatten the top.
- Cut candy in alternating diagonal lines to form candy corn shapes. Finish shaping individual kernels by hand until smooth.
- Candy can be refrigerated in layers of waxed paper to better maintain its shape.
- Makes 1 3/4 pounds of candy.

40. Candy Easter Eggs Recipe

Serving: 12 | Prep: | Cook: 5mins | Ready in:

Ingredients

- 1 box confectioners' sugar
- 2 cups coconut
- 1 stick butter
- 1/3 cup white corn syrup
- 1/2 teaspoon salt
- 1 teaspoon vanilla

Direction

- Mix, chill and shape into balls.
- For potatoes roll in cinnamon.
- For eggs dip in chocolate and 1/4 teaspoon of paraffin wax.

41. Candy Strawberries Recipe

Serving: 16 | Prep: | Cook: | Ready in:

Ingredients

- 2 (3 oz.) pkgs. strawberry gelatin
- 1 c. flaked coconut
- 1 c. chopped pecans
- 3/4 c. Eagle Brand milk
- 1/2 tsp. vanilla
- Red decorators sugar

Direction

- Mix gelatine, coconut and pecans.
- Stir in vanilla and milk.
- Mix well.
- Chill in refrigerator for 1 hour.
- Shape into small balls or into the shape of strawberries.
- Roll in red sugar.

42. Candy Train A Candy Craft Recipe

Serving: 1 | Prep: | Cook: | Ready in:

Ingredients

- 1 roll of Lifesavers Candy
- 1 small package of gum
- 1 chocolate rollo Candy
- 1 Hershey's Kiss
- 1 mini Hershey's chocolate bar
- 1 Starburst candy
- 4 Round peppermint candies
- Fancy string or Ribbon for the ornament hanger
- Low temp. hot glue gun

Direction

- If you want to use your train as an ornament - take your ribbon and tie into a loop around the Lifesavers.
- Glue the roll of Lifesavers candy to the package of gum with the ribbon loop in-between.
- Glue the peppermint candies on each side to make the wheels of the Candy Train.
- Glue the Hershey's Kiss on the end of the Lifesavers to make the train smokestack. (I do mine with the flat side up but I have seen them the other way)
- On the other end of the train glue a Rollo candy to make the engineer's room - glue a small candy on top for the roof (use a Starburst candy or mini chocolate bar)
- Take your mini Hershey's bar and run a bead of glue the entire length and place on back end of the Candy Train.
- *These are adorable additions to holiday gift baskets or part of your ribbon and bow decorations on gift boxes or gift bags. They are also good stocking stuffers.

43. Candy Box Caramels Recipe

Serving: 48 | Prep: | Cook: 5mins | Ready in:

Ingredients

- 12 ounces chocolate- and/or vanilla-flavor candy coating*, coarsely chopped
- 1 cup toffee pieces, crushed; finely chopped pistachios; and/or nonpareils
- 48 short plastic or wooden skewers (optional)
- 1 14-ounce package vanilla caramels (about 48), unwrapped
- 2 ounces chocolate- and/or vanilla-flavor candy coating*, coarsely chopped (optional)

Direction

- In a microwave-safe 4-cup measure, place the 12 ounces candy coating.
- Microwave on 100% power (high) for 3 minutes or just until melted, stirring every 30 seconds.
- Place toffee pieces, nuts, or nonpareils in a shallow dish.
- If desired, insert a skewer into each caramel.
- Dip one caramel into melted candy coating; turn to coat as much of the caramel as desired, allowing excess coating to drip off caramel. (If not using skewers, use a fork to lift caramel out of candy coating, drawing the fork across the rim of the glass measure to remove excess coating from caramel.)
- Place dipped caramel in toffee pieces, nuts, and/or nonpareils, turning to coat.
- Place coated caramel on a baking sheet lined with waxed paper. Repeat with remaining caramels.
- Let caramels stand about 1 hour or until coating dries.
- If desired, microwave 2 ounces of a contrasting color of candy coating in a microwave-safe bowl on 100% power (high) for 2 minutes or just until melted, stirring every 30 seconds.
- Cool slightly.
- Transfer coating to a small, heavy plastic bag; cut a small hole in one corner of bag and drizzle additional coating over coated caramels.
- Let caramels stand until set.
- To Store:
- Layer caramels between waxed paper in an airtight container; cover. Store at room temperature for up to 1 week or freeze for up to 3 months.
- *If desired, substitute milk chocolate, dark chocolate, and/or white chocolate baking squares with cocoa butter for candy coating.

44. Caramel Apple Smores Recipe

Serving: 1 | Prep: | Cook: 2mins | Ready in:

Ingredients

- One green apple
- 1 package caramels
- 1 bag marshmallows
- chocolate chips(optional)

Direction

- Slice apple into round slats, the edges work especially well but the whole apple can be used to make more s'mores!
- Melt caramel using stove or microwave.
- Roast a marshmallow as would for a s'more.
- Place half of the apple slices on wax paper.
- Top each apple slice with a roasted marshmallow.
- Drizzle caramel over top of marshmallow.
- Top with other apple halves.
- If desired melt chocolate chips and drizzle over top!

45. Caramel Candy Pretzel Rods Two Ways Recipe

Serving: 20 | Prep: | Cook: 5mins | Ready in:

Ingredients

- 1 14-oz. package individually wrapped caramels
- 1 tbsp. water
- About 20 long pretzel rods (ie: Rold Gold)
- about 1 cup mini-candy coated chocolate pieces (ie: M&M's)
- About 3/4 cup crushed toffee bits
- About 3/4 cup mini chocolate chips
- 1/2 cup white chocolate chips
- 1/2 cup semi-sweet chocolate chips

Direction

- Unwrap caramels and place in a large microwave safe bowl with the water; microwave on high 1 minute or until smooth. Heat in additional 15 second increments if necessary. Let cool until bowl is just barely warm to the touch (will help caramel set quicker on the pretzels)
- Line a tray or baking sheet with parchment paper.
- Dip each pretzel in the caramel and/or spread with a butter knife so that all but 1" to 1 1/2" of the pretzel is covered. Let set for a minute, then dip or roll in either M&M's OR toffee bits/mini chocolate chips, pressing into caramel with your hand. Place on parchment paper line sheet.
- When done, place sheet in refrigerator for at least 10 minutes to set.
- Meanwhile, melt white chocolate chips and semi-sweet chocolate chips in separate bowls in the microwave (takes about a minute).
- Drizzle each pretzel with white chocolate, then dark chocolate and place on tray.
- Return to refrigerator for at least 15 minutes to set completely.
- Wrap in plastic wrap or cellophane bags and secured with a ribbon.

46. Caramel Kisses Recipe

Serving: 20 | Prep: | Cook: 20mins | Ready in:

Ingredients

- Waxed paper or deep baking trays
- butter
- 4-5 cups chopped pecans
- 2 cups sugar
- 1 cup light Karo or other corn syrup
- 1/4 tsp salt
- 16 oz. cream

Direction

- Spread several sheets of waxed paper on table or cabinet; butter the paper, then sprinkle pecans over it. Or butter the baking trays and sprinkle nuts in them. (You'll need more nuts for the waxed paper method.)
- Mix sugar, syrup, salt, and half of cream. Stir mixture until it boils then turn down heat.
- Add remainder of cream and cook slowly, stirring constantly, until mixture forms a firm ball in cool water.
- Pour mixture over pecans in trays, or on waxed paper.
- Cover with more waxed paper, if using.
- Cool completely and cut into pieces.

47. Caramel Peanut Butter Fudge Recipe

Serving: 32 | Prep: | Cook: | Ready in:

Ingredients

- 3 tbsp corn syrup
- 1 cup sugar
- ¾ cup dark brown sugar

- ¾ cup Amoré almonds + Dairy beverage (or whole milk)
- 1 tsp kosher salt
- pinch baking soda
- 10 soft caramel candies, chopped
- ½ cup creamy peanut butter

Direction

- Line a 9" pan with parchment and set aside.
- In a medium saucepan, combine corn syrup, sugars, milk, salt, and baking soda. Bring to a boil over medium-high heat, stirring occasionally.
- Cook until the mixture reads 237F on a candy thermometer.
- Remove saucepan from heat and stir in the caramels and peanut butter.
- Continue stirring until completely smooth.
- Pour mixture into prepared pan. Set aside and let fudge set.

48. Caramelized Party Mix Recipe

Serving: 8 | Prep: | Cook: 10mins |Ready in:

Ingredients

- ¼ cup butter (no substitutes here, please!)
- ¾ cup packed brown sugar
- 2 tablespoons corn syrup
- dash of salt
- 3 cups Rice Chex cereal
- 2 cups thin pretzel sticks
- 1 cup mixed nuts (I use cashews, but use whatever you like)

Direction

- Melt butter in a large skillet (I use my electric skillet for this, but stove top would be fine, I'm sure).
- Add brown sugar, corn syrup and salt.
- Cook for 1 minute, then shut off electric skillet or remove pan from burner.
- Using a large mixing spoon or spatula (coated with butter or cooking spray first), immediately stir in cereal, pretzels and nuts.
- Stir gently to coat well, and then spread the warm mixture on a large piece of waxed paper that you have sprayed with some cooking spray.
- When cool, break into chunks and store in covered container.

49. Cashew Brittle Recipe

Serving: 2 | Prep: | Cook: 45mins |Ready in:

Ingredients

- 1 C, sugar
- 1/2 c. light corn syrup
- 1/4 c hot water
- 2 c. salted cashews (pieces are fine, and cheaper!)
- 1 tbsp butter
- 1 tsp baking soda
- You really should have a candy thermometer for this. Otherwise, use a cup of ice cold water: when you drop some of the liquid into it and it becomes a spindly piece that cracks, that is the right stage (hardcrack) to stop and spread it out to cool.
- Have ready a flat sheet pan (like an airbake cookie sheet so no lip is in the way) that is greased well, plus a flat spreader or long flat heat resistant spatula

Direction

- In a heavy 3 qt. saucepan mix sugar, corn syrup and water.
- Stir over medium heat until sugar dissolves (no gritty stuff on bottom of pan).
- Add cashews, and continue stirring - constantly - over medium heat until the mixture reaches 295 degrees (see note above about hard crack stage).

- {The other thing to note here is as the mixture approaches the right temperature, the cashews start to get really toasty brown and the syrup is so bubbly it doesn't seem like a liquid anymore}.
- Remove from heat and add butter and baking soda (this is really cool - it gets all foamy!)
- Stir rapidly until butter melts and soda dissolves.
- Spread immediately and quickly onto greased pan.
- When cool enough to handle, grab pieces and stretch (ouch!) by hand to desired thinness.
- Cool completely before breaking into pieces.
- Will keep in airtight container for up to 2 mos.
- Like it would still be around that long!!
- MERRY CHRISTMAS!

50. Cashew Truffles Recipe

Serving: 1 | Prep: | Cook: 6mins | Ready in:

Ingredients

- 1 cup plus 2 tablespoons whipping cream
- 1/4 cup butter
- 12 ounces semisweet chocolate, cut into chunks
- 6 ounces milk chocolate, cut into chunks
- 1 teaspoon vanilla extract
- 2 cups finely chopped cashews

Direction

- In small saucepan, bring cream and butter to a boil. Remove pan from heat. Add chocolates and vanilla and stir until mixture is creamy and smooth. Refrigerate about 3 hours* until firm enough to handle.
- Form into 1-inch balls, then roll in cashews.
- Store in refrigerator.

51. Cereal Bars Recipe

Serving: 8 | Prep: | Cook: 120mins | Ready in:

Ingredients

- 1 cup rolled oats
- 1 cup dessicated coconut
- 1/4 cup wheat germ
- 1 cup sesame seeds
- 1/2 cup pepitas
- 1/2 cup sunflower seed kernels
- 1 cup sultanas
- 125g butter
- 1/2 cup honey
- 1/3 cup brown sugar

Direction

- Dry-roast all the dry ingredients in a fry pan for 5 minutes, add the sesame seeds and coconut last as they cook quicker. Let cool and stir in sultanas
- Melt the butter over low temperature, add the brown sugar and stir to dissolve. Add honey, stir until bubbling, and simmer for 6-7 minutes. (When a drop turns solid in cold water it's ready) remove from the heat and combine with dry ingredients in bowl.
- Press into a large slab tin. Cut into squares and leave to set for 2 hours. Enjoy

52. Champagne Truffles Recipe

Serving: 12 | Prep: | Cook: 10mins | Ready in:

Ingredients

- 6 ounces semisweet chocolate coarsely chopped
- 1/4 cup butter cut into small pieces
- 3 tablespoons whipping cream
- 1 beaten egg yolk
- 3 tablespoons champagne

- unsweetened cocoa powder or powdered sugar

Direction

- In a heavy medium saucepan combine semisweet chocolate, butter and whipping cream. Stirring constantly cook over low heat until chocolate is melted. Add in egg yolk mixture and stir. Cook and stir over medium low heat for 2 minutes. Remove from heat. Stir in champagne and transfer truffle mixture to a bowl. Cover and refrigerate for 1 hour or until cool and smooth stirring occasionally. Beat cooled truffle mixture with electric mixer over medium for 1 minute. Refrigerate for 30 minutes or until mixture holds its shape. Line a baking sheet with waxed paper. Use a small scoop or spoon to form 1 inch balls. Place each piece on the prepared baking sheet. Cover and chill in the refrigerator until firm. Roll truffles in cocoa or powdered sugar and serve.

53. Chattanooga Chew Chews Recipe

Serving: 32 | Prep: | Cook: 25mins | Ready in:

Ingredients

- Crust: 2 cups all purpose flour
- 1 cup brown sugar
- 1 cup pecans, chopped
- 1/2 cup salted butter (NO SUBSTITUTES)
- caramel topping : 1 cup butter
- 3/4 cup brown sugar 1 (12 oz. package semi-sweet chocolate

Direction

- Preheat oven to 350 degrees F.
- In bowl mix flour, butter, and brown sugar. Press into ungreased 9x13-inch pan. Sprinkle pecans evenly over unbaked crust.
- For caramel topping: Melt brown sugar and butter in a saucepan. Bring to a boil and continue to boil for 1 min., stirring constantly.
- Pour caramel mixture over crust and pecans. Bake for 20-25 min. or until surface is bubby.
- Remove from oven sprinkle chocolate chips over hot surface. Gently swirl melted chocolate chips with a spatula for a marbled effect.
- Cool at least 5 hours. Cut into small squares (very rich candy!)

54. Chewy Chocolate Nut Candies Recipe

Serving: 24 | Prep: | Cook: 30mins | Ready in:

Ingredients

- 1 1/2 cups candy corn
- 1 tbsp chocolate fudge frosting
- 1 1/2 tbsp nutella
- 1/4 cup smooth peanut butter
- 1 tbsp salted butter
- Optional:
- Add 1/4 cup crushed Rice Krispies cereal to the freshly melted dough mixture and knead in for "crispy" candy

Direction

- In a bowl, combine the candy corn, frosting, Nutella and peanut butter.
- Microwave until everything is melted together, about 2 minutes, stirring halfway through.
- Stir in the butter until smooth.
- Press into chocolate / candy moulds or a 9" square pan.
- If in the square pan, let sit 2 minutes then score with a bench scraper or sharp knife. Let cool completely.
- If desired, coat in chocolate after they have set completely.

55. Chipotle Fudge Recipe

Serving: 12 | Prep: | Cook: 30mins | Ready in:

Ingredients

- 2 cups granulated sugar
- 2 tablespoons honey
- 2 ounces unsweetened chocolate broken in pieces
- 1/4 teaspoon salt
- 3/4 cup milk
- 1/2 teaspoon ground chipotle pepper
- 1 teaspoon ground cinnamon
- 3 tablespoons unsalted butter in pieces
- 1/2 teaspoon vanilla extract

Direction

- In a large heavy saucepan combine sugar, honey, chocolate, salt and milk.
- Place over medium-high heat and stir constantly for 3 minutes.
- Cover with a lid and heat until mixture comes to a full boil about 1 minute longer.
- Uncover and cook until mixture becomes shiny and thick about 4 minutes stirring often.
- Remove from heat and stir in the chipotle pepper and cinnamon.
- Place butter on the fudge and set aside to cool.
- When the fudge has become tepid after about 20 minutes add vanilla and stir until fudge starts to firm.
- Pour into a loaf pan and even the top.
- Set aside until firm.
- Cut into squares.

56. Chocolate Billionaires Recipe

Serving: 28 | Prep: | Cook: 5mins | Ready in:

Ingredients

- 1- package caramels unwrapped (about 14 ounces)
- 3- tablespoons water
- 1 1/2 - cups of chopped pecans
- 1- cup crisp rice cereal....like (Rice Krispies)
- 3- cups milk chocolate chips
- 1 1/2 - teaspoons shortening

Direction

- Line 2 baking sheets with waxed paper, grease the paper and set aside.
- In a large heavy saucepan, combine the caramels and water, cook and stir over low heat until smooth.
- Stir in pecans and rice cereal until all is coated.
- Drop by teaspoonfuls onto prepared pans.
- Refrigerate for 10 minutes or until firm.
- Meanwhile melt chocolate chips and shortening, stir until smooth.
- Dip candy into chocolate coating entire candy and place back onto waxed paper.
- Refrigerate until set.
- Then store in airtight containers.
- Yields approx. 2 pounds.

57. Chocolate Orange Sesame Truffles Recipe

Serving: 21 | Prep: | Cook: | Ready in:

Ingredients

- 4 oz stevia-sweetened bittersweet chocolate (I used CocoPolo), chopped finely
- zest of 1 blood orange*
- 3 tbsp fresh blood orange juice*
- ¼ cup agave nectar (I used Amoretti Organolicious Blood Orange Flavored Blue Agave Nectar)
- 1 tbsp tahini
- 3 tbsp sesame seeds, for coating
- Blood oranges give these an exotic, rich sweetness, but navel oranges work just as well.

Direction

- Place chocolate in a small bowl, set aside.
- Combine zest, juice and agave in a small pot and bring to a brisk simmer.
- Reduce heat to low, add tahini and beat well.
- Cook, stirring constantly, for 30 seconds.
- Remove from heat and set aside for 1 minute.
- Pour over the chocolate and cover for 1 minute, then stir until chocolate is completely melted.
- Pour into a shallow pan and refrigerate at least 2 hours, until firm.
- Place sesame seeds in a shallow dish.
- Scoop 1" balls of ganache and roll into balls. Roll in the seeds to coat, then transfer to a plate.
- Chill at least 1 hour before serving.

58. Chocolate Bourbon Truffles Recipe

Serving: 26 | Prep: | Cook: 15mins | Ready in:

Ingredients

- 1 can (14 ounces) sweetened condensed milk
- 3 cups semisweet chocolate chips
- 1 Tablespoon vanilla extract
- 2 Tablespoons bourbon (if you don't like bourbon you can substitute it with Frangelico, Bailey's Irish Creme, Kahlua coffee liqueur, Cointreau, Grand Marnier, creme de menthe or any other liqueur.)
- 1/2 to 3/4 cup pecans, finely chopped
- granulated sugar, unsweetened cocoa, or very finely chopped pecans

Direction

- Combine chocolate chips and sweetened condensed milk in a saucepan over low heat.
- Heat, stirring, until melted and smooth.
- Remove from heat.
- Stir in the vanilla, bourbon, and 1/2 to 3/4 cup pecans.
- Transfer to a small bowl.
- Cover and chill for 3 to 4 hours, or until mixture is firm.
- Working with fingertips, shape into 1-inch balls.
- Roll in finely chopped pecans, sugar, coconut or unsweetened cocoa.
- Place on a tray or baking sheet, cover loosely, and chill for at least 1 hour.
- If desired, put each truffle in a decorative fluted paper or foil cup and keep in tightly covered container in the refrigerator until giving or serving.
- Keep these refrigerated, tightly covered.

59. Chocolate Butter Toffee Recipe

Serving: 15 | Prep: | Cook: 30mins | Ready in:

Ingredients

- 1 - cup (2 sticks) butter. (margarine is never a good thing for (humans.) hahaha........ In addition, for this recipe, it will not work................
- 1 - c upsugar
- 1 - cup semi sweet chocolate chips
- 1/4 - cup finely chopped toasted almonds

Direction

- Cook butter and sugar in a heavy 2 quart saucepan over medium heat, stirring occasionally until small amount of mixture dropped into ice water forms brittle globs or candy thermometer reaches 300 degrees – about 25-30 minutes.
- If stirred too often, the toffee may separate.
- Spread quickly into 15x10x1 inch pan.
- Sprinkle chocolate chips over hot candy.
- Let stand for 5 minutes.

- Spread melted chocolate over candy, then sprinkle with almonds. Cool and break into pieces

60. Chocolate Buttercream Cherry Candies Recipe

Serving: 48 | Prep: | Cook: |Ready in:

Ingredients

- Buttercream:
- About 48 maraschino cherries with stems, well drained
- 1/4 cup (1/2 stick) butter, softened
- 2 cups powdered sugar
- 1/4 cup cocoa
- 1 to 2 tablespoons milk, divided
- 1/2 teaspoon vanilla extract
- 1/4 teaspoon almond extract
- White Chip Coating (recipe follows)
- chocolate Chip Drizzle (recipe follows)
- White Chip Coating:
- 1 (12 oz.) pkg. white chocolate chips
- 2 tbsp. vegetable oil
- chocolate Chip Drizzle:
- 1/4 C. chocolate chips
- 1/4 tsp. shortening (do not use butter, margarine, spread or oil)

Direction

- Buttercream Cherries:
- 1. Cover tray with wax paper. Lightly press cherries between layers of paper towels to remove excess moisture.
- 2. Beat butter, powdered sugar, cocoa and 1 tablespoon milk in small bowl until well blended; stir in vanilla and almond extract. If necessary, add remaining milk, one teaspoon at a time, until mixture will hold together but is not wet.
- 3. Mold scant teaspoon mixture around each cherry, covering completely; place on prepared tray. Cover; refrigerate 3 hours or until firm.
- 4. Prepare White Chip Coating. Holding each cherry by stem, dip into coating. Place on tray; refrigerate until firm.
- 5. About 1 hour before serving, prepare Chocolate Chip Drizzle; with tines of fork drizzle randomly over candies. Refrigerate until drizzle is firm. Store in refrigerator.
- White Chip Coating:
- Place White Chips in small microwave-safe bowl; drizzle with vegetable oil. Microwave at HIGH (100%) 1 minute; stir. If necessary, microwave at HIGH an additional 15 seconds at a time, stirring after each heating just until chips are melted and mixture is smooth. If mixture thickens while coating, microwave at HIGH 15 seconds; stir until smooth.
- Chocolate Chip Drizzle:
- Place Chocolate Chips and teaspoon shortening in another small microwave-safe bowl. Microwave at HIGH (100%) 30 seconds to 1 minute; stir until chips are melted and mixture is smooth.

61. Chocolate Cappuccino Candy Recipe

Serving: 0 | Prep: | Cook: 15mins |Ready in:

Ingredients

- 1 TBSP. instant coffee granules.... get a good coffee
- 1 TBSP. hot water
- 2 cups sugar
- 1 cup evaporated milk
- 1/2 cup butter
- 1 (12-ounce) bag of semisweet chocolate morsels
- 1 (7-ounce) jar marshmallow cream
- 1 cup chopped pecans
- 1 TBSP. finely grated orange rind
- 2 teasp. orange or orange extract

- 2 teasp. brandy extract

Direction

- Combine the coffee granules and the water.
- Stir until the granules are dissolved. Set aside.
- Combine the sugar, milk, and butter in a large saucepan.
- Cook over medium heat until mixture comes to a boil, stirring constantly.
- Boil 10 minutes, stirring constantly. Remove from heat after the 10 minutes.
- Add chocolate morsels and the marshmallow cream. Stirring until melted.
- Stir in coffee mixture, pecans, orange rind and the orange and brandy extracts. Mix well.
- Spread mixture evenly in a well-buttered 13 x 9 x 2-inch pan.
- Cover and chill.
- Cut into squares.
- Store in refrigerator.
- Yields: 2 3/4 pounds

62. Chocolate Caramel Walnut Fudge Recipe

Serving: 1 | Prep: | Cook: 5mins | Ready in:

Ingredients

- Yield: 2 pounds
- 3 cups semisweet chocolate morsels
- 1 14-ounce can condensed milk
- 1/8 teaspoon salt
- 1 cup chopped walnuts
- 1/2 cup caramel ice cream topping
- 1-1/2 teaspoons vanilla extract

Direction

- Line an 8x8-inch baking pan with aluminum foil; spray lightly with non-stick vegetable spray.
- In a large saucepan, combine chocolate morsels, condensed milk, and salt. Heat, stirring constantly, until chocolate melts. Remove from heat. Stir in walnuts, caramel topping, and vanilla. Spread evenly in prepared baking pan. Chill for 2 hours or until firm.
- Invert onto a cutting board; peel off foil. Cut into squares.

63. Chocolate Cherry Sweets Recipe

Serving: 24 | Prep: | Cook: 240mins | Ready in:

Ingredients

- 1 cup semi-sweet chocolate chips
- 1/3 cup evaporated milk
- 1 1/2 cups sifted powdered sugar
- 1/3 cup chopped nuts
- 1/3 cup chopped maraschino cherries, well drained
- 1 1/4 cups coconut or chopped nuts

Direction

- Melt chocolate and milk over low heat.
- Remove from heat.
- Stir in powdered sugar, nuts and cherries, mix well.
- Chill until cool enough to handle.
- Shape into 1-inch balls and roll in nuts or coconut.
- Chill at least 4 hours.
- Keep chilled till time to serve.

64. Chocolate Chip Cookie Brittle Recipe

Serving: 48 | Prep: | Cook: 20mins | Ready in:

Ingredients

- 1 cup (2 sticks) softened butter
- 1 teaspoon salt

- 2 cups all-purpose flour
- 1 1/2 teaspoons vanilla
- 1 cup granulated sugar
- 1 cup semi-sweet chocolate chips

Direction

- Preheat oven to 350 degrees.
- In a large mixing bowl, cream together softened butter, vanilla, and salt.
- Add granulated sugar and mix well.
- Add flour and stir until well-blended.
- Mix in chocolate chips until thoroughly combined.
- Press evenly into ungreased baking sheet.
- Bake for approximately 20 minutes or until lightly browned.
- Remove from oven and cool completely.
- Break into irregular pieces.
- May substitute peanut butter chips, milk chocolate chips, or white chocolate chips for variation.
- Store in tightly-covered container.

65. Chocolate Coated Macaroon Balls Recipe

Serving: 54 | Prep: | Cook: 5mins | Ready in:

Ingredients

- BALLS:
- 2 1/2 cups powdered sugar
- 2 1/2 cups flaked coconut
- 3 tablespoons milk
- COATING:
- 1 cup chocolate chips
- 1/4 cup corn syrup
- 2 tablespoons shortening

Direction

- In large bowl, combine powdered sugar and coconut. Gradually stir in milk.
- Knead mixture on powdered sugar-dusted surface for 1-2 minutes or until smooth.
- Roll mixture into 3/4" balls.
- Refrigerate balls while preparing coating.
- In small saucepan over low heat, melt coating ingredients, stirring constantly. Remove from heat.
- Set saucepan in pan of warm water to maintain dipping consistency.
- Insert toothpick in ball; dip in melted chocolate. Place balls on waxed paper-lined cookie sheet or insert toothpicks in piece of Styrofoam.
- Refrigerate balls 15 minutes or until chocolate is set. Place in candy cup papers. Store in fridge.
- Makes 54.

66. Chocolate Covered Cherries Recipe

Serving: 24 | Prep: | Cook: 5mins | Ready in:

Ingredients

- 2 cups powdered sugar
- 1/4 cup butter
- 1/4 cup sweetened condensed milk
- 1 teaspoon vanilla or 1/2 teaspoon almond extract
- 1 pinch salt
- 10 ounce jar of maraschino cherries, drained
- 12 ounce bag chocolate chips

Direction

- Combine the first 5 ingredients until well blended and smooth and place in fridge until firm.
- Meanwhile spread out the drained cherries on a cookie sheet and freeze for at least 1 hours.
- Scoop out about 1-2 teaspoon of filling and form into a ball, flatten it and form around a cherry.

- Place on a wax paper lined cookie sheet and freeze for 1 hr. after you have formed them all.
- Melt chocolate and using a small fork dip each cherry placing it on a wax paper or foil lined cookie sheet and chill in fridge until chocolate is solid.
- Remove cherries carefully as not to break them open and lose the center.
- Place in an airtight plastic container and keep in a cool dry place for up to 1 month.

67. Chocolate Covered Easter Eggs Recipe

Serving: 48 | Prep: | Cook: 150mins | Ready in:

Ingredients

- ·1/2 cup butter, softened
- ·1 teaspoon vanilla extract
- ·1 (8 ounce) package cream cheese, softened
- ·2 1/2 pounds confectioners' sugar
- ·1 cup creamy peanut butter (optional)
- ·1 cup flaked coconut (optional)
- ·1 cup unsweetened cocoa powder (optional)
- 1 cup chopped dried cherries (optional)
- ·2 cups semisweet chocolate pieces
- ·2 tablespoons shortening or vegetable oil (optional)

Direction

- In a large bowl, mix together the butter, vanilla, and cream cheese. Stir in confectioners' sugar to make a workable dough. For best results, use your hands for mixing.
- Divide the dough into four parts. Leave one of the parts plain. To the second part, mix in peanut butter. Mix coconut into the third part, and cocoa powder into the last part. Roll each type of dough into egg shapes, and place on a waxed paper lined cookie sheet. Refrigerate until hard, at least an hour.
- Melt chocolate chips in a heat-proof bowl over a pan of simmering water. Stir occasionally until smooth. If the chocolate seems too thick for coating, stir in some of the shortening or oil until it thins. Dip the chilled candy eggs in chocolate, and return to the waxed paper lined sheet to set. Refrigerate for 1/2 hour to harden.

68. Chocolate Cream Cheese Fudge Recipe

Serving: 14 | Prep: | Cook: 20mins | Ready in:

Ingredients

- 4 squares unsweetened chocolate
- 8 oz. cream cheese
- 4 cups confectioners' sugar
- 1-1/2 tsps. vanilla extract
- Note: Instead of vanilla extract I add liqueur ie. Baileys or Frangelico or whatever.
- 1/2 cup pecans or walnuts, chopped

Direction

- Melt chocolate in microwave, then cool to room temperature.
- With cream cheese at room temperature, mix cream cheese with melted chocolate.
- Add confectioners' sugar and vanilla extract.
- Pour into an 8 x 8 inch pan.
- Refrigerate for a couple of hours before cutting.
- If you want to add a peanut butter flavour, add 1/2 cup peanut butter and increase sugar to 5 cups.

69. Chocolate Dipped Caramallows Recipe

Serving: 70 | Prep: | Cook: | Ready in:

Ingredients

- FOR THE caramel LAYERS
- vegetable oil cooking spray
- 4 cups heavy cream
- 4 cups sugar
- 2 cups light corn syrup
- 6 ounces (1 1/2 sticks) unsalted butter
- 1 1/2 teaspoons salt
- 1 teaspoon pure vanilla extract
- FOR THE marshmallow LAYER
- 2 1/2 teaspoons unflavored gelatin (one 1/4 ounce envelope)
- 1/3 cup plus 1/4 cup cold water
- 1 cup sugar
- salt
- FOR FINISHING candies
- Tempered chocolate
- White nonpareils, for sprinkling

Direction

- Make first caramel layer: Coat a rimmed baking sheet with cooking spray. Line with parchment, leaving a 2-inch overhang on 2 sides, then coat parchment with spray.
- Place 2 cups cream, 2 cups sugar, 1 cup corn syrup, and 6 tablespoons butter in a large pot. Bring to a boil, stirring until sugar dissolves and butter melts, about 5 minutes. Cook over medium heat, stirring often, until mixture registers 245 degrees on a candy thermometer, about 20 minutes. Remove pot from heat, and stir in 3/4 teaspoon salt and 1/2 teaspoon vanilla. Pour into prepared pan without scraping bottom of pot. Let stand.
- Make the marshmallow layer: Sprinkle gelatine over 1/3 cup water in a mixer bowl, and let soften, about 5 minutes.
- Mix sugar and remaining cup water in a small saucepan over medium-high heat, stirring until sugar dissolves. Wash down sides of pan with a wet pastry brush to prevent sugar crystals from forming. Cook, undisturbed, until mixture registers 238 degrees on a candy thermometer, about 10 minutes. (You may have to tilt pan to get an accurate read.) Remove pan from heat, and whisk sugar syrup and a pinch of salt into gelatine. Pour into a mixer bowl, and whisk on medium-high until cool and thick, about 10 minutes. Spread marshmallow evenly over caramel to cover, and let stand for 30 minutes.
- Prepare second caramel layer with remaining ingredients as in step 2. Pour over marshmallow layer, covering entire surface, and let stand, uncovered, until set, about 8 hours.
- Using a 1 1/4-inch round cutter, cut out 70 rounds. Using a fork, dunk each round in chocolate. Scrape bottom of fork against edge of bowl to remove excess, and place dipped candies on a parchment-lined baking sheet. Sprinkle nonpareils on top, and let stand until set. Caramallows will keep, covered and refrigerated, for up to 5 days
- Helpful Hint
- These indulgent treats include two caramel layers, and each layer must be made separately at different times. Start the second one after the marshmallow layer has set on top of the caramel.

70. Chocolate Filled Strawberries Recipe

Serving: 1 | Prep: | Cook: 15mins | Ready in:

Ingredients

- You will need:
- Punnet of strawberries
- milk or dark chocolate chips

Direction

- 1. Cut the stems off your washed strawberries and scoop out the center of the berry.
- 2. In a glass bowl, heat the chocolate chips in the microwave, stirring every 30 seconds until completely melted.
- 3. Spoon/pipe the melted chocolate into the strawberries - you can use an egg carton to hold them upright.

- 4. Place in the refrigerator for about 10 minutes until they harden a bit. Enjoy!

71. Chocolate Marshmallow Cashew Fudge Recipe

Serving: 6 | Prep: | Cook: 40mins | Ready in:

Ingredients

- 2 cups sugar
- 4 Tbsp cocoa powder
- 1 cup milk
- 1 Tbsp butter
- Dash of salt (not needed if you use salted cashews)
- 1 tsp vanilla essence
- 10 large or 25 miniature marshmallows (white or colored)
- 4 oz cashews, crushed into large pieces
- veg oil

Direction

- Oil a cookie sheet with the veg oil (for thin fudge) or a square jelly roll or cake pan (for thicker fudge)
- In a saucepan combine the sugar, cocoa powder and milk
- Cook to the soft ball stage*
- *Bring to a rapid boil, stirring occasionally. Boil until the mixture becomes the thickness of thin pudding. The mixture will be foamy. Put a drop on a cold saucer and wait for a few minutes. When mixture on plate is shiny and doesn't stick to your finger, it's ready. Don't give up. Keep boiling! It will be thin for a while but will thicken up eventually. Be patient!
- Turn down the heat to very low and stir in the butter. This will immediately cut the foam and make the mixture shiny.
- Stir in the salt (if you are using unsalted nuts) and vanilla.
- Stir in the marshmallows. You can melt them completely or not. It's up to you. I melt the large ones, but don't melt the miniatures.
- Stir in the nut pieces.
- Turn off the heat and pour QUICKLY into the prepared pan. Make sure you use a wooden spatula to scrape and spread the fudge.
- Allow to cool before cutting or breaking into squares.

72. Chocolate Mint Candy Recipe

Serving: 12 | Prep: | Cook: 10mins | Ready in:

Ingredients

- 10 squares of semi-sweet chocolate baking bar (1oz each)
- 1 can of Eagle Brand sweetened condensed milk
- 2 Tsp of vanilla extract
- 1 package of White baking chocolate 170 grams
- 1 TB peppermint extract
- 4-6 drops of green food coloring

Direction

- Melt the semi-sweet chocolate chips with one cup of the Eagle Brand milk in the microwave for one minute, stir to blend.
- Remove from microwave and stir in vanilla extract
- Spread half of the mixture into a parchment paper-lined 8 inch square pan.
- Chill in the refrigerator until firm for 10 minutes.
- Keep the remaining semi-sweet chocolate at room temperature!
- Melt the white chocolate in remaining Eagle Brand in microwave for one minute. Stir to blend.
- Stir in Peppermint extract and food coloring. You can add more color if you want a deeper green color. The color is up to you!

- Spread over the chilled semi-sweet chocolate layer.
- Chill for 10 minutes in the refrigerator.
- Spread the reserved semi-sweet chocolate over the mint layer.
- Chill again but for 2 full hours or until solid to the touch.
- Lift from pan and peel off paper.
- Cut into squares and serve!

73. Chocolate Mint Fudge Recipe

Serving: 12 | Prep: | Cook: 10mins | Ready in:

Ingredients

- 1 cup milk chocolate chips
- 1 cup semisweet chocolate morsels
- 1 cup green mint flavored chocolate chips
- 14 ounce can sweetened condensed milk
- 1 cup chopped walnuts
- 1 teaspoon vanilla extract

Direction

- Line square baking pan with foil.
- Combine milk chocolate and semisweet morsels and milk in medium heavy duty saucepan.
- Warm over lowest possible heat stirring until smooth.
- Remove from heat then stir in nuts and vanilla extract.
- Put mint chips over warmed mixture and spread evenly.
- Spread evenly into prepared pan the refrigerate 2 hours or until form.
- Lift from pan then remove foil and cut into pieces.

74. Chocolate Orange Truffles Recipe

Serving: 0 | Prep: | Cook: 5mins | Ready in:

Ingredients

- 1/3 cup whipping cream
- 2 tablespoons unsalted butter
- 1 1/2 tablespoons orange flavoring
- 8 ounces bittersweet chocolate, broken into chunks
- cocoa powder
- 6 ounces bittersweet chocolate
- 2 tablespoons solid vegetable shortening

Direction

- 1. Heat the whipping cream and butter together just to a simmer, then add chocolate. Remove from heat while chocolate melts. Add flavoring. Stir until glossy and pour into a chilled bowl. Set aside until firm.
- 2. Once firm, use a small melon baller and scoop ganache out. Roll by hand, using cocoa powder to reduce stickiness. Chill until firm.
- 3. Melt 6 ounces bittersweet chocolate with 2 tablespoons solid vegetable shortening in the microwave for about 1 minute. Stir until melted; microwave additional seconds as needed. Drop each ball individually into chocolate, roll with a fork until coated, then use the fork to lift out and place on parchment paper. Chill and keep refrigerated.

75. Chocolate Peanut Butter Cake Eggs Recipe

Serving: 15 | Prep: | Cook: 2hours | Ready in:

Ingredients

- 1 recipe for a single-layer chocolate cake, baked (I used a half batch of chocolate-cake.html">One Bowl chocolate cake)

- 245g smooth peanut butter (don't use natural), warmed slightly
- pinch sea salt
- bittersweet chocolate, for dipping

Direction

- Crumble the cake into a bowl and allow to dry out at room temperature overnight.
- Stir in the peanut butter and salt, "mashing" the mixture with a spatula until "doughy".
- Scoop out 15 balls of the mixture and shape into eggs.
- Place on a tray or plate and freeze until solid.
- Melt the bittersweet chocolate in a double boiler or microwave and dip the eggs to coat.
- Allow to harden completely at room temperature.

76. Chocolate Peanut Butter Fudge Recipe

Serving: 12 | Prep: | Cook: 10mins | Ready in:

Ingredients

- 2 cups semisweet chocolate morsels
- 14 ounce can sweetened condensed milk
- 1 cup peanut butter chips
- 1 cup chopped peanuts
- 1 teaspoon vanilla extract

Direction

- Line square baking pan with foil.
- Combine chocolate morsels and milk in medium heavy duty saucepan.
- Warm over lowest possible heat stirring until smooth.
- Remove from heat then stir in nuts and vanilla extract.
- Spread peanut butter chips over top and spread.
- Spread evenly into prepared pan the refrigerate 2 hours or until form.
- Lift from pan then remove foil and cut into pieces.

77. Chocolate Peanut Sweeties Recipe

Serving: 60 | Prep: | Cook: | Ready in:

Ingredients

- 1 cup peanut butter
- 1/2 cup butter-softened
- 3 cups confectioners' sugar
- 60 miniature pretzels(about 3 cups)
- 1 1/2 cups milk chocolate chips
- 1 tablespoon shortening

Direction

- In a small mixing bowl, beat peanut butter and butter until smooth.
- Beat in confectioners' sugar until combined.
- Shape into 1" balls. Press on each pretzel.
- Place on waxed paper lined baking sheets. Refrigerate until peanut butter is set.
- In a microwave safe bowl or heavy saucepan, melt chocolate chips and shortening, stirring until smooth.
- Dip peanut butter balls into chocolate. Return to baking sheet. Pretzel side down.
- Refrigerate at least 30 minutes before serving.
- Store in an airtight container in the refrigerator.

78. Chocolate Raspberry Truffles Recipe

Serving: 12 | Prep: | Cook: 60mins | Ready in:

Ingredients

- 1/2 cup heavy cream

- 12 ounces of semi-sweet chocolate, chopped fine
- 1/4 cup unsalted butter, cut into bits and softened
- 1/2 cup seedless red raspberry jam
- 2 tablespoons Chambord
- pinch of salt
- 1/2 cup sifted unsweetened cocoa powder

Direction

- In a saucepan bring cream just to a boil over medium heat.
- Remove the pan from the heat.
- Add the chocolate.
- Stir the mixture until chocolate is melted completely and mixture is smooth.
- Let the mixture cool slightly and then add butter, bit by bit.
- Stir the mixture until it is smooth.
- Stir in the jam, the Chambord and a pinch of salt.
- Transfer mixture to bowl.
- Chill it, covered, for 4 hours. or until it is firm.
- Make teaspoon sized balls out of the mixture and roll the balls in the cocoa powder.
- Chill the truffles on a baking sheet lined with wax paper for 1 hour or until they are firm.
- Keep them in an airtight container, chilled, for 2 weeks.
- Makes about 40 truffles

79. Chocolate Truffles Recipe

Serving: 10 | Prep: | Cook: 45mins | Ready in:

Ingredients

- 150g dark cooking chocolate, melted
- 1 can x 170g Cream
- 175g cake crumbs
- 1/2 cup ground almonds
- chocolate vermicelli or cocoa powder to finish

Direction

- Melt the chocolate in a medium bowl over a medium saucepan a quarter full of simmering water, while stirring
- Allow the melted chocolate to cool slightly, then fold in the cream and mix until smooth
- Gradually add the cake crumbs and ground almonds, stirring continuously. Then chill for 30 - 45 minutes
- Divide the mixture into 20-25 pieces and roll into balls.
- Take the balls and roll them in the chocolate vermicelli or cocoa powder then place in petit four cases
- After you roll the mixture you can open a whole and add nuts, hazelnuts, cherries, a piece of orange etc. or have them plain then roll them in the cocoa or the vermicelli chocolate, or roll them in nuts. Use your imagination and taste.
- Serve these truffles with coffee or pack them into pretty boxes to give as presents.

80. Chocolate Peanut Butter Truffles Recipe

Serving: 18 | Prep: | Cook: 1mins | Ready in:

Ingredients

- 8 (1 ounce) squares Semi-Sweet baking chocolate
- 1/2 cup peanut butter
- 1 (8 ounce) tub Cool Whip, thawed
- *Suggested coatings, such as powdered sugar, unsweetened cocoa, finely chopped peanuts, multi-colored sprinkles, coconut, finely crushed cookies or Semi-Sweet baking chocolate

Direction

- Microwave chocolate in large microwaveable bowl on HIGH 2 min. or until chocolate is almost melted, stirring every 30 sec. Stir until chocolate is completely melted.

- Add peanut butter; stir until well blended.
- Cool to room temperature. Gently stir in whipped topping. Refrigerate 2 hours.
- Scoop truffle mixture with melon baller or teaspoon, then roll into 1-inch balls.
- Roll in suggested coatings.
- Store in tightly covered container in refrigerator.

81. Chocolate Coconut Candiesmounds Like Recipe

Serving: 5 | Prep: | Cook: 15mins | Ready in:

Ingredients

- (Candy)….
- 3/4C. mashed potatoes (Homemade are the best.. NO spices or milk..
- Just Plain potatoes!!
- 1 Pound flaked coconut
- 1 Pound Confectioners sugar
- 1t. vanilla or almond extract (I'm allergic to almonds that are
- Concentrated in any way)!
- (Coating)….
- 1 16 oz. bag semi-sweet chocolate chips
- 1/8 bar of paraffin (for added glossiness)
- Melted in double boiler….

Direction

- Candy)
- Mix all ingredients together.
- Drop by heaping teaspoons onto waxed paper (refrigerate for an hour if you cannot roll into balls.)
- Roll into balls and refrigerate until firm and can withstand dipping.
- (I usually refrigerate twice before rolling and after rolling. I've even covered and left over night after rolling then dipped the next day.)
- (Coating)
- In a double boiler melt chocolate and paraffin to smooth & glossy.

- Dip, making sure all sides are covered. I use a fork then let set-up. Can put in chill chest at this point. Even overnight. These candies freeze very well and are first sellers at craft shows and bake sales.
- Remember. Warn people that there is Coconut in these!!! Enjoy!!!!

82. Chocolate Coconut Truffles Recipe

Serving: 48 | Prep: | Cook: 10mins | Ready in:

Ingredients

- 1 cup (2 sticks) real butter, softened
- 1 pound confectioner's sugar
- 1/2 can sweetened condensed milk
- 1 11-ounce package shredded coconut
- 1 cup chopped pecans (optional)
- 1/2 teaspoon vanilla extract
- 1/4 bar paraffin wax
- 1 16-ounce package semi-sweet chocolate chips
- waxed paper

Direction

- In large mixing bowl, combine softened butter, confectioner's sugar, sweetened condensed milk, coconut, and vanilla, and chopped pecans, if desired. Mix until well blended.
- Refrigerate until firm enough to form balls. (Approximately 1 hour)
- Roll into small balls and place on waxed-paper lined baking sheet.
- Chill once again until firm.
- In double-boiler, melt paraffin wax and chocolate chips until melted and smooth.
- Dip coconut balls into chocolate mixture using toothpicks and place on waxed paper to set.
- May sprinkle additional coconut on top as garnish!
- Refrigerate in plastic container with lid.

- We make several layers with waxed paper to prevent sticking together.
- These also freeze well!

83. Chocolate Dipped Peanut Butter Balls Recipe

Serving: 36 | Prep: | Cook: 15mins | Ready in:

Ingredients

- 4 1/4 cups confectioners' sugar
- 2 cups creamy peanut butter
- 1 stick (4 ounces) unsalted butter, at room temperature
- 3 cups crisp puffed rice cereal
- 12 ounces semisweet chocolate, coarsely chopped
- 12 ounces milk chocolate, coarsely chopped
- 2 tablespoons vegetable oil

Direction

- Have ready several large baking sheets lined with parchment paper.
- In a large bowl, using an electric mixer on low speed or by hand, combine the confectioners' sugar, peanut butter and butter until well blended. Add the puffed rice cereal and mix well. Using your hands, form the mixture into walnut-size balls (about 1 generous tablespoon each) and place them on a tray. Cover and refrigerate for about 1 hour, or until firm.
- Melt the chocolates in a bowl set over a saucepan of barely boiling water or in the microwave. Add the oil and stir until smooth. Using a fork and working with 1 chilled peanut butter ball at a time, dip the balls into the melted chocolate mixture, rolling to coat evenly. Shake off any excess chocolate and transfer to the lined baking sheets. Set aside for at least 2 hours to set.
- The peanut butter balls can sit for as long as 8 hours at room temperature before serving.

Refrigerate in an airtight container for up to 2 weeks.
- A variation I found that looks yummy as well!
- Ingredients:
- 2 c. crushed graham crackers
- 2 c. powdered sugar
- 2 c. peanut butter (creamy or chunky, your choice)
- 1/4 c. butter (barely melted in the microwave)
- Dipping chocolate
- Mix together the first 4 ingredients as you would a pie crust. Chill in the fridge for at least 1 hour.
- Melt the dipping chocolate. Roll peanut butter mixture into small balls, and dip into the chocolate. Allow to set on wax paper. Chill until served.

84. Christmas Cracker Candy Recipe

Serving: 4 | Prep: | Cook: 12mins | Ready in:

Ingredients

- 1/4 lb saltine crackers
- 1/2 lb (2 sticks; 1 cup) butter
- 1 cup sugar
- 12 oz white chocolate chips
- 1/2 cup finely chopped pistachio nuts
- Red and green sugar crystals, opt.

Direction

- Preheat oven to 350 degrees. Line a large cookie sheet (with sides) with saltine crackers, having edges touching. In a medium saucepan, melt butter and sugar together. Bring to low boil, and simmer until mixture is white and frothy. Pour butter mixture over saltines, using a spatula to spread and cover all crackers. Bake 10 minutes or until golden brown. Remove from oven and sprinkle chips over crackers. Return baking sheet to oven for 1-2 minutes until chips soften. Remove from oven and spread white chocolate evenly over saltines. Sprinkle with nuts, and if desired, red and green sugar crystals. Refrigerate or freeze until hard. Break into small pieces.

85. Christmas Gift Chocolate Fudge Recipe

Serving: 5 | Prep: | Cook: |Ready in:

Ingredients

- 4-1/2 C sugar
- 1-2/3 C evaporated milk
- 1/2 pound butter or margarine
- 3- 6 oz pkgs semi-sweet chocolate pieces
- 1 Tbsp vanilla
- **1- 8 oz jar marshmallow crème
- 2 C nuts
- **Can substitute with 2 C mini mallows or 31 large mallows

Direction

- "Combine sugar, milk & butter in a deep saucepan.
- Cook to softball stage, stirring constantly & scraping sugar crystals from sides of pan; 9 min.
- Remove from heat.
- Stir in chocolate until partially melted, blend in vanilla & marshmallow.
- Stir in nuts.
- Turn into buttered 9" x 13"x 2" pan.
- Cool.
- Refrigerate for 3 to 4 hours or overnight.
- Cut in squares.

86. Christmas Rum Balls Recipe

Serving: 15 | Prep: | Cook: |Ready in:

Ingredients

- 225g arrow root or rich tea biscuits crushed.
- 1.5 cups/75g Rice Krispies or Cornflakes
- 2 tbsps /20g cocoa
- 3 tbsp /20g rum
- 1 tsp cinnamon
- 1 tsp mixed spice (all spice)
- 1.5 cups /150g mixed fruit
- 1 cup /75g shredded/desiccated coconut
- 1 x 395g can sweetened condensed milk
- ice with white icing and red and green sweets.

Direction

- Crush the biscuits- I put them in a large bowl and bash them with the end of a rolling pin. Then crumble the big bits with my hands.
- Add the Rice Krispies, cocoa, spices and coconut. Mix.
- In a separate bowl mix the rum and the mixed fruit. (Leaving it for a while is best so the fruit absorbs the rum). Then add to the dry ingredients.
- Mix everything well and add condensed milk.
- Mix well until all coated.
- Roll into balls using wet hands.
- Makes 20 good-sized rum-balls.
- No cooking required!
- These are best kept for a few days or even a couple of weeks (yes!) Store in an air tight container in the fridge and decorate when needed.
- Decorate with white icing sugar (mixed with a little water) and red and green sweets.
- Happy Christmas!

87. Christmas Strawberries Recipe

Serving: 60 | Prep: | Cook: |Ready in:

Ingredients

- 1 pkg. shredded coconut
- 5 oz. walnuts (about 1-1/4 cups)

- 14 oz. can sweetened condensed milk 2 Tbsp. sugar
- 1 (3 oz. pkg.) strawberry Jell-O ®
- red and green colored sugars

Direction

- In a food processor or blender mix together coconut and nuts. Place in large mixing bowl.
- Combine dry Jell-O ®, sugar and milk. Pour over coconut mixture. Mix well.
- Take about a teaspoon of mixture and shape into a strawberry. (I roll in a ball first then shape) The trick to these is to not make them too big or it will take away the strawberry effect.
- Gently roll in red sugar, then dip top of strawberry into green sugar. Place on a waxed paper covered cookie sheet to dry overnight.
- Store in airtight container. These freeze well.
- Makes about 5 or 6 dozen.
- * Note* these are sticky. Wet hands a bit before shaping.

88. Cobblestone Candy Recipe

Serving: 123 | Prep: | Cook: 10mins | Ready in:

Ingredients

- 3-6 ounce packages of semi-sweet chocolate morsel (3 cups)
- 2 cups miniature marshmallows
- 1 cup coarsely chopped nuts; walnut, pecan, peanut, macadamia

Direction

- Melt the semi-sweet morsels in a double boiler.
- Stir until melted and smooth.
- Add marshmallows and nuts.
- Line an 8-inch square pan with aluminum foil.
- Turn chocolate mixture onto the foil-lined pan.
- Let stand until firm.
- Cut into squares.
- Makes 1-2/3 pounds candy.

89. Coconut Bon Bons Recipe

Serving: 4 | Prep: | Cook: | Ready in:

Ingredients

- 15 oz sweetened condensed milk
- 1/2 c butter, or margarine
- 2 c confectioners' sugar
- 12 oz coconut, grated dried
- 24 oz Semi-sweet chocolate
- 4 tb shortening

Direction

- Mix together condensed milk, butter, sugar and coconut.
- Cover with wax paper and chill for 24 hours.
- Melt chocolate with shortening.
- Roll coconut mixture into balls and using a fork dip the balls into the chocolate.
- Drop on wax paper to cool and dry.

90. Coconut Bon Bons My Way Recipe

Serving: 12 | Prep: | Cook: | Ready in:

Ingredients

- 1 pound flaked coconut
- 1 can Eagle Brand sweetened condensed milk
- 1 pound powdered sugar
- 1/4 cup butter, melted
- whole almonds (optional) for those who like Almond Joy's
- Syrup:
- 3 packages (6 ounces each) chocolate chips
- 1/4 pound paraffin wax

Direction

- Combine coconut, milk, powdered sugar and butter. Roll into balls; (this is where you can place an Almond on each ball and press enough to stick) chill 4 hours.
- Combine chips and paraffin in double boiler. Dip balls into chocolate mixture. Place on wax paper to dry.

91. Coconut Candy Recipe

Serving: 20 | Prep: | Cook: 25mins | Ready in:

Ingredients

- 2 cups superfine white sugar
- 1 1/2 cups light corn syrup
- 2 TBSP. water
- 6 cups shredded coconut
- 2 TBSP. whipped cream
- 1 TBSP. butter

Direction

- Line a 13 x 9 inch baking pan with foil, extending foil over the edges of pan.
- Butter foil; set aside
- In a heavy large saucepan or Dutch oven; combine sugar, corn syrup, and water.
- Cook and stir over medium heat until the sugar dissolves and the mixture starts to boil
- Stir in coconut.
- Clip a candy thermometer to the side of the pan
- Cook over medium high heat until the mixture reaches 238'F
- Coconut should be lightly golden
- Stir in cream
- Continue cooking till mixture again reaches 238'F
- Stir in butter
- Pour into prepared pan. Cool slightly
- Fluff with a fork, cool. Cut candy into squares
- Wrap in waxed paper. DO NOT stack the candy

92. Coconut Creams Recipe

Serving: 24 | Prep: | Cook: 90mins | Ready in:

Ingredients

- 3 oz. cream cheese, softened
- 1/3 c. powdered sugar
- 1 tsp. vanilla
- 1 c. coconut
- 1/2 c. chopped nuts
- 12 oz. semi-sweet chocolate chips

Direction

- ***Cook time includes chill time***
- Mix all ingredients together except chocolate. Chill 1 hour.
- Shape into small balls.
- Melt chocolate in double-boiler or metal (or glass) bowl set over pan of simmering water. Do not get water in the chocolate! Dip centers in the chocolate on place on waxed paper to set.
- Keep in airtight container in the fridge for up to one week.

93. Coconut Curry Macadamia Nuts Recipe

Serving: 12 | Prep: | Cook: 30mins | Ready in:

Ingredients

- 1-1/2 teaspoons ground ginger
- 1-1/2 teaspoons ground cumin
- 1-1/2 tablespoons curry powder
- 1/2 teaspoon cayenne pepper
- 1/4 cup firmly packed dark brown sugar
- 3/4 teaspoon kosher salt

- 2 egg whites
- 5 cups macadamia nuts
- 1 cup sweetened coconut flakes

Direction

- Preheat oven to 300.
- Combine ginger, cumin, curry powder, cayenne, brown sugar and salt then set aside.
- Beat egg whites with small whisk until frothy then whisk in reserve spice mix.
- Stir in nuts and coconut then spread in a single layer onto 2 lightly greased baking sheets.
- Bake stirring nuts and rotating pans halfway through cooking for 25 minutes.
- Transfer to parchment paper to cool then store in airtight container at room temperature.

94. Coconut Fudge Recipe

Serving: 24 | Prep: | Cook: 7mins | Ready in:

Ingredients

- 1 12 oz can evaporated milk
- 4 1/2 cups sugar
- 2 tablespoons butter, sweet
- 1 1/2 -2 pounds white chocolate
- 2 cups marshmallow creme
- 1 - 1 1/2 cups coconut

Direction

- Bring milk and sugar, butter to a boil in a large saucepan, over medium heat.
- Reduce heat and cook for 7 minutes.
- Remove from heat stir in chocolate until melted then stir in marshmallow and fold in coconut spread in large shallow pan and cut into squares. I use an 8 x8 pan.

95. Coconut Kisses Recipe

Serving: 6 | Prep: | Cook: 5mins | Ready in:

Ingredients

- 1 cup skimmed powdered milk
- 1/2 cup water
- 2 tbsp margarine
- 1/2 cup skimmed milk
- 3/4 cup dessicated coconut
- 1 dsp cornflour
- 4 tbsp cooking powdered sweetener
- Dessicated coconut to roll
- cloves

Direction

- In a blender, mix well the powdered milk, water, margarine, milk, coconut and cornflour.
- Pour into a pan.
- Cook, mixing all the time, until you can see the pan bottom.
- Add the sweetener.
- Pour onto a lightly greased plate.
- Let it cool.
- Mould little "balls" the size of a small walnut.
- Roll in the coconut to coat.
- Stick a clove on top of each.
- Put on small paper cases and serve.

96. Coconut Patties Recipe

Serving: 18 | Prep: | Cook: 10mins | Ready in:

Ingredients

- 1 1/4 C Confectioners sugar
- 1/2 C unsalted butter, cut into small pieces
- 1 egg white
- 1/8 tsp salt
- 1 1/4 C coconut , packed (sweetened or unsweetened)
- 1 1/2 tsp vanilla

- 4 ounce semi-sweet or milk chocolate (I found that 4 wasn't enough & would recommend 8 oz just to be safe)

Direction

- Make the coconut filling: In a medium heatproof bowl set over a pan of simmering water, whisk together the confectioner's sugar, butter, egg white and salt until very liquid and warm to the touch, about 10 minutes.
- Remove from heat and, with a spoon, stir in the coconut and vanilla until well combined. Cover with plastic wrap and refrigerate for 1 to 2 hours, up to overnight.
- When ready to coat the coconut, in a small heatproof bowl set over a pan of simmering water melt the chocolate. When almost melted, turn off the heat and let the chocolate continue to melt completely, stirring occasionally. Keep the bowl over the warm water. If you are using milk chocolate, you will need to add 1 tsp. of vegetable oil while melting.
- Form the balls: Line a small tray with parchment paper. Using a scant ounce of the coconut mixture, roll into a small ball and place on the parchment-paper lined tray. (I used a small scoop to form the balls, to ensure they were uniform in size). Repeat with remaining mixture, forming 18 balls.
- Arrange 18 paper or foil mini-cups on the tray. Gently place one of the balls into the warm melted chocolate and, using two forks, roll the ball in the chocolate until well coated. Life (do not pierce) the coated coconut ball with one of the forks, allowing some of the chocolate to drip back into the bowl, and carefully place in one of the prepared cups. Repeat with the remaining coconut balls and melted chocolate. Refrigerate until the chocolate has hardened and use as desired.
- To Prepare ahead: the rounds can be prepared ahead and will keep for at least 1 week, refrigerated in a covered container.
- I would refrigerate for 1/2 hour or so until they are firm to the touch. The heat from my hands made these soft when I rolled them and it was semi-disastrous when trying to roll them in chocolate. Also, I place just a tad bit of coconut on top, I think it's a little preview of what the eater can expect to find inside. I'm not sure why these are called patties, as they are clearly balls, but I'm sure they would be good too if you gave them a bit of a smush. Or you can make these into a square pan cool and coat in chocolate. To make the real patties.

97. Copycat Pay Day Candy Bars Recipe

Serving: 8 | Prep: | Cook: 30mins | Ready in:

Ingredients

- Copycat Pay Day Candy Bars
- ~~~~~~~~~~~~~~~~~~~~~~~~~~~~~~~
- Level (estimated) Intermediate to Advanced
- ~~~~~~~~~~~~~~~~~~~~~~~~~~~~~~~
- 5 caramel squares
- 1/4 cup milk
- 1 teaspoon peanut butter
- 1 tablespoon corn syrup
- 1/2 teaspoon vanilla
- 1/2 teaspoon salt
- 1 1/4 cups powdered sugar
- 20 caramel squares
- 1 tablespoon water
- 2 cups dry roasted peanuts (slightly crushed)

Direction

- Combine the first six ingredients in a sauce pan.
- Cook over low heat until the caramel has melted and stirs smooth. Add 3/4 cup powdered sugar and stir to mix in. Reserve the remaining sugar.
- Turn heat to medium high. Using a candy thermometer, cook caramel mixture until exactly 230F while stirring often.

- Remove from heat, let cool for a few minutes, and add remaining powdered sugar. Use a hand mixer to beat in the sugar for a couple minutes. Let candy cool for 20 minutes. Divide candy into eight equal pieces and form each into 4 inch logs.
- Place on wax paper and let cool for one hour.
- In a double boiler, add remaining caramels and water.
- Melt until smooth. Remove from heat, but keep hot water under the caramel so it doesn't firm up.
- Use a pastry brush to coat one of the logs with hot caramel.
- Roll in peanuts in a shallow dish. If any spots are not completely covered in peanuts, apply more caramel and stick back in peanuts. Repeat with the remaining logs.
- Allow to cool completely before eating.

98. Cornflake Chewies Recipe

Serving: 20 | Prep: | Cook: 25mins | Ready in:

Ingredients

- 6 cups cornflakes (or 5-1/2 cups original Kellogg's Special K)
- 1 cup sugar
- 1 cup clear Karo, or other light corn syrup (actually Blackburn syrup tastes the best, if you can find it)
- 1 Tablespoon butter
- 1 tsp vanilla extract
- 1-1/4 cup smooth peanut butter (best is the kind you mix up yourself)

Direction

- Pour cornflakes into a big bowl. Lightly spray 13x9 casserole dish.
- If using unmixed peanut butter, spoon into bowl with 1 to 1-1/2 tablespoons sugar and mix with hand mixer.
- Combine sugar and syrup in small pot. Heat on low, stirring constantly, until sugar is melted.
- Remove from heat; stir in butter and vanilla.
- Add peanut butter and stir well.
- Pour mixture over cornflakes and stir gently until well coated.
- Spread in prepared dish.
- When completely cool, cut into squares.

99. Cotlets Recipe

Serving: 24 | Prep: | Cook: 20mins | Ready in:

Ingredients

- 2 envelopes unflavored gelatin
- 1 1/4 cups apricot juice, divided
- 2 cups sugar
- 1 tsp. vanilla
- 1 drop rose water
- 1 cup finely chopped walnuts
- powdered sugar

Direction

- Soak the gelatine in 1/2 cup apricot juice for 10 minutes.
- In a heavy saucepan, pour in remaining apricot juice and sugar and bring to a boil. Add gelatine mixture and boil for 15 minutes, stirring constantly. Remove from heat. Allow to cool 20 minutes. Then add vanilla, rose water and nuts. Stir well. Pour into a greased 11x7" pan. Cover and let set 48 hours before cutting into squares and rolling in powdered sugar.

100. County Fair Cream Candy Recipe

Serving: 6 | Prep: | Cook: 20mins | Ready in:

Ingredients

- 2 cups granulated sugar
- 3/4 cup sour cream
- 1/2 tsp vanilla extract WITH
- 1/4 tsp almond extract OR 1/4 tsp peppermint flavoring
- 1/2 cup broken nut meats
- 10 candied cherries, sliced

Direction

- In a 2-quart saucepan combine sugar and cream, stirring well. Place on heat, then continue stirring to dissolve sugar.
- Cover pan; bring mixture to a boil; cook 1 minute or until steam inside pan has melted all sugar crystals down from the sides.
- Remove cover; continue cooking without stirring over gentle heat to a soft-ball stage (235 degrees F), about 12 minutes.
- Let cool without stirring or moving until lukewarm (110 degrees F).
- Add flavoring, nutmeats and cherries.
- Stir-beat with heavy spoon until candy becomes creamy and loses its gloss, about 8 minutes.
- Pour into a lightly greased, 8-inch square pan.
- Cut while still warm.
- Makes about 1 pound.

101. Cranberry Candy Recipe

Serving: 50 | Prep: | Cook: 10mins | Ready in:

Ingredients

- 1 can jellied cranberry sauce
- 2 - 3 oz. packages of strawberry jello (or raspberry)
- 1 cup sugar
- 2/3 cup chopped pecans
- sugar

Direction

- Heat jellied cranberry sauce in medium saucepan until melted. Remove from heat and slowly add Jell-O until it is dissolved, then add sugar until it is dissolved. Heat to boiling for 2 minutes. Remove from heat and add pecans, stir well.
- Spray an 8"X8" pan lightly with Pam - don't use a flavored Pam. Pour in cranberry mixture and let it set for 12 hours on the counter in a cool place. Cut in 1" squares and roll in sugar - coating them well.
- Let them ripen for 2 days before eating.

102. Cream Cheese Fudge Recipe

Serving: 25 | Prep: | Cook: | Ready in:

Ingredients

- 1 - 3 oz. package cream cheese, softened
- 2 cups sifted confectioners sugar
- 1/4 tsp. vanilla flavoring
- a dash of salt
- 1/2 cup chopped pecans
- 2 - 1 oz. squares unsweetened chocolate, melted

Direction

- Cream, cream cheese until smooth.
- Gradually add the sifted confectioners' sugar. Blending well.
- Add melted chocolate and blend well.
- Add vanilla, salt and pecans. Stir well.
- Turn into a well-greased square pan and chill in refrigerator for 30 minutes or until firm.
- Cut into squares.

103. Cream Cheese Pumpkin Truffles Recipe

Serving: 24 | Prep: | Cook: 240mins | Ready in:

Ingredients

- 2½ cups white chocolate chunks
- 1/3 cup gingersnap cookie crumbs, plus more for garnish
- 1/4 cup canned pumpkin purée
- 1/4 cup graham cracker crumbs, plus more for garnish
- 1 tablespoon confectioners' sugar
- 1/2 teaspoon orange zest
- 1/8 teaspoon ground cinnamon
- Pinch of fine salt
- 2 ounces cream cheese, softened
- *I added some chopped walnuts to sprinkle on top!

Direction

- Melt 1/2 cup of the chocolate in a double boiler over medium-low heat or in the microwave for about 1 minutes.
- Stir often to keep the chocolate from burning.
- Transfer to a large bowl.
- Add gingersnap crumbs, pumpkin, graham cracker crumbs, sugar, zest, cinnamon, salt and cream cheese and beat with an electric mixer until smooth.
- Transfer to a shallow bowl, cover and chill until just solid enough to roll into balls, about 2 hours.
- Line a large sheet tray with parchment paper.
- Melt remaining 2 cups chocolate and transfer to a small, deep bowl. Roll 1 heaping teaspoon of the pumpkin mixture into a ball in your hands, then drop into the chocolate.
- Working quickly, gently spoon chocolate over to coat.
- Using a small spoon or fork, lift the truffle out of the chocolate, shake off excess and transfer to prepared sheet tray.
- Dollop a bit of extra chocolate on any parts that remain exposed, then sprinkle a few gingersnap or graham cracker crumbs over the top, if you like.
- Repeat process with remaining pumpkin mixture and chocolate, then chill truffles until chocolate is completely set, about 1 hour.
- ***You could add a few tablespoons of Pumpkin Liqueur or rum to the cream cheese before rolling for a more "adult" flavor... These would look great in any gift basket!

104. Cream And Butter Toffee Recipe

Serving: 8 | Prep: | Cook: 20mins | Ready in:

Ingredients

- 350 ml measure granulated sugar
- 2 heaping Tbsp salted butter
- 250 ml whipping cream
- 2 Tbsp light corn syrup

Direction

- Boil everything to 300 degree/hard crack stage on a candy thermometer.
- Pour onto a tinfoil lined baking sheet.
- Let cool and break up and eat.
- You can grease the tinfoil if you want but it's not really necessary.
- In Shanghai this stuff gets sticky and gooey (from the humidity) way too fast, so if you live in a humid climate best to eat it quickly :)

105. Creole Candy Recipe

Serving: 0 | Prep: | Cook: | Ready in:

Ingredients

- One 1 pound box confectioner's sugar
- 1/2 cup (1 stick) butter (do not substitute margarine)

- 1/8 teaspoon salt
- 2 cups pecan halves
- 1/2 cup boiling water
- 1 teaspoon vanilla extract

Direction

- In a large saucepan, combine all the ingredients except the vanilla. Place over medium heat, bring to a boil, then reduce the heat slightly and continue cooking, stirring only enough to prevent scorching, to the soft-ball stage, 238* on a candy thermometer. Remove from the heat, add the vanilla, and stir until the mixture begins to thicken.
- Pour 1 teaspoon of the mixture into each of 36 tiny muffin papers. Allow to cool completely.
- 36 pieces

106. Crock Pot Candy Recipe

Serving: 2 | Prep: | Cook: 180mins | Ready in:

Ingredients

- 2-lbs of almond bark
- 12-oz. bag of chocolate chips
- 1 4-oz. bar of German chocolate
- 2-lbs of nuts (can use peanuts, mixed, cashews, etc)

Direction

- Put everything in a crock pot. Set to low setting. Cover and do no open for 3 hrs. After 3 hrs. open and stir all together. Drop by spoonfuls on waxed paper. They will harden in a few minutes.
- Makes approximately 200 peanut clusters and they are very, very good.
- Can also add some dried cherries if you would like.

107. Crock Pot Chocolate Fritos Candy Recipe

Serving: 4 | Prep: | Cook: 180mins | Ready in:

Ingredients

- 2 cups Fritos
- 2 cups pretzels
- 1 stick (1/2 cup) butter
- 1/2 cup brown sugar
- 2 tablespoons peanut butter
- 12 ounces chocolate chips
- 1/2 cup peanuts or honey roasted nuts

Direction

- Smash Fritos and pretzels in plastic bag.
- Line a 13 x 9-inch pan with foil or parchment paper.
- Place butter, brown sugar, peanut butter and chocolate chips in crock pot and cook on HIGH for 1 - 2 hours until melted and mixed well.
- Stir in Fritos and pretzels and pour into pan. Sprinkle peanuts on top and refrigerate until set. Break into pieces.

108. Crockpot Peanut Clusters Recipe

Serving: 100 | Prep: | Cook: 3hours | Ready in:

Ingredients

- These ingredients are layered in the slow cooker as listed
- 2 # of dry roasted peanuts
- 1-----4oz pkg of German sweet chocolate squares
- 1 pkg semi sweet chocolate chips
- 2 and a half pound of white almond bark

Direction

- Layer these ingredients as listed in the bottom of a 6 qt. slow cooker. Break up the German chocolate in squares and put them over the peanuts.
- Also, break up the almond bark in squares as you put them over the chocolate chips.
- Cook on Low 3 hrs. Do not raise the lid during this time. After 3 hrs. stir until smooth with a wooden spoon.
- When smooth, put them in small candy or tart paper cups. You can get 100 or more clusters this size. You can make them larger if you want. You can spoon them out on parchment paper the size you like. They are very cute done in the papers. My friend who gave me this recipe took them out of the papers after they cooled. The chocolate breaks up a little when they are removed from the paper. She did not want the chocolate on her carpet or causing a mess for anyone.
- These will make very nice gifts.

109. Crockpot White Chocolate Candy Recipe

Serving: 4 | Prep: | Cook: 120mins | Ready in:

Ingredients

- 16 oz jar unsalted dry roasted peanuts
- 16 oz jar salted dry-roasted peanuts
- 4 oz German chocolate squares
- 12 oz chocolate chips
- 24 oz bark* white chocolate
- Pam spray

Direction

- Spray Pam in crock pot.
- Put into the crock pot in order as written. Cook on low for 2 hours. Stir mixture and dip out by spoonfuls onto wax paper.
- *Barks are slabs of chocolate used for candy making.

110. DATES WITH SESAME SEEDS Recipe

Serving: 810 | Prep: | Cook: 10mins | Ready in:

Ingredients

- 2 lbs. soft dates
- 1/4 cup corn oil
- 1/2 lb. almonds
- 1 tablespoon ground cardamom seeds
- 1 cup sesame seeds

Direction

- Blanch, skin and split the almonds in two. Fry them in oil until golden brown. Remove, drain and spread out on a paper towel.
- Brown the sesame seeds in a pan without oil, until golden, stirring constantly. Spread sesame seeds on a tray.
- Remove the seeds from the dates and mix into the cardamom seeds to form a dough; take pieces the size of a date and stuff with a piece of almond. Close and mold into a finger shape. Roll in the sesame seeds and arrange on a serving dish.

111. Darianas Easy Chocolate Truffles Recipe

Serving: 60 | Prep: | Cook: 120mins | Ready in:

Ingredients

- Two 12 oz. packages semi-sweet chocolate chips
- Three 4 oz. sweet chocolate bars (chopped)
- One 7 oz. jar marshmallow cream
- 4 1/2 cups sugar
- 2 Tablespoons butter
- One 12 oz. can evaporated milk

Direction

- FILLING:
- Place one 12 oz. package of chocolate chips, plus all the chocolate bars and the marshmallow cream into a heat-proof bowl.
- Heat sugar, butter, and evaporated milk in a heavy-bottomed sauce pan until sugar dissolves and mixture comes to a full boil.
- Boil mixture for 5 minutes, stirring constantly.
- Pour hot mixture into the bowl of chocolate and mix well. (The resulting mixture will become firm and cool enough to scoop.)
- Line one cookie sheet with Saran Wrap.
- Using a small scoop, form individual balls and place on cookie sheet.
- Refrigerate until firm and chilled.
- CHOCOLATE COATING:
- In the top part of a double boiler melt the second package of chocolate chips and stir until smooth.
- Using your hands, roll the refrigerated chocolate balls until smooth and then place back in the refrigerator to chill for a few minutes. (Chilling sets the chocolate to make dipping easier.)
- Rest each ball on a fork and dip into the melted chocolate. Then gently place the ball on a clean cookie sheet lined with wax paper.
- Refrigerate the truffles or serve immediately at room temperature.

112. Dark Chocolate ButterCrunch Recipe

Serving: 24 | Prep: | Cook: 20mins | Ready in:

Ingredients

- 1 cup (2 sticks, 1/2 pound) butter*
- 1 1/2 cups (12 ounces) sugar
- 3 tablespoons water
- 1 tablespoon light corn syrup
- 2 cups (8 ounces) diced pecans or slivered almonds, toasted
- 1 pound semisweet or bittersweet chocolate, finely chopped (chocolate chips are an easy solution here; you'll need about 2 2/3 cups)
- *If you use unsalted butter, add 1/2 teaspoon salt.

Direction

- In a large, deep saucepan, melt the butter. Stir in the sugar, water and corn syrup, and bring the mixture to a boil. Boil gently, over medium heat, until the mixture reaches hard-crack stage (300°F on an instant-read or candy thermometer), about 20 minutes. The syrup will seem to take a long time to come to the hard-crack stage, but be patient; all of a sudden it will darken, and at that point you need to take its temperature and see if it's ready. (If you don't have a thermometer, test a dollop in ice water; it should immediately harden to a brittleness sufficient that you'll be able to snap it in two, without any bending or softness). Pay attention; too long on the heat, and the syrup will burn. And what a waste of good butter and sugar that would be!
- While the sugar mixture is gently bubbling, spread half of the nuts, in a fairly closely packed, even single layer, on a lightly greased baking sheet. Top with half the chocolate. When the syrup is ready, pour it quickly and evenly over the nuts and chocolate. Immediately top with the remaining chocolate, then the remaining nuts. Wait several minutes, then gently, using the back of a spatula, press down on the chocolate-nut layer to spread the chocolate around evenly.
- While the candy is still slightly warm, use a spatula to loosen it from the baking sheet. When cool, break it into uneven chunks.
- Yield: about 24 big bite-sized pieces, if you want to be scientific about it.

113. Dark Chocolate Cococans Recipe

Serving: 30 | Prep: | Cook: 10mins | Ready in:

Ingredients

- 1 14 ounce bag of sweetened shredded coconut
- 1 bag of dark chocolate chips-you can use semi-sweet
- 6 ounces of sweetened condensed milk
- 1/2 tsp vanilla extract
- 1/2 tsp almond extract
- 2 cups of powdered sugar
- 1 pound of large pecan halves
- 1/4 cup of honey
- 1/4 tsp. salt
- (butter for your hands!)

Direction

- Mix the condensed milk with the sugar
- Add extracts and salt and mix well.
- Press this mixture evenly into a 13x9 pan covered in Release aluminum foil with extra foil on sides for easy removal.
- Place in the freezer for one hour.
- Remove the pan from the freezer and remove the candy from the pan using the foil.
- Cut into small 2 inch squares
- Using buttered hands, roll the candy into small log-shaped pieces, rounding off the edges slightly.
- Dip only the bottom of one pecan half lightly into the honey and press on top of each coconut log or piece. (Honey is the glue!)
- Place all of the candy on wax paper or a silicon mat (or use the foil!)
- Melt the dark chocolate in a glass bowl or large glass measuring cup.
- Using 2 forks, quickly dip each candy and pecan into the chocolate and allow excess to drip off.
- Place dipped candy back on foil or waxed paper to dry and set.

114. Deep Fried Candy Bars Recipe

Serving: 4 | Prep: | Cook: 10mins | Ready in:

Ingredients

- 1 egg
- 1 cup milk
- 1 tbsp vegetable oil
- 1 cup flour
- 1 tsp baking powder
- Pinch of salt
- Candy bars of your choice.

Direction

- Chill or freeze the candy bars.
- Combine egg, milk and vegetable oil in a cup.
- In a bowl, combine flour, baking powder and salt. Pour the wet ingredients into the dry ingredients and mix well with a wire whisk. Cover and chill for a few minutes while the oil heats.
- Remove batter from the refrigerator and adjust the consistency if necessary. Heat about 4 cups of oil or shortening to 375 degrees F.
- Dip the chilled candy bar in the batter and gently place into the oil. Cook only until the outside is golden. Remove and drain on brown paper. Allow to cool for a minute as the inside can easily burn your mouth.

115. Delicious Copycat Almond Joy Bars Recipe

Serving: 26 | Prep: | Cook: 10mins | Ready in:

Ingredients

- Copycat almond Joy Bars
- (26 servings)
- 4 c (8 1/2-oz) shredded coconut

- 1/4 c light corn syrup
- 1 pk (11 1/2-oz) milk chocolate pieces
- 1/4 c vegetable shortening
- 26 Whole natural almonds (1-oz)

Direction

- Line two large cookie sheets with waxed paper.
- Set large wire cooling rack on paper; set aside.
- Place coconut in large bowl; set aside.
- Place corn syrup in a 1-cup glass measure. Microwave on high (100%) 1 minute or until syrup boils.
- Immediately pour over coconut. Work warm syrup into coconut using the back of a wooden spoon until coconut is thoroughly coated.
- This takes a little time, there is enough syrup.
- Using 1 level measuring tablespoon of coconut, shape into a ball by squeezing coconut firmly in palm of one hand, then rolling between both palms.
- (HINT: Measure out all of the coconut then roll into balls.)
- Place 2 inches apart on wire racks. Let dry 10 minutes.
- Reroll coconut balls so there are no loose ends of coconut sticking up.
- Place milk chocolate and shortening in a 4-cup glass measure or 1 1/2 quart microwave-safe bowl. Microwave on high 1 to 2 minutes or until mixture can be stirred smooth and is glossy; stirring once or twice.
- Working quickly, spoon 1 level measuring tablespoon of the chocolate over each coconut ball, making sure chocolate coats and letting excess chocolate drip down onto waxed paper.
- While chocolate coating is still soft, lightly press whole almond on top of each.
- Let stand to set or place in refrigerator. Store in a single layer in airtight container.
- Keeps best if refrigerated.

116. Delicious Homemade Creme Filled Chocolate Candy Recipe

Serving: 24 | *Prep:* | *Cook:* 5mins | *Ready in:*

Ingredients

- Centers:
- 1 cup of sweetened condensed milk
- 1/4 lb softened margarine
- 2 1/2 lbs powdered sugar
- 1 tsp vanilla (or any extract you'd like! mint or maple are great inside chocolates!)
- 1/2 cup of ground up pecan or walnut halves- optional

Direction

- Blend ingredients, then shape into 1" balls and chill for a few hours or overnight.
- Using a toothpick, dip each ball into the chocolate (recipe below) and cool on waxed paper or tin foil.
- (Cover the toothpick hole with a little teensy bit more of the chocolate, using the toothpick)
- Chocolate:
- 12 oz. of semi-sweet bits
- 6 oz. unsweetened chocolate
- Melt in microwave or in a double boiler to dip the centers (above) in! Keep the chocolate warm while dipping centers.

117. Diabetic Chocolate Candy Recipe

Serving: 30 | *Prep:* | *Cook:* 10mins | *Ready in:*

Ingredients

- 3 oz. package cream cheese (softened)
- 2 tablespoons skim milk
- 1 1/2 teaspoons white vanilla extract
- 1 cup powdered sugar replacement (Splenda)
- 1 recipe semisweet dipping chocolate (below)

- Beat cream cheese, milk and vanilla until fluffy; stir
- in powdered sugar replacement. Form into 30 balls and
- dip each one in chocolate.
- Yield: 30 creams
- Calories 1 cream: 31
- Exchange 1 cream: 1/4 low fat milk
- Semisweet Dipping chocolate is Below

Direction

- Semisweet Dipping Chocolate
- 1 cup non-fat dry milk powder
- 1/3 cup cocoa
- 2 tablespoons paraffin wax
- 1/2 cup water
- 1 tablespoon liquid shortening
- 1 tablespoon liquid sugar replacement
- Combine milk powder, cocoa and wax in food processor or blender; blend to soft powder.
- Pour into top of double boiler and add water, stirring to blend. Add liquid shortening.
- Place over hot (not boiling) water, and cook and stir until wax pieces are completely dissolved and mixture is thick, smooth and creamy.
- Remove from heat. Stir in sugar replacement and let cool slightly.
- Dip candies according to recipe. Shake off excess chocolate. Place on very lightly greased waxed paper and allow to cool completely. (If candies do not remove easily, slightly warm the waxed paper over electric burner or with clothes iron.)
- Store in a cool place.
- Yield: 1 cup
- Calories full recipe: 427
- Exchange full recipe: 3 low fat milk

118. Dipped Chocolate Graham Sticks Recipe

Serving: 40 | Prep: | Cook: 3mins | Ready in:

Ingredients

- 1 box chocolate Graham Sticks (I use honey Maid)
- 12 ounces white chocolate chips, or any white chocolate candy coating
- holiday cookie decorations, optional

Direction

- Melt the white chocolate in the microwave. I use a 1 cup measuring cup, so that I have a narrow, deep container, making it easier to dip the sticks. I just fill it with the white chocolate chips, melt it, and keep adding more chips and melting it as I need more coating.
- Have a large piece of waxed paper on the counter.
- Dip each graham stick halfway into the melted white chocolate.
- Set it on the waxed paper, and sprinkle with holiday edible decorations (tinted sugars or any of the cute decorations that are now available for sprinkling on cookies, etc.).
- Once the melted white coating has hardened back up, the sticks will peel right off the waxed paper and you can store them in a container.

119. Double Nut English Toffee Recipe Recipe

Serving: 30 | Prep: | Cook: |Ready in:

Ingredients

- • 2 - cups butter softened and divided
- • 2 cups sugar
- • 1- package (12 ounces) semi-sweet chocolate chips...... (I needed another 12 ounces)
- • 2- cups pecans or you can use walnuts.... divided .... (I liked the pecans), I had about 1/4 cup left over.
- • Wooden spoon (I prefer bamboo spoons)

- Here is Tinks link if you want to comment on this recipe she posted.
- Double Nut English Toffee

Direction

- Butter a 15 inch x 10 inch x 1 inch pan with 1 1/2 teaspoons butter set aside. I took it I was to spread out the butter using my fingers per the picture, or maybe just getting the thinnest layer and only using 1/2 teaspoon….. Once made, the bottom seemed greasy; I would like to try just spraying canola oil on the bottom, a very light coat and spreading it out very thin. There is so much butter in the recipe I wonder if it would really stick inside the pan?
- In a heavy saucepan, combine sugar and remaining butter
- Cook and stir over medium heat until a candy thermometer reads 290 degrees (soft crack stage). I used my 2 quart copper bottom and after 30 minutes on medium and medium high my candy thermometer would not go past 225. At 30 minutes it had been bubbling and started to change consistency, it began balling up on the wooden spoon. I decided that was it, and poured it on the buttered sheet. It spread out very nice.
- Sprinkle with 1 cup (I think another 6-8 ounces) of the chocolate chips, let stand until the chips become glossy……..spread evenly over the top. I think it would have been better to nuke the chips and soften them a little; about 30-45 seconds so they would melt better on the mixture and spread out easier and more even. If you look closely there are areas where the chips didn't fill the whole mix. They did get glossy per the original recipe. Add nuts
- I placed the whole tray in the refrigerator for 1 hour to set up.
- Remove from refrigerator.
- It does make over 3 lbs. and is quite thick. It has incredible flavor, but then how could 2 lbs. of real butter and 2 cups of sugar not taste good. This was totally low cal and non-fatting good stuff.
- Break into 2 inch pieces or whatever and store in an airtight container
- Yields 3 1/2 pounds candy.

120. Dr Pepper Fudge Recipe

Serving: 24 | Prep: | Cook: 30mins | Ready in:

Ingredients

- 4 cups of sugar
- 1 1/3 cups dr. pepper
- 4 oz grated unsweetened chocolate
- 4 tbsp white corn syrup
- 1/2 cup butter or margarine
- 2 tsp vanila
- 1 to 2 cups chopped nuts. (optional)

Direction

- Mix sugar, dr. pepper, chocolate and corn syrup in a heavy sauce pan.
- Cook very slowly, stirring constantly until sugar is dissolved and chocolate is melted.
- Continue cooking on low to med heat until 236 degree's is reached on a candy thermometer or soft ball stage.
- Remove from heat and cool to 110 degree's then add butter and vanilla.
- Beat until candy loses its shiny look.
- Add nuts and pour into slightly buttered pan.
- When cool, cut into squares.

121. Dressed Up Chocolate Bark Recipe

Serving: 12 | Prep: | Cook: 10mins | Ready in:

Ingredients

- chocolate (milk or semi-sweet)
- Classic Toppings: dried fruits such as apricots, raisins, candied orange peel, cranberries, and

cherries. toasted nuts including hazelnuts, pecans, almonds, and pistachios.
- Contemporary Toppings: caramelized cocoa nibs (see recipe), cereal, candied ginger, and dried fruits such as pineapple, blueberries, and strawberries. toasted pumpkin seeds and pine nuts.

Direction

- Line a chilled baking sheet with parchment paper. Pour warm (not hot), melted chocolate into the prepared pan.
- Spread the chocolate evenly to about 1/8 inch thick using a small offset spatula. Sprinkle toppings on the chocolate and place in the freezer to set, approximately 20 minutes.
- For even-sized pieces, cut up bark before it sets completely. If you like a more rustic look, allow the bark to harden completely before breaking it up into pieces. Store in a cool, dry place.

122. Drunk Gummie Bears Recipe

Serving: 0 | Prep: | Cook: 2mins | Ready in:

Ingredients

- Gummy Bears
- vodka
- Sierra Mist Cranberry Splash
- or Any kind of juice

Direction

- Marinade gummy bears in Vodka mixed with Sierra Mist Cranberry Splash or other juice or pop. So Yummy.

123. Dulce De Leche For Non Cheaters Recipe

Serving: 8 | Prep: | Cook: 120mins | Ready in:

Ingredients

- 2 litres (1/2 gallon) whole milk
- 500 g (1 cup) sugar
- 1 teaspoon of sea salt
- 2 vanilla pods (optional*)

Direction

- Add milk, sugar, and salt into a pot large enough that there are a few inches between the level of the milk and the top of the pot.
- If using vanilla, cut the vanilla pods lengthwise, scrape the seeds from the pods and add everything into the pot - this is the French version called "Confiture de Lait"
- Turn the heat to medium high, whisk or stir the mixture constantly until it comes to a full boil.
- Turn the heat down to barely simmer, and continue to cook, uncovered, for 3 hours.
- When the mixture gets to the desired consistency, remove the vanilla pods, and whisk until smooth.
- Pour into small jars and let cool. When it cools down completely, put the lid on the jars and keep in the fridge.
- NOTE: When in doubt, turn the heat lower. If the heat is too high your milk will boil over and develop a skin, which you won't be able to get rid of later. If the heat is too low you'll just have to cook it longer.
- ANOTHER NOTE: Check the consistency at about 2.5 hours. The consistency you are looking for is a loose caramel. It thickens a bit after cooling.

124. Dulce De Leche Under Pressure Recipe

Serving: 1 | Prep: | Cook: 20mins | Ready in:

Ingredients

- sweetened condensed milk

Direction

- Submerge the can completely in the water and cook in pressure-cooker for 20 to 30 minutes.
- Pour into small jars, seal and keep in fridge.

125. EASTER COOKIES Recipe

Serving: 8 | Prep: | Cook: 20mins | Ready in:

Ingredients

- 3 OZ. CRUSHED WHOLEWHEAT biscuits
- 3 OZ caster sugar
- 1 egg yolk
- 1/2 OZ CHOPPED PEEL
- 1 OZ. currants
- 1/4 TEASPOON mixed spice 6 OZ. flour
- PINCH OF salt

Direction

- CREAM THE FAT AND SUGAR TOGETHER.
- BEAT IN THE EGG.
- ADD THE PEEL AND CURRANTS, SPICE AND SALT, THEN BEAT IN THE FLOUR.
- MIX TO A STILL DOUGH, USING A LITTLE MILK IF REQUIRED.
- ROLL OUT ON TO A FLOURED BOARD.
- PRICK THE SURFACE ALL OVER WITH A FORK.
- CUT OUT WITH A BISCUIT CUTTER.
- BAKE ON A PREVIOUSLY GREASED BAKING TRAY.
- GAS MARK 6 FOR 20 MINUTES UNTIL LIGHTLY COLOURED.
- LEAVE TO COOL SLIGHTLY BEFORE LIFTING FROM THE TRAY.

126. Easiest Fudge In The World Recipe

Serving: 10 | Prep: | Cook: 4mins | Ready in:

Ingredients

- 12 oz. pkg. semisweet chocolate chips
- 14 oz. can sweetened condensed milk

Direction

- Place chips and milk in microwave safe bowl.
- Microwave on medium power for 2-3 minutes, stirring after 2 minutes.
- Microwave, stirring at 1 minutes intervals, until chips are melted and mixture is smooth and thick.
- Pour into greased 8" square pan and cool.
- You can also melt the chips and milk in a heavy saucepan over low heat.

127. Easter Baskets Recipe

Serving: 2 | Prep: | Cook: | Ready in:

Ingredients

- ¾ c peanut butter
- ¾ c butterscotch chips
- 4 Shredded wheat biscuits, crumbled

Direction

- Mix peanut butter and butterscotch chips over low heat or place in microwave until melted; add shredded wheat.

- Cool slightly, then mold into baskets (try shaping over back of bowl).
- Place baskets in fridge to set.
- Fill baskets with Easter eggs, candies, miniature chocolate bars, etc.
- Another alternative is to make little nests instead of bowls and fill them with little candy Easter eggs.

128. Easy Apricot Balls Recipe

Serving: 1 | Prep: | Cook: | Ready in:

Ingredients

- 8 ounces dried apricots, finely chopped
- 1 cup sweetened flaked coconut
- 1/2 cup chopped walnuts
- 2 tab fresh squeesed orange juice
- 1/4 cup sweetened condensed milk
- more flaked coconut or finely chopped pecans for rolling
- Optional (dip cold balls in melted chocolate and roll in coconut or chopped nuts)

Direction

- Process chopped apricots, walnuts and coconut in a food processor until thoroughly combined. Add OJ and sweetened condensed milk; process until combined. Pour mixture into a dish; refrigerate until firm, about 30 to 45 minutes. Place waxed paper on a baking sheet; set aside. Place additional coconut or finely chopped pecans in a shallow bowl. Shape apricot mixture into balls about 1-inch in diameter. Roll in coconut or pecans; place on waxed paper. Refrigerate until firm. Store in an airtight container in the refrigerator. Makes about 24 balls.

129. Easy Breezy Fudge Recipe

Serving: 8 | Prep: | Cook: 3mins | Ready in:

Ingredients

- 1 pound box of powdered sugar
- 3 eggs (beat with sugar)
- ½ teaspoon vanilla
- Mix together with mixer
- 1 Large package (12oz.) real chocolate chips
- 1 cube of real butter

Direction

- Melt together (butter and chips) over low heat (do not over heat).
- Mix together with sugar mixture.
- Add nuts as many as desired, pour into an 8x8 pan and refrigerate.
- Note: I have doubled this recipe and it makes a 9x13 pan very nicely.

130. Easy Chocolate Cashew Clusters Recipe

Serving: 18 | Prep: | Cook: | Ready in:

Ingredients

- 2 cups semisweet or milk chocolate chips
- 1 tablespoon shortening-optional
- 2 cups unsalted or lightly salted cashews- whole or very roughly chopped.

Direction

- In a small saucepan over medium low heat, combine chocolate chips and shortening.
- Stir constantly until melted.
- Remove from heat immediately and let stand for 5 minutes.
- Add cashews and stir until well coated.

- Drop in tablespoons onto wax paper lined cookie sheet.
- Chill until set.
- If using microwave to melt chocolate, shortening may be omitted.
- Keep refrigerated.

131. Easy Chocolate Dipped Coconut Creams Recipe

Serving: 96 | Prep: | Cook: 10mins | Ready in:

Ingredients

- 1 (14-ounce) can sweetened condensed milk
- 1/4 cup butter, melted
- 1 TBSP. lemon juice
- 8 cups sifted powdered sugar
- 1 (7-ounce) can flaked coconut
- 1/2 cup toasted almonds, finely chopped
- 16 ounces chocolate-flavored candy coating

Direction

- Combine the condensed milk, butter, and the lemon juice. Stir well.
- Gradually stir in the powdered sugar. Mix well.
- Add coconut and the almonds. Mix well.
- Shape into 3/4-inch balls.
- Cover and freeze 4 hours or until firm.
- Put candy coating in top of a double boiler. Bring water to a boil.
- Reduce heat to low. Cook until the coating melts.
- Remove from the heat but leave the coating over the water.
- Using 2 forks dip frozen candy balls in melted coating.
- Allow the excess to drip off.
- Cool on wax paper.
- Store in the refrigerator.
- ....

- To make a nice presentation but the candies in paper candy cups.
- Yields 8 dozen

132. Easy Chocolate Mint Truffles Recipe

Serving: 10 | Prep: | Cook: 3mins | Ready in:

Ingredients

- * 1/3 cup semisweet mint-chocolate morsels or plain or Raspberry flavor.
- * 4 ounce cream cheese
- * 1-16 ounce package powdered sugar, sifted
- * 1/4 cup unsweetened cocoa
- * 1/4 cup additional powdered sugar

Direction

- PREPARATION:
- Place 1/3 cup morsels in a medium glass bowl and microwave at high 1 minute or until morsels are almost melted, stirring until smooth. Let cool. Add the softened cream cheese to melted morsels, beat at medium speed of mixer until smooth.
- Add powdered sugar and beat until well blended. Press mixture into a 6 inch square on heavy duty plastic wrap, cover and chill at least one hour.
- Cut mixture into 48 squares. Roll each square into a ball and place on wax paper. Roll half in unsweetened cocoa and half in powdered sugar. Melt 2T mint chips and drizzle each ball. Serve at room temperature. Can be frozen.

133. Easy Chocolate Truffles Recipe

Serving: 60 | Prep: | Cook: 2mins | Ready in:

Ingredients

- 1 1/2 pk chocolate;semi sweet; 12 squares
- 1 8 ounces Pkg Cream Cheese; softened
- 3 c powdered sugar
- 1 TB coffee liqueur
- 1 TB orange liqueur
- 1 TB almond liqueur
- Nuts; chopped
- unsweetened cocoa
- flake coconut
- Sprinkles; colored

Direction

- Cook chocolate in large microwave-safe bowl on HIGH for 2 minutes, stirring halfway through heating time. Stir until chocolate is melted.
- Beat cream cheese in large bowl with electric mixer on medium speed until smooth. Gradually beat in sugar until well blended. Stir in chocolate until blended. Divide mixture into thirds, add 1 flavor liqueur to each third; mix well. Refrigerate about 3 hours or until firm. Shape into 1-inch balls. Roll in nuts, cocoa, coconut or sprinkles. Keep in refrigerator. Makes 5 dozen

134. Easy Fudge Yummy Recipe

Serving: 10 | Prep: | Cook: 5mins | Ready in:

Ingredients

- 3 cups semi-sweet chocolate chips
- 1 can Eagle Brand Condensed Milk
- Dash of salt
- 1 1/2 - 2 cups chopped nuts
- 1 1/2 teaspoon vanilla

Direction

- Melt Chips and milk together when melted put in dash of salt. Remove from heat then add 1 1/2 to 2 cups nuts and 1 1/2 teaspoons Vanilla.
- Stir well and pour into square pan lined with wax paper. Chill 2 hours.

135. Easy Ham Bake Recipe

Serving: 8 | Prep: | Cook: 50mins | Ready in:

Ingredients

- 1 bag (1 lb) frozen broccoli cuts
- 1 can (10 3/4 oz) condensed 98% fat-free cream of mushroom soup
- 1 can (10 3/4 oz) condensed cheddar cheese soup
- 1 cup fat-free (skim) milk
- 3 cups cut-up cooked ham, chicken, turkey or beef
- 2 cups Bisquick mix
- 1 1/2 cups fat-free (skim) milk

Direction

- Heat oven to 425°F. Spray 13x9-inch (3-quart) glass baking dish with cooking spray. In large microwavable bowl, mix broccoli, soups, 1 cup milk and the ham. Microwave on High 5 minutes, stirring after 3 minutes. Pour into baking dish.
- In medium bowl, stir Bisquick mix and 1 1/2 cups milk until blended. Pour evenly over soup mixture.
- Bake uncovered 25 to 30 minutes or until light golden brown. Let stand 5 minutes before serving.

136. Easy Microwave Pralines Recipe

Serving: 24 | Prep: | Cook: 8mins | Ready in:

Ingredients

- 1 1/2 cups brown sugar
- 2/3 cup heavy cream
- 2 tablespoons butter
- 1 cup pecan halves

Direction

- In a large, microwave safe bowl, combine sugar, cream, butter, pecans.
- Microwave 8 minutes on high, stirring once.
- Let rest 1 minute
- Then stir 3 minutes more.
- Drop by teaspoonfuls on buttered waxed paper (If mixture is runny, allow to cool 30 seconds more and try again.)

137. Easy Peanut Butter Fudge

Serving: 8 | Prep: | Cook: 30mins | Ready in:

Ingredients

- 2 teaspoons butter, softened
- 2 cups sugar
- 1/2 cup whole milk
- 1-1/3 cups peanut butter
- 1 jar (7 ounces) marshmallow creme

Direction

- Line an 8-in. square pan with foil; grease with butter.
- In a heavy saucepan, combine sugar and milk; bring to a boil over medium heat, stirring constantly. Boil 3 minutes, stirring constantly. Remove from heat.
- Stir in peanut butter and marshmallow creme until blended. Immediately spread into prepared pan; cool slightly.
- Refrigerate until firm. Using foil, lift fudge out of pan. Remove foil; cut into squares. Store between layers of waxed paper in an airtight container.
- Tips:
- Drizzle individual fudge squares with melted chocolate to add some easy holiday glam.
- We tasted six popular kinds of chunky peanut butter. Here's the brand we like best.
- Nutrition Facts
- 1 piece: 67 calories, 3g fat (1g saturated fat), 0 cholesterol, 28mg sodium, 10g carbohydrate (9g sugars, 0 fiber), 1g protein.

138. Easy Tiger Butter Candy Recipe

Serving: 72 | Prep: | Cook: 10mins | Ready in:

Ingredients

- 1 pound white chocolate
- 1-12 ounce jar chunky peanut butter
- 1 pound semisweet chocolate, melted

Direction

- For melting, combine white chocolate and peanut butter, either in double-boiler or microwave safe bowl
- Stir OFTEN whether melting in double-boiler or melting in microwave
- When melted, spread onto a waxed paper-lined 15- x 10- x 1-inch jellyroll pan.
- Pour semisweet melted chocolate over peanut butter mixture.
- SWIRL through with a knife*
- Chill until firm.
- Cut into 1-1/2 inch pieces.
- Store in refrigerator.
- *ATTN: Don't go on a kitchen gadget search for *knife* :) Meant to type *knife*, but, I'm not

going to change it because it gave Pink (see comments) and me such a great laugh! Hope you get a laugh too! I will never be able to make these again without thinking about swirling through with a *knife*!! LOL

139. Easy Peasey Rocky Road Fudge Recipe

Serving: 48 | Prep: | Cook: 2mins | Ready in:

Ingredients

- 2 cups Semi-sweet chocolate Morsels
- 1 can (14 oz.) CARNATION sweetened condensed milk
- 1 teaspoon vanilla extract
- 3 cups miniature marshmallows
- 1 1/2 cups coarsely chopped walnuts

Direction

- LINE 13 x 9-inch baking pan with foil; grease lightly.
- MICROWAVE morsels and sweetened condensed milk in large, uncovered, microwave-safe bowl on HIGH (100%) power for 1 minute; STIR. Morsels may retain some of their shape. If necessary, microwave at additional 10- to 15-second intervals, stirring until smooth. Stir in vanilla extract. Fold in marshmallows and nuts.
- PRESS mixture into prepared baking pan. Refrigerate until ready to serve. Lift from pan; remove foil. Cut into pieces.

140. Eggnog Fudge Recipe

Serving: 40 | Prep: | Cook: 10mins | Ready in:

Ingredients

- 1/8- cup butter, chilled
- 3 -cups sugar
- 1- cup eggnog
- 6- ounces white chocolate chips
- 1- 1/2- cup mini-marshmallows
- 1 cup almonds, chopped
- 1/2 -teaspoon nutmeg
- 1/2- teaspoon cinnamon

Direction

- Line a 9 x 9-inch cake pan with aluminum foil and set aside.
- Spray the sides of a large saucepan with butter-flavor non-stick spray.
- Add the eggnog and sugar, and bring to a rolling boil over medium to medium-high heat, stirring constantly
- Boil for two full minutes.
- Fold in the marshmallows, cinnamon, and nutmeg.
- Bring back to a rolling boil for another 6 minutes, stirring constantly. The mixture will start to turn brown, which is normal, but if you see brown flakes in the mixture then turn down the heat a little.
- Remove from heat and add the butter, chips, and nuts.
- Stir until thoroughly mixed or until the mixture starts to lose its glossy appearance.
- Pour into prepared pan.
- Cool at room temperature.
- Remove from pan, remove foil, cut into 1-inch squares.
- Makes about 40 pieces or more

141. Egyptian Stuffed Colorful Sweet Peppers Filfil Rumi Mahsi Maaa Lon Recipe

Serving: 3 | Prep: | Cook: 30mins | Ready in:

Ingredients

- 3 large sweet peppers, green, yellow, orange or red
- 2 Tb. unsalted butter
- 2/3 c. corn kernels off the cob or canned
- 1 small onion chopped
- ¾ lb. italian sausage turkey links, sweet or hot
- 2 c. crumbled corn bread (approx)
- ¾ c. shredded pepper jack cheese*

Direction

- Heat over to 350F. Slice peppers in half from stem to bottom and remove stem. Also remove seeds and membranes, and set aside.
- Melt butter in skillet. Add onion, corn and sausage, breaking the sausage apart with a spoon or spatula, and cook until the sausage is no longer pink. Add crumbled corn bread and a little water if mixture seems too dry.
- Divide filling among peppers evenly and top with shredded cheese. Bake peppers at 350F, covered, for about 30 minutes or until cheese is melted and peppers are tender.
- * If pepper jack cheese is unavailable, use shredded mozzarella and add hot peppers to taste.

142. Elegant Marshmallows Recipe

Serving: 20 | Prep: | Cook: 10mins | Ready in:

Ingredients

- 1 bag of fresh large marshmallows
- 3 cups of your choice of chocolate for dipping
- *Toppings:
- Finely chopped pecans, walnuts, macadamia nuts or peanuts
- toasted and finely chopped almonds
- Dark or milk chocolate sprinkles
- graham cracker crumbs
- toasted coconut
- Colored sugar crystals
- Toffee bits, finly chopped

Direction

- Prepare your work area first by laying down either sheets of wax paper or aluminum foil to catch any drips. Have some paper-lined trays and some wire racks ready.
- You'll need two forks.
- Put your toppings into cereal or soup-sized bowls. You will need room to roll the chocolate-dipped marshmallows into your toppings.
- Put your chocolate into the microwave for one minute.
- Remove and stir until melted.
- If the chocolate hasn't melted, cook for 30 more seconds and stir.
- Drop one marshmallow directly into the chocolate and dip it quickly, rolling it around until completely covered.
- Let the excess chocolate drip off and place on wire rack.
- If at any time, your chocolate gets too firm to roll, place it back in the microwave for about 10 seconds and stir.
- If you want to dip the marshmallow into one of your toppings, as soon as it is covered in chocolate, with the two forks, drop the marshmallow directly into the topping and roll until covered in nuts, crumbs or sprinkles and place on tray to dry.
- That's all there is to it!
- - I enjoy using the Lindt chocolate candy bars that come out during the holidays as the chocolate is fantastic and very creamy. You have to make sure that you don't over heat it in the microwave or it can burn. Better chocolate makes for a better dipped marshmallow!
- I place several varieties of marshmallows in clear cellophane bags and give them out to as gifts for the holidays. These can be shipped in candy boxes well during the cooler months.
- -

143. Elizabethan Orange Cakes Recipe

Serving: 12 | Prep: | Cook: 300mins | Ready in:

Ingredients

- oranges
- superfine or "baker's" sugar

Direction

- Peel and section the oranges and remove as much as possible of the membrane so you have only pulp left.
- Crush thoroughly and drain as dry as possible. (You can save the juice for other uses)
- To each half-cup of drained pulp, add one cup of sugar and mix until all the sugar is dissolved.
- Spread out thinly onto parchment paper in circles about the diameter of a saucer. Let dry until the top is fairly solid, then turn upside down onto another piece of parchment paper and use a knife blade to peel the paper away.
- Continue to let dry until the "cakes" are dry through. This process can be speeded up by placing in an oven with a pilot light, but still expect it to take several hours. (Or try it in a food dehydrator on the "Fruit" heat setting.)
- Break or cut into small pieces and store in an airtight container.

144. English Toffee Recipe

Serving: 100 | Prep: | Cook: 30mins | Ready in:

Ingredients

- 2-2/3 cups sugar
- 2 cups butter
- 6 Tblsp. water
- 2 Tblsp. light corn syrup
- 1 cup finely chopped almonds, toasted
- 1 cup coarsely chopped almonds, untoasted
- 2 cup chocolate chips (or more, to taste)

Direction

- Butter two cookie sheets, or spray with non-stick spray.
- In a heavy saucepan, combine sugar, butter, water, corn syrup and untoasted almonds.
- Cook over medium heat, stirring occasionally, to hard crack stage (300 degrees).
- Quickly pour mixture into prepared sheets and spread as thinly as possible, approx. 1/4 inch thick. Using the back of two forks, keep spreading the candy until it fits all the way to each side, then spread more from the middle, where it will be thicker.
- Sprinkle the chocolate chips evenly over the hot candy and wait about one minute, until melted.
- Spread chocolate over candy and then sprinkle with toasted almonds.
- Chill until completely hardened and then break into bite-sized pieces.
- Hints: I undercook this just slightly, not more than about 5 degrees, so that it is easier on the teeth.

145. Extravagant Old Fashioned Fudge Dated 1942 Recipe

Serving: 12 | Prep: | Cook: 20mins | Ready in:

Ingredients

- 2 cups granulated sugar
- 1 cup milk
- 1/2-teaspoon salt
- 2 squares unsweetened chocolate
- 2 tablespoons white corn syrup
- 2 tablespoons butter
- 1/2 teaspoon vanilla extract
- 1/2 cup chopped pecans

Direction

- In saucepan combine sugar, milk, salt, chocolate and corn syrup.
- Stir over low heat until sugar dissolves.
- Cook gently stirring occasionally until a mixture dropped into cold water forms soft ball.
- Remove from heat and drop in butter but do not stir then cool without stirring.
- Add vanilla then with spoon beat until candy loses gloss then add nuts.
- Turn into greased loaf pan then cool and cut into squares.

146. Fabulous 5 Minute Prep Fudge Recipe

Serving: 24 | Prep: | Cook: 5mins | Ready in:

Ingredients

- 1 12-ounce package semisweet chocolate pieces (2 cups)
- 2/3 cup sweetened condensed milk (one-half of a 14-ounce can)
- 1 tablespoon water
- 3/4 cup chopped walnuts, toasted if desired
- 1 teaspoon vanilla

Direction

- Line a cookie sheet with waxed paper; set aside.
- In a medium microwave-safe bowl, combine chocolate pieces, sweetened condensed milk, and water.
- Use double boiler or Microwave, uncovered, on 100% power (high) for 1 minute; stir.
- Microwave about 1 minute more, or until chocolate is melted and mixture is smooth, stirring every 30 seconds.
- Stir in nuts and vanilla.
- Pour mixture onto prepared cookie sheet and spread it into a 9x6-inch rectangle, or drop mixture by rounded teaspoons onto prepared cookie sheet.
- Chill fudge about 30 minutes or until firm.
- Cut fudge into 1-1/2-inch squares.

147. Famous Chocolate Bourbon Balls Recipe

Serving: 12 | Prep: | Cook: 10mins | Ready in:

Ingredients

- chocolate bourbon Balls
- 6 ounces semi-sweet chocolate morsels
- 3 T. corn syrup
- 1/2 cup bourbon
- 2 1/2 cups vanilla wafer crumbs
- 1/2 cup sifted confectioners' sugar
- 1 cup nuts, finely chopped
- Granulated sugar

Direction

- Melt chocolate morsels over simmering water.
- Remove from heat. Add corn syrup and bourbon; set aside.
- In large bowl, combine vanilla wafer crumbs, confectioners' sugar and nuts.
- Add chocolate mixture; mix well. Let stand 30 minutes.
- Form into 1-inch balls. Roll in granulated sugar. Let season in covered container for several days.

148. Fancy Coffee Cup Truffles Recipe

Serving: 18 | Prep: | Cook: 10mins | Ready in:

Ingredients

- Use the best chocolate you can find!
- 9 oz. bittersweet or semisweet chocolate broken into pieces

- 2/3 c. heavy cream
- 1/3 vanilla bean
- 2 tbsp. unsalted butter
- Pinch of cinnamon
- 3 tbsp. unsweetened cocoa powder
- Sm. pinch of salt
- 1 c. confectioners' sugar, sifted

Direction

- Line the inside of 8 x 4 inch loaf pan with wax paper.
- In top of double boiler over gently simmering water, melt chocolate, stir occasionally. Remove from heat, stir until smooth. Set aside.
- STIR CHOCOLATE SMOOTHE...DO NOT BURN!!
- (Alternatively, microwave chocolate in medium glass or plastic bowl at medium power for 60 seconds, stirring between heating well, until chocolate can be stirred smooth.)
- In small pan warm cream with the vanilla bean over low heat.
- First place cream in a glass measuring cup, then split vanilla bean, scrape it and add bean scrapings to cream.
- Microwave full power 60 seconds. Remove from heat and remove vanilla bean. Gradually stir in cream into the melted chocolate until smooth. Add butter, cinnamon, cocoa and salt. Stir until well mixed. Scrape mixture into prepared pan and smooth top. Cover - refrigerate. (Truffles can be prepared up to 3 days ahead.)
- To unmold run a thin knife around edges. Cut chocolate crosswise into 3/4 inch strips. DO NOT draw knife out by pulling toward you, pull straight up after making cut, holding down chocolate.
- Cut into cubes, place on baking sheet lined with waxed paper. (Can be frozen up to 1 week at this point.)
- Place confectioners' sugar in a bag. Add frozen chocolate cubes to bag in batches, shake. Place on small decorative plate or sugar bowl. Serve with fresh coffee and pitcher of warm milk.

149. Fannie Mae Caramels Recipe

Serving: 108 | Prep: | Cook: | Ready in:

Ingredients

- 2 C. light corn syrup
- 1(14oz) can sweetened condensed milk
- 1 1/2 C. milk
- 1 C. whipping cream
- 1 C. butter
- 4 C. sugar
- 2 tsp. vanilla
- 2 C. nuts (walnuts)
- Tempered dipping chocolate if preferred or wax paper cut into rectangles

Direction

- Butter a 9X 13 baking pan. In heavy 6 quart Dutch oven, combine sugar, corn syrup, condensed milk, milk, cream and butter. Place over medium heat and stir occasionally with wooden spoon until comes to boil. Clip on candy thermometer. Cook stirring constantly until reaches 240 degrees or soft ball stage. Remove from heat. Stir in vanilla and nuts. Pour without scraping into pan. Allow to stand overnight. Cut into 1-inch rectangles or squares. Wrap in wax paper or dip in chocolate.

150. Fantasy Fudge Recipe

Serving: 12 | Prep: | Cook: 5mins | Ready in:

Ingredients

- 3 cups sugar
- 3/4 cup margarine
- 1 can (5 oz.) evaporated milk
- 1 pkg. (12 oz.) semisweet chocolate pieces

- 1 jar (7 oz.) marshmallow creme
- 1 cup chopped nuts
- 1 tsp. vanilla

Direction

- Combine sugar, margarine and milk in heavy 2 to 3-quart saucepan. Bring to a full rolling boil, stirring constantly. Continue boiling 5 minutes over medium heat or until candy thermometer reaches 234° F., stirring constantly to prevent scorching. Remove from heat.
- Stir in chocolate pieces until melted. Add marshmallow crème, nuts and vanilla. Beat until well blended. Pour into a greased 13-by-9-inch pan.
- Cool at room temperature. Cut into squares.

151. Five Minute Fudge Recipe

Serving: 24 | Prep: | Cook: 5mins | Ready in:

Ingredients

- 12-ounce package semisweet chocolate pieces (2 cups)
- 2/3 cup sweetened condensed milk (one-half of a 14-ounce can)
- 1 tablespoon water
- 3/4 cup chopped walnuts, toasted if desired
- 1 teaspoon vanilla

Direction

- Line a cookie sheet with waxed paper; set aside. In a medium microwave-safe bowl, combine chocolate pieces, sweetened condensed milk, and water.
- Microwave, uncovered, on 100% power (high) for 1 minute; stir. Microwave about 1 minute more, or until chocolate is melted and mixture is smooth, stirring every 30 seconds. Stir in nuts and vanilla. Pour mixture onto prepared cookie sheet and spread it into a 9x6-inch rectangle, or drop mixture by rounded teaspoons onto prepared cookie sheet.
- Chill fudge about 30 minutes or until firm. Cut fudge into 1-1/2-inch squares.

152. Foolproof Microwave Fudge Recipe

Serving: 64 | Prep: | Cook: 5mins | Ready in:

Ingredients

- 18 oz. (3 cups) semi-sweet chocolate chips
- 1 can sweetened condensed milk
- 1 tsp. vanilla
- 1/2 c. chopped nuts, optional

Direction

- Butter 8 x 8 inch baking pan.
- In medium glass bowl, mix together chocolate chips and milk. Microwave on high for 3 minutes, stirring after each minute or until melted and smooth. If still not melted, microwave in 30 second intervals until melted and smooth.
- Remove from microwave, stir in vanilla and nuts, if using. Pour into prepared pan and let set until cool. Cut into 1-inch squares.

153. French Caramels Recipe

Serving: 36 | Prep: | Cook: 60mins | Ready in:

Ingredients

- 1 cup half and half (no substitutions)
- 1 cup salted butter (2 sticks)
- 1/2 tsp. fleur de sel salt
- 2 3/4 cups superfine sugar
- 1/4 corn syrup

- (Optional addition of another 1/2-1 tsp of salt sprinkled over the top of the cooling caramel)

Direction

- Bring the half and half, butter and salt to a boil in a heavy saucepan or pot.
- Set aside after mixture reaches boil.
- In another pot, cook the sugar and corn syrup over a medium heat to a temperature of 293 degrees on a candy thermometer.
- As the sugar begins to melt, swirl the pan often until all of the sugar has melted.
- Once melted, remove from heat and add the half and half mixture stirring once or twice.
- Set the pan back over a medium flame and cook until the mixture reaches 248 degrees, stirring frequently. This should take from 10 to fifteen minutes and the mixture will look like a caramel sauce.
- Remove from heat and pour into an 8x8 inch pan and let it cool for 2 hours. (Before it sets, I sprinkle the caramel evenly with a bit more fleur de sel (salt).
- After 2 hours, the caramel should have set and can now be removed from the pan. You can pour hot water over the bottom of the pan for about a minute to loosen it up or use the non-stick aluminum and line the pan in advance. I use a silicone pan and just bend the candy out and then slice into small pieces which are wrapped later in wax paper or cellophane wrap.

154. Frito Munch Candy Recipe

Serving: 12 | Prep: | Cook: 15mins | Ready in:

Ingredients

- 4 cups of thin pretzels, broken up into 1/2 pieces
- ** I used a bag of the peanut butter filled pretzels with great success instead of the pretzels.
- 4 cups Fritos, broken in pieces (I use Scoops)
- 20 mini Reese's peanut butter cups cut in half
- 1 1/2 stick of salted butter
- 1 cup packed brown sugar
- 2 cups bittersweet chocolate chips
- 2 cups salted "cocktail" peanuts

Direction

- Preheat 350 degrees
- Line a jelly roll pan with non-stick aluminum foil.
- Place the Fritos and pretzels in the pan.
- Sprinkle with the Reese's cups and 1 cup of the peanuts.
- Melt the butter in a pan over medium heat and then add the brown sugar.
- Bring the mixture to a boil and boil for two minutes.
- Stir several times to make sure that the sugar is dissolving well.
- Pour the sugar mix over the dry ingredients in the pan and bake for 10 minutes.
- Remove pan from oven and using a wooden spoon, push the dry ingredients closer together on the pan.
- Sprinkle with the chocolate chips and place the pan back in the oven for 2 minutes.
- Remove pan and spread the now melted chocolate over the dry ingredients.
- Sprinkle with the remaining 1 cup of peanuts.
- Let the mixture cool for several hours until the chocolate sets.
- Cut into squares or break into pieces and serve.

155. Frosted Walnuts Recipe

Serving: 12 | Prep: | Cook: 5mins | Ready in:

Ingredients

- 4 cups of walnut halves
- 1 1/2 cups of granulated sugar
- 1/2 cup of fresh sour cream
- 2 tsp. vanilla extract
- 1 tsp. cinnamon

Direction

- Put the walnuts into a heat-proof glass bowl or ceramic bowl.
- Add the sugar and sour cream to a medium-sized sauce pan and bring to a boil over medium heat, stirring constantly until sugar melts.
- Cook for four minutes and add the vanilla extract and cinnamon.
- Stir and cook for one more minute.
- Pour the mixture over the walnuts.
- Stir until the walnuts are coated.
- Pour on to a pan either coated with butter or on to waxed paper.
- *In this day and age, you can use the Release aluminum foil or a large silicone baking mat.

156. Frozen Peppermint Patties Recipe

Serving: 15 | Prep: | Cook: 15mins | Ready in:

Ingredients

- 1 pkg unflavored gelatine
- 1 T boiling water
- 1 cup heavy cream
- 3 drops peppermint flavor
- 1 ounce cream cheese
- 1 ounce unsweetened chocolate, melted
- 1/2 tsp vanilla extract
- 2 T sugar(10 packs of splenda)

Direction

- Soften gelatine in boiling water.
- Add all ingredients into a blender and blend well.
- Chill for 10 minutes.
- Spoon onto parchment paper. Freeze till solid.
- Pack in an airtight container.

157. Fruit Leather Recipe

Serving: 4 | Prep: | Cook: 3mins | Ready in:

Ingredients

- Any fresh,ripe fruit,washed,peeled,pitted,chopped.
- I'm partial to a combination of kiwi,pineapple,strawberry,apple(for pectin)
- water(or)fruit juice.
- Fresh lemon juice
- Sugar
- spices

Direction

- In a saucepan, add your fruit and water.
- If using 4 cups of chopped fruit, then add 1/2 cup water or fruit juice.
- Cover and simmer mixture for about 20 minutes or until cooked.
- Uncover, stir and mash with potato masher.
- If your cooking 4 cups of fruit, then add sugar, 1 Tablespoon at a time, depending on how sweet the fruit is before, will depend on how much sugar you will add.
- Add the lemon juice 1 teaspoon at a time to spark the flavor of the fruit.
- May add a pinch or two of spices (I don't, unless I am making all apple or peach, then I add pie spice.)
- Continue to cook until the sugar is dissolved and fruit is thickened, about 15 to 20 minutes, on simmer.
- Place fruit puree in blender and blend until smooth, dust it to your taste with more sugar, lemon juice or spices.
- Line a jelly roll pan with heavy duty plastic wrap.

- Pour fruit puree into pan to a thickness of about 1/8 "to 1/4".
- Place in a 140 degree oven, for about 8 to 12 hours, or until the fruit is dried out, no longer sticky, and smooth on the surface.
- Peel up, roll up, in its plastic wrap, and store in an airtight container in the refrigerator.
- Note: The ideal option is a dehydrator.

158. Fruit And Nut Chocolate Chunk Candy Recipe

Serving: 36 | Prep: | Cook: 5mins | Ready in:

Ingredients

- • 1 1/4 lb fine-quality bittersweet chocolate (not unsweetened), broken into small pieces
- • vegetable oil for greasing pan
- • 2/3 cup dried cranberries
- • 2/3 cup raisins
- • 2/3 cup salted roasted shelled pistachios (3 oz)
- • 2/3 cup salted roasted cashews (3 oz)

Direction

- Melt chocolate in top of a double boiler or metal bowl set over a saucepan of barely simmering water, stirring occasionally until smooth.
- While chocolate is melting, line bottom and sides of an 8-inch square baking pan with foil, leaving a 2-inch overhang, then lightly oil foil.
- Remove chocolate from heat and stir in fruit and nuts, then spread evenly in baking pan. Freeze until firm, about 20 minutes. Lift candy in foil from pan using overhang and transfer to a cutting board. Peel off foil and cut candy with a long heavy knife into 36 pieces.
- Cooks' notes: • If you have more time, chill the candy in the refrigerator (instead of in the freezer) until firm, about 1 hour. • Candy keeps, wrapped well in foil and chilled, 2 weeks.

159. Fudge Recipe

Serving: 1 | Prep: | Cook: 40mins | Ready in:

Ingredients

- 3 ounces unsweetened chocolate, coarsely chopped (3 1-ounce squares)
- 3 cups sugar
- 1 cup half-and-half
- 1 tablespoon corn syrup
- 1/4 teaspoon salt
- 3 tablespoons butter
- 2 teaspoons vanilla extract
- 1 cup nuts and/or dried fruit, chopped (optional)
- ~~~~~~~~~~~~~~~~~~~~~~~~~~~~~~~~~~~~~~~
- an 8-inch-square pan
- waxed paper
- a large (3- to 4-quart) saucepan
- a wooden spoon
- a candy thermometer
- a pastry brush
- a marble slab (optional)
- a spatula (optional)
- a cutting board

Direction

- Prepare your square pan by greasing it with butter or lining it with waxed paper.
- Mix together chocolate, sugar, half-and-half, corn syrup, and salt in the saucepan.
- Stir over medium-low heat with a wooden spoon until the chocolate melts and the mixture begins to boil.
- As soon as the syrup starts to boil, stop stirring and clip the candy thermometer to the side of the saucepan, being careful not to let it touch the bottom.
- Let the syrup cook, undisturbed, until it reaches the soft-ball stage, about 235° F–240° F.

- While it cooks, wash down the sides of the saucepan with a pastry brush dipped in a small amount of warm water to loosen and dissolve any sugar crystals clinging to the sides.
- Carefully remove the saucepan from the heat and let the mixture rest, undisturbed.
- Let it cool to approximately 110° F.
- At this point, a slight skin should have formed on the top.
- Be patient—this may take a while!
- (Alternatively, you may pour the mixture onto a marble slab at this point and allow it to cool on the slab—this is the way that professionals make fudge.)
- Add the vanilla and butter and begin to stir with a wooden spoon.
- (If you are adding nuts or dried fruit, add them just before the mixture completely loses its gloss.)
- You don't need to use a lot of force, but you should keep stirring constantly until the fudge "sets up."
- You will be able to see the mixture gradually change from glossy to dull, lighten in color, and stiffen.
- Again, patience (and a strong arm) is needed—this change can take from 15 to 20 minutes to occur!
- (Be careful not to beat too long or too hard—this can result in a coarse, grainy fudge, as can stirring while the fudge is still too hot.)
- ~ ~
- If you're adding nuts or fruit, you may want to warm them slightly in a microwave before adding them.
- If they are too cold, the temperature difference may "shock" the fudge and cause it to solidify too quickly.
- ~~~~~~~~~~~~~~~~~~~~~~~~~~~~~~~~~~~~~~~
- Soft-Ball Stage
- 235° F–240° F
- Sugar concentration: 85%
- At this temperature, sugar syrup dropped into cold water will form a soft, flexible ball. If you remove the ball from water, it will flatten like a pancake after a few moments in your hand.
- ~~~~~~~~~~~~~~~~~~~~~~~~~~~~~~~~~~~~~~~
- Did You Know?
- Fudge was invented in the United States around 100 years ago.
- The exact origins are disputed, but all accounts claim that the first batch of fudge was accidentally created by failing to make another type of candy—possibly caramels.
- Many stories also claim that fudge was invented by students at a women's college—Vassar, Smith, or Wellesley.
- ~~~~~~~~~~~~~~~~~~~~~~~~~~~~~~~~~~~~~~~
- Why do I add corn syrup?
- Corn syrup acts as an "interfering agent" in this and many other candy recipes.
- It contains long chains of glucose molecules that tend to keep the sucrose molecules in the candy syrup from crystallizing.
- In fudge, the addition of "interfering agents" can be a double-edged sword: you want crystals to form, but not until the cooked mixture has cooled down to a certain degree.
- ~~~~~~~~~~~~~~~~~~~~~~~~~~~~~~~~~~~~~~~
- Why do I add vanilla?
- Vanilla is often added to chocolate candies or other chocolate recipes because it complements and accents the flavor of chocolate.
- ~~~~~~~~~~~~~~~~~~~~~~~~~~~~~~~~~~~~~~~
- Why do I need to stop stirring after the syrup begins to boil?
- At this point, you have dissolved the crystal structure of the sugar.
- Stirring or other agitation is one of the many factors that can encourage the fructose and glucose molecules in your syrup to re-join and form sucrose—crystals of table sugar.
- ~~~~~~~~~~~~~~~~~~~~~~~~~~~~~~~~~~~~~~~
- Why do I wash down the sides of the pan?

- The sugar crystals are dissolved at this point in the process.
- But a single seed crystal of sugar clinging to the side of the pan might fall in and encourage recrystallization.
- ~~~~~~
- Why does the fudge need to cool for such a long time?
- The key to a smooth and creamy texture is a fudge that's full of thousands of tiny sugar crystals.
- Heating the syrup to a high temperature and then allowing it to cool, undisturbed, produces a supersaturated solution — this means that the solution contains more sugar molecules than would normally be possible at room temperature.
- A supersaturated solution is highly unstable, and any agitation will cause crystallization to occur throughout the solution.
- If fudge is stirred while it's still hot, fewer crystals form, and they grow larger as the syrup cools, resulting in a coarse, grainy candy.
- ~~~~~~
- Why is it so important to keep stirring until the fudge "sets"?
- Stirring helps control the size of the sugar crystals that form — it keeps them from growing too large, which would produce gritty fudge.

160. Fudge For ONE Recipe

Serving: 1 | Prep: | Cook: 1mins | Ready in:

Ingredients

- Makes 1 individual serving
- 1/3 cup sugar (I use 1/2 Splenda)
- 1 heaping tablespoon cocoa
- 1 tablespoon and 2 teaspoons milk
- 1 scant tablespoon butter or margarine
- 1/2 teaspoon vanilla
- 1 tab. chopped nuts (optional)

Direction

- Mix sugar, cocoa and milk in 1 quart glass measuring cup. Microwave on high 1 minute. Stir down sides of cup and microwave 40 seconds more. Add butter and vanilla. Beat until thick and eat. Let set up and cut into squares or eat warm right out of the bowl.

161. Fun Taffy Pull Recipe

Serving: 12 | Prep: | Cook: 10mins | Ready in:

Ingredients

- 1 cup granulated sugar
- 1/4 cup light corn syrup
- 2 tablespoons butter
- 2/3 cup water
- 1 teaspoon salt
- 1 tablespoon cornstarch
- 1 teaspoon vanilla extract
- 8-10 drops food coloring
- extra butter for hands

Direction

- Have ready a well-buttered 10 inch pan for it to cool in.
- Combine in a two quart pot: sugar, corn syrup, butter, water, salt and corn starch.
- Mix very well and once it's boiling you can check to see when it's ready by dropping a little bit off a spoon into cold water. If a hard ball forms, it's time to remove from heat and add a teaspoon of vanilla extract and 8 or 10 drops of food coloring. Place in the buttered pan and allow to cool enough to handle it. Now butter your hands and go have some fun. Pull it, bend it, flatten it and fold it until it is stiff and lightly colored like pastels. Cut into

desired shapes and sizes and wrap in wax paper. If you work fast enough with it, you can even attempt ribbons or twisted pieces. It's a blast. This recipe will make about a pound of taffy. The more people you have playing with the soft candy, the more you may want to double or triple the ingredients.

- Caution: Children must wait until an adult says it's okay to handle it, as it is quite hot and can leave some nasty burns if touched when it first comes out of the pan. Keep checking though. You don't want to allow it to get so cool that it's no longer pliable.

162. Ganache Recipe

Serving: 12 | Prep: | Cook: 3mins | Ready in:

Ingredients

- Semi-sweet chips or bittersweet chips
- Fresh heavy whipping cream only
- Flavored extracts of your choice

Direction

- I'm just going to post the basic steps for making a ganache which is the ultimate formula for making truffles, some frostings and glazes and or chocolate mousses that do not require eggs as part of the ingredients.
- ...Truffles
- 1/2 cup cream
- 1 cup chocolate chips or chopped chocolate.
- (Never use milk chocolate)
- Put chocolate in a glass bowl with the cream.
- Using a 1000 watt microwave, melt for one minute and stir.
- If the chocolate has melted completely, stir until you have satiny "sauce" adding a teaspoon of whichever flavored extract you wish to use at this point.
- Let the mixture cool for an hour or more depending on the temp of your kitchen. When cooled enough to be solid yet soft enough to make balls, remove teaspoonfuls of ganache and roll into balls, setting on wax paper or foil while continuing to make more. You can eat them this way or roll the ganache in chopped nuts, chocolate, powdered cocoa, coconut, chopped candies or anything else that your heart desires. Try some of those flavored coffee powders sold in all of the markets.
- ...Glazes
- 1/3 cup cream
- 1 cup chocolate
- Melt for one minute in microwave until mixture is blended and let cool until your cakes or cookies have cooled completely. Pour the glaze over your baked products once it too, has cooled.
- ...Mousses
- 1 cup cream
- 1 cup chocolate
- Mix with whipped toppings such as Cool Whip and use in parfait glasses with layers of puddings or more whipped cream. This is also great as a sauce for ice cream.
- As far as the extracts go, you can flavor the ganache with many of them with great success.
- Peppermint extract will give you wonderful mint truffles or a lovely mint sauce if used with the glaze. Use sparingly as the mint extract is very strong and a little goes a long way in a truffle. Use a 1/4 of a teaspoon first and taste it. I once used a full teaspoon and ended up with something that tasted like chocolate toothpaste. So start with small amounts and taste it all before adding more.
- Orange extract makes really lovely flavored truffles and a chocolate sauce as well.
- Lemon extract is fabulous!
- You can also add a tablespoon of flavored liqueurs such as coffee flavored and almond flavored liqueurs. There are fruit flavored liquors as well that are worth trying. Rum, cognac and champagne also make flavorful truffles.
- For a treat, make brownies and place a scoop of ice cream over the brownie and add some of

- the ganache with some whipped cream on top of that. YUM!
- Now that I'm in a chocolate mood, here's one last suggestion for a great treat. If you do make brownies, add a layer of the truffle recipe over the warm brownies and let the whole pan cool. Do not refrigerate this. Just let it cool for a few hours. This is my version of Death by Chocolate! (This can also be used on top of plain cheesecakes (and it's so good on top of a lemon cheesecake. omg!)
- *I am using a pic I found on the web! I confess!

163. Glacé Orange Slices Dipped In Dark Chocolate Recipe

Serving: 0 | Prep: | Cook: | Ready in:

Ingredients

- 3 and a half cups of white sugar
- 4 oranges
- 300g dark chocolate (if you wish to dip the orange slices in chocolate)
- 2/3 cup extra caster sugar (if you wish to coat the orange slices with caster sugar)

Direction

- 1. Cut the four oranges into slices about 1cm thick.
- 2. Put orange slices in a container and cover completely with boiling water. Cover the container then leave for 24 hours.
- 3. Put 3 and a half cups caster sugar in a large pot with 5 cups of water. Simmer for 2 – 3 minutes till sugar has dissolved.
- 4. Place orange slices in the pot and simmer. Then reduce heat to the lowest it can go and leave for 3 – 4 hours.
- 5. Lift orange slices out of pot and place on a tray with a rack and place into a preheated oven at 90°C for an hour.
- 6. Cut each orange slice in half. Roll in caster sugar if desired.
- 7. (Optional) - Melt chocolate in a bowl over simmering water. Dip the straight side of each orange slice about 2/3 of the way into the chocolate.
- 8. Transfer to non-stick paper and leave to cool. Do not cool in fridge/freezer as chocolate will develop water molecules.
- Tips:
  - • Melt the chocolate and leave to cool but not harden. This is similar to tempering and will prevent white specs from developing on the chocolate.
  - • Store orange slices neatly in a container in layers with waxed paper.

164. Goobers Recipe

Serving: 60 | Prep: | Cook: 90mins | Ready in:

Ingredients

- 1 cup peanut butter
- 1/2 cup butter (no substitutes), softened
- 3 cups confectioners' sugar
- 5 dozen miniature pretzel twists (about 3 cups)
- 1 1/2 cups milk chocolate chips
- 1 tablespoon vegetable oil

Direction

- In a mixing bowl, beat peanut butter and butter until smooth. Beat in confectioners' sugar until combined.
- Shape into 1-in. balls; press one on each pretzel. Place on waxed paper-lined baking sheets. Refrigerate until peanut butter mixture is firm, about 1 hour.
- In a microwave-safe bowl or heavy saucepan, melt chocolate chips and oil.
- Dip the peanut butter ball into chocolate. Return to baking sheet, pretzel side down. Refrigerate for at least 30 minutes before serving. Store in the refrigerator.

165. Grand Marnier Truffles Recipe

Serving: 48 | Prep: | Cook: 10mins | Ready in:

Ingredients

- 1/4 cup heavy cream
- 2 tablespoons Grand Marnier liqueur
- 6 ounces sweet chocolate
- 4 tablespoons sweet butter softened
- Powdered unsweetened cocoa

Direction

- Boil cream in a small heavy pan until reduced to 2 tablespoons.
- Remove from heat then stir in grand marnier and chocolate.
- Return to low heat and stir until chocolate melts.
- Whisk in softened butter.
- When mixture is smooth pour into a shallow bowl and refrigerate about 40 minutes.
- Scoop chocolate up with a teaspoon and shape into 1" balls.
- Roll balls in unsweetened cocoa.
- Store truffles covered in the refrigerator.
- Let truffles stand at room temperature for 30 minutes before serving.

166. Grand Marnier And Chocolate Truffles Recipe

Serving: 20 | Prep: | Cook: 10mins | Ready in:

Ingredients

- 1/2 cup double cream
- 6 oz dark chocolate, broken into pieces
- 4 tbsp Grand Marnier
- Zest of 1/2 orange
- 1 1/2 cup dark chocolate to dip, or sifted cocoa powder to roll

Direction

- Line a baking sheet with non-stick paper.
- Put the cream into a pan and bring to boil. Remove the pan from the heat and add the chocolate pieces, the Grand Marnier and the orange zest. Stir until really well mixed. Cool and chill for 15 min.
- Beat the mixture for around 5 min until it gets a consistency like fudge. Shape into small balls and place them on the baking sheet. Freeze for 1 hour.
- Melt a cup of the dipping chocolate in a bowl in bain-marie. Lift the bowl off the pan and add the remaining chocolate and stir until melted.
- Using a fork, dip the truffles into the chocolate, then place on the lined baking sheet.
- Alternatively you can roll the truffles in sifted cocoa powder or grounded nuts.
- Use your imagination! :)

167. Grandma's Strawberry Candies Recipe

Serving: 10 | Prep: | Cook: 5mins | Ready in:

Ingredients

- 2 strawberry jello powders (use sweetened or unsweetened, 7 ounze packages)
- 1 can condensed milk (not evaporated)
- 1 pound dessicated coconut
- 1 tablespoon lemon juice
- 2 tablespoons white sugar
- red food coloring (about 20 drops)

Direction

- Combine 1 1/2 packages of jelly powder with coconut, condensed milk, lemon juice and sugar.
- Add food coloring to this mixture
- Shape mixture into strawberries; roll these strawberries gently in the remaining jelly powder
- Make leaves on stem end of strawberries with green butter icing
- Chill. Makes 3 dozen.

168. HAYSTACKS Recipe

Serving: 24 | Prep: | Cook: 20mins | Ready in:

Ingredients

- 12 OZ PACKAGE chips (chocolate, butterSCOTCH, peanut butter OR mint, OR ANY COMBINATION)
- 1/2 (5 1/2 OZ) CAN CHINESE CHOP SUEY noodles
- 1/2 CUP walnuts
- 1/2 CUP coconut

Direction

- DO NOT TRY AMD MAKE TOO MUCH AT ONE TIME.
- MELT CHIPS IN THE TOP OF A DOUBLE BOILRT.
- STIR IN NOODLES, NUTS AND COCONUT.
- DROP BY SPOONFULS ONTO WAX PAPER AND COOL.
- EAT THEM ALL UP.

169. HOT Hot Chocolate Espresso Beans Recipe

Serving: 16 | Prep: | Cook: 60mins | Ready in:

Ingredients

- 1 lb fine espresso beans
- 8 oz semisweet chocolate, chopped
- 1 cup heavy cream
- 1 tsp instant espresso powder
- 1 habanero chili, halved and seeded

Direction

- In a double boiler, melt chocolate. Stir until smooth.
- In a small heavy saucepan, heat cream, espresso powder, and habanero over a low flame until habanero is tender. Do not scorch cream.
- Transfer cream mixture to a blender and puree habanero. You may strain mixture afterwards if you like.
- Gradually stir cream mixture into melted chocolate until smooth and creamy. It should be fluid enough to coat your beans, and thick enough to stick.
- In batches, mix in espresso beans until coated and remove to parchment paper to cool in an even, single layer. Avoid touching beans as they will harden together.
- Drizzle coated beans with remaining chocolate mix and allow to cool completely. Store in an airtight container and share with everyone!

170. Halloween Candy Bark

Serving: 24 | Prep: | Cook: 30mins | Ready in:

Ingredients

- 2 teaspoons butter
- 1-1/2 pounds white candy coating, coarsely chopped
- 2 cups pretzels, coarsely chopped
- 10 Oreo cookies, chopped
- 3/4 cup candy corn
- 3/4 cup dry roasted peanuts
- 1/2 cup milk chocolate M&M's
- 1/2 cup Reese's Pieces

Direction

- Line a 15x10x1-in. baking pan with foil; grease foil with butter. In a microwave, melt candy coating; stir until smooth. Spread into prepared pan. Sprinkle with remaining ingredients; press into candy coating. Let stand about 1 hour.
- Break or cut bark into pieces. Store in an airtight container.
- Nutrition Facts
- 1 ounce: 152 calories, 7g fat (5g saturated fat), 1mg cholesterol, 84mg sodium, 21g carbohydrate (18g sugars, 0 fiber), 1g protein.

171. Harvest Moon Lollipops Recipe

Serving: 12 | Prep: | Cook: 1mins | Ready in:

Ingredients

- Materials:
- 12 (10- to 12-inch-long) lollipop sticks
- 1 (24-ounce) package chocolate Flavor MoonPies
- 1 (14-ounce) package orange candy melts
- 1 zip-top plastic bag
- Scissors
- wax paper
- Halloween candies
- Halloween sugar cake decorations
- Decorator icing
- Ribbon (optional)

Direction

- Step 1: Insert 1 lollipop stick 2 to 3 inches into marshmallow center of Moon Pie.
- Step 2: Microwave candy melts in a glass bowl at MEDIUM (50% power) 1 minute or until melted, stirring once; spoon into plastic bag, and seal.
- Step 3: Snip a small hole in 1 corner of the bag; pipe melted candy around where stick meets Moon Pie to secure. Lay flat on wax paper, and let stand until firm.
- Step 4: Pipe fun border of melted candy around edges. Attach candies and/or cake decorations with decorator icing. Tie ribbons around tops of sticks, if desired.

172. Hazelnut Fantasy Fudge Recipe

Serving: 0 | Prep: | Cook: 10mins | Ready in:

Ingredients

- 3 cups sugar
- 3/4 cup (1 1/2 Sticks) butter (unsalted)
- 1 small can (5oz.) evaporated milk
- 1 13oz. jar Ferrero "Nutella" (Hazelnut Spread with skim milk & cocoa)
- 1 7oz. jar Kraft's Jet-Puffed marshmallow cream
- 1 tsp. vanilla
- 1 cup Sliced (in Half) "Fresh Hazelnut's (optional)

Direction

- 1 Heat Sugar, Butter, and Evaporated Milk to Full roaring Boil in three Quart Heavy Sauce pan over medium heat, Stirring Constantly!
- Boil on medium heat until candy thermometer reaches 234 deg, F about 4 minutes, stirring constantly!
- Remove from heat!
- Stir in "Ferrero!" Nutella and "Kraft!" Marshmallow cream until properly blended until smooth and consistent in texture and appearance! Then add Vanilla and Hazelnut's until well blended! Spread into 9x13 foil lined pan!
- Cool at room temperature at least 4 hours, cut into squares, store in air tight container!

173. Hazelnut Truffles Recipe

Serving: 120 | Prep: | Cook: 10mins | Ready in:

Ingredients

- 1 14-ounce can sweetened condensed milk
- 1 13-ounce jar (about 1-1/4 cups) chocolate-hazelnut spread
- 4 ounces unsweetened chocolate, chopped
- 1 tablespoon irish cream liqueur or vanilla
- 2/3 cup halved hazelnuts (filberts), toasted*
- Finely or coarsely chopped toasted hazelnuts (filberts)
- unsweetened cocoa powder

Direction

- 1. In a heavy medium saucepan combine sweetened condensed milk, chocolate-hazelnut spread, and unsweetened chocolate. Cook over low heat until chocolate melts, stirring constantly. Remove saucepan from heat. Cool slightly. Stir in liqueur or vanilla until smooth. Transfer to a mixing bowl; cover and chill about 3 hours or until firm.
- 2. Line a baking sheet with waxed paper. For each truffle, form about 1 teaspoon of the chocolate mixture around 1 toasted hazelnut half to make a 3/4-inch ball. Roll in chopped toasted nuts or cocoa powder.
- 3. Store in a tightly covered container in the refrigerator for several weeks or freezer up to 3 months.
- Makes 120 candies.
- To Toast Hazelnuts
- Place nuts in a skillet. Cook over medium-low heat, stirring or shaking skillet often for 7 to 10 minutes or until skins begin to flake and nuts are light golden brown. Watch carefully to avoid overbrowning. Remove nuts from skillet and place on a clean kitchen towel. When hazelnuts are cool enough to handle, rub the nuts together in the towel, removing as much of the brown skin as possible.

174. Home Made "mozart Kugel" Recipe

Serving: 0 | Prep: | Cook: 60mins | Ready in:

Ingredients

- 150 g marzipan
- 200 g marzipan
- 40 g pistachio nut, not salted (grounded)
- 1 teaspoon maraschino (wild cherry brandy)
- 50 g hazelnut
- 50 g sugar (white)
- 300 g chocolate
- 40 g butter

Direction

- Ground pistachio in a coffee blender and add into first 150 g marzipan and add one teaspoon of maraschino. Mix well to get green paste. Make small balls.
- Cover the green balls with 200g marzipan to make a little bigger ball.
- Melt sugar in a pan (Teflon) until brown. Roast the hazelnut. Add roasted hazelnut into still warm sugar and let it cool.
- When cooled put sugar with hazelnut into blender and make rough mixture of sugar and hazelnut.
- Now cover the marzipan balls with hazelnut/sugar mixture. If it won't stuck, you may use some kind of hazelnut cream (I use Nutella) and then roll the balls into hazelnut/sugar.
- When done, melt chocolate (with some butter) on steam and using toothpick dip the balls into chocolate. Keep them in cool place, but not refrigerator.

175. Homemade Caramels Recipe

Serving: 35 | Prep: | Cook: 30mins | Ready in:

Ingredients

- 1 cup butter or margarine
- 1 lb bag of brown sugar
- Dash of salt
- 1 cup of light corn syrup
- 1 can (15 oz) sweetened condensed milk
- 1 tsp vanilla

Direction

- Melt butter in heavy 3 qt. saucepan.
- Add brown sugar and salt stirring until thoroughly combined.
- Blend in corn syrup.
- Gradually add sweetened condensed milk.
- STIR CONSTANTLY OVER MED HEAT UNTIL CANDY REACHES 245 DEGREES.
- Remove from heat.
- Stir in vanilla.
- Pour into a buttered 9 x 13 pan.
- Cool.
- Cut into small pieces and wrap in wax paper.

176. Homemade Cinnamon Praline Pecans Recipe

Serving: 20 | Prep: | Cook: 30mins | Ready in:

Ingredients

- 2 lbs pecan or walnut halves
- 2 egg whites
- 2 tsp water
- 1 cup sugar
- 1 tsp cinnamon
- a dash of salt
- 1/2 tsp cocoa-or more
- cayenne pepper to taste

Direction

- Preheat oven to 325.
- Beat egg whites and water together.
- Stir in pecans and toss quickly.
- In the meantime, have mixed the sugar, cinnamon, salt and cocoa. Pour over the pecans and toss quickly.
- Pour pecans into a greased baking sheet.
- Bake about 30 minutes, stirring every ten minutes.
- Using a spatula, loosen the pecans from the sheet immediately. Cool.
- Can be stored in an airtight container for up to two weeks.
- You can use any nuts you like, really. I love cashews done this way, too.

177. Homemade Gum Drops Recipe

Serving: 36 | Prep: | Cook: 15mins | Ready in:

Ingredients

- 4 cups white sugar
- 1-1/2 cups boiling water
- 2 envelopes knox gelatin
- flavorings and food colorings
- use the candy flavorings.they have so many like watermelon, cotton candy, lemon strawberry, tutti frutti, banana creme and so on

Direction

- Soak gelatine in 1/4 cup cold water for 5 minutes.
- Add boiling water, when dissolved, add sugar, and boil slowly for 15 minutes.
- Prior to pouring candy into the pans dip bottom of pans into cold water for a minute. Then take pans out
- Then divide in 2 pans add flavoring and coloring, as desired.
- Let stand overnight.
- Then cut into small squares or any shape roll in powdered sugar.

- Eat and enjoy store with container with lid. Use wax paper to layer candies. Unless you eat them all.

178. Homemade Marshmallows Recipe

Serving: 80 | Prep: | Cook: 40mins | Ready in:

Ingredients

- powdered sugar
- 3 1/2 envelopes unflavored gelatin (2 tablespoons + 2 1/2 teaspoons
- 1/2 cup cold water (125 ml)
- 2 cups sugar (500ml)
- 1/2 cup light corn syrup
- 1/2 cup hot water
- 1/4 teaspoon salt
- 3 egg whites, room temperature
- 2 teaspoons vanilla extract

Direction

- Line the bottom and sides of a 13- by 9- inch baking pan with plastic wrap.
- Oil and then generously dust with powdered sugar.
- In a large bowl of an electric mixer, sprinkle gelatine over the cold water.
- Let stand to soften.
- In a large, heavy saucepan, cook sugar, corn syrup, hot water and salt over low heat.
- Stir until sugar is dissolved.
- Increase heat to medium-high.
- Boil about 4 to 5 minutes without stirring.
- Boil until a candy or digital thermometer registers 240 deg F or until syrup reaches firm ball stage.
- Immediately remove from heat.
- Pour hot sugar mixture over gelatine mixture.
- Stir until gelatine is dissolved.
- Beat mixture on high speed until white, thick and nearly tripled in volume (5-6 minutes)
- In another large bowl with clean beaters, beat whites until they just hold stiff peaks.
- Beat whites and vanilla into sugar mixture until well combined.
- Pour into prepared baking pan.
- Sift 1/4 cup powdered sugar evenly over top.
- Refrigerate uncovered until firm (at least 3 hours)
- Run a thin knife around edges of pan.
- Invert pan onto a large cutting board.
- Sprinkle top with 1/4 cup powdered sugar.
- With a large knife, trim edges of marshmallows.
- Cut into 1-inch cubes.
- Lightly grease the blade of your knife with vegetable shortening.
- Cover new edges in powdered sugar.
- Store.
- For a delicious treat, cover with melted chocolate.

179. Homemade Mini Peanut Butter Cups Recipe

Serving: 24 | Prep: | Cook: 10mins | Ready in:

Ingredients

- 1 1/2 cups milk or semisweet chocolate chips
- 2/3 cup creamy or chunky peanut butter
- 1/4 cup sifted powdered sugar
- 1/4 cup whipping cream

Direction

- Over double boiler, melt chocolate chips.
- Place over bowl of hot water.
- Using pastry brush, coat bottoms and sides of 24-1 inch mini paper liners.
- Set aside remaining chocolate.
- Freeze cups until firm.
- Repeat coating procedure.

- In mixing bowl, add peanut butter, powdered sugar and whipping cream and mix until well blended.
- Spoon 1 tsp. peanut butter mixture into center of each cup.
- Chill.
- Spoon remaining chocolate over peanut butter mixture and spread evenly.
- Chill completely.

180. Homemade Tootsie Rolls Recipe

Serving: 10 | Prep: | Cook: 20mins | Ready in:

Ingredients

- 1 cup granulated sugar
- 1/2 cup light corn syrup
- 2 tablespoons shortening
- 4 teaspoons cocoa
- 2 tablespoons evaporated skim milk
- 1/2 teaspoon vanilla

Direction

- Combine sugar, corn syrup, shortening and cocoa in medium saucepan over medium/high heat.
- Bring mixture to boil then reduce heat and simmer candy until temperature reaches 275 degrees.
- Remove saucepan from heat and when bubbling stops add evaporated milk.
- Beat candy with an electric mixer in the pan for about 30 seconds.
- Add vanilla then continue to beat candy until it begins to firm up and you can no longer beat it.
- Pour candy out onto wax paper and when it is cool divide into several portions.
- Roll portions into long ropes that are approximately 1/2" thick.
- Use a sharp knife to slice candy into 1" long pieces.
- Arrange the candy on a plate and let it sit out overnight so that it firms up.

181. Homemade Twix Bars Recipe Recipe

Serving: 6 | Prep: | Cook: 1hours | Ready in:

Ingredients

- Ingredients:
- * For the cookie part:
- 1 cup (2 sticks) salted butter, at room temperature
- 1 cup confectioners' sugar
- 2 teaspoons vanilla extract
- 2 cups all-purpose flour
- * For the caramel layer:
- 2 cups caramel, cut into small chunks
- 3 tablespoons heavy cream
- * For the chocolate layer:
- 3 cups chopped milk chocolate, melted
- 1 tablespoon vegetable shortening (if the chocolate is too thick)

Direction

- Directions:
- Preheat your oven to 300F. Spray a 9 x 13 inch pan lightly with cooking spray, or line with parchment paper, and set aside.
- In a medium-sized bowl, beat together the butter, sugar and vanilla. Add the flour. At first the mixture may seem dry, but will come together as you continue to beat at medium speed.
- Take the dough, it will be somewhat stiff, and press it evenly into the pan. Lightly flouring your fingertips will help with any sticking.
- Prick the crust all over with a fork. The holes will allow steam to escape and the crust will bake evenly with fewer bubbles.
- Bake the crust until it's lightly golden brown on top and the edges are deeper golden brown, about 35 to 45 minutes.

- Remove from the oven and immediately run a knife around the edges to loosen the crust. Set it aside to cool completely.
- Melt the caramel and cream over low heat in a small saucepan. Pour the caramel over the cooled crust and set in the refrigerator for 30 minutes to chill and firm up.
- Melt the milk chocolate slowly in a double boiler or over very low heat. If it seems very thick, add a tablespoon of shortening to thin it.
- After the caramel layer has chilled firm, cut down the length of the pan, splitting the bars into two long, narrow bars. Then cut each long strip into "fingers". Dip the chilled bars into melted chocolate and place on parchment paper to set for several hours.
- OR
- Pour chocolate evenly over the chilled caramel layer and spread to cover all of the caramel. Return to the fridge until the chocolate is well set. Cut bars into 2 x 2 squares to serve.
- The second option is easier and quicker than the first one, but both ways will give you the yummy treat!
- It's best to store bars in the refrigerator.
- ENJOY!!!

182. Honey Caramels With Pistachios Recipe

Serving: 36 | Prep: | Cook: 20mins | Ready in:

Ingredients

- 1 1/2 cups honey
- 1/4 cup water
- 1 tbl lemon juice
- 1/2 teaspoon salt
- 1/2 cup tahini (sesame seed paste)
- 1/2 cup chopped pistachios or almonds(Optional if you do not want nuts)
- Equipment: candy thermometer, parchment paper, wax paper

Direction

- Line a square baking pan with parchment paper and grease the paper with some oil.
- Place honey, water, lemon juice, and salt in a heavy bottomed saucepan and bring to a boil.
- Let boil over medium heat until it reaches hard ball stage, 260F on a candy thermometer (about 15-20 minutes).
- Remove from the heat and quickly whip in the tahini.
- Pour the mixture into the prepared pan.
- Sprinkle the pistachios over the surface.
- Set aside in the refrigerator to cool and harden (a couple of hours)
- Use a greased knife to cut the caramels into pieces. (If they start to get soft or sticky, quick-chill them in the freezer before continuing).
- Wrap each piece in a square of wax paper and twist the ends to secure. Store in the refrigerator, as they tend to be a little melty at room temperature.
- _____

183. Honey Maple Mac Nuts Recipe

Serving: 6 | Prep: | Cook: 10mins | Ready in:

Ingredients

- 1/2 cup honey
- 1/2 cup maple syrup
- Pinch salt
- 4 tablespoons milk
- 1 teaspoon vanilla
- 1 cup roasted macadamia nuts

Direction

- Combine ingredients, except nuts, in a large pot.
- Bring to a boil over medium heat and cook until mixture thickens. Remove from heat, then beat until soft and creamy.

- Add nuts; mix well to coat.
- Spread on wax paper and allow to harden.
- From the Honolulu Star-Bulletin 7/2001

184. Incredible Brown Sugar Or Penuche Fudge Recipe

Serving: 12 | Prep: | Cook: 30mins | Ready in:

Ingredients

- 3 cups brown sugar
- 1 cup evaporated milk
- 1 tablespoon light corn syrup
- 1 teaspoon vanilla
- 1 cup chopped nuts, optional
- 3 tablespoons butter

Direction

- In a medium saucepan (2 to 3-quart size), combine brown sugar with evaporated milk and corn syrup; bring to a boil, stirring constantly. Continue boiling, stirring frequently, to soft ball stage or when candy thermometer registers 234° to 238°.
- Remove from heat and add vanilla and butter; do not stir. Let cool for about 25 minutes, then beat with a wooden spoon until the fudge just begins to thicken. Add chopped nuts and beat for a few more minutes, until it begins to lose its gloss but is not too thick. Pour or spread in a greased pie plate or 8-inch square pan. Score when set and cut into squares when firm.
- To test for soft ball stage:
- Use fresh cold water each time you test the candy. In about 1 cup of cold water, spoon about 1/2 teaspoon of hot candy. Put you hand into the water and push the candy to form a ball. Gently pick the formed ball up (if it will not form a ball, it is not done) - the soft ball will flatten slightly when removed from water.

185. Irish Potato Candy Recipe

Serving: 10 | Prep: | Cook: | Ready in:

Ingredients

- 1/2 C (about 1 small to medium potato). mashed potatoes
- 2 1/4 C. confectioner's sugar
- 1-12 oz. jar peanut butter

Direction

- Place potatoes in mixer bowl.
- Add sugar a little bit at a time beating well after each addition.
- Spread onto a big piece of waxed paper about 12"x18" and make a rectangle about 10"x15".
- Spread peanut butter over top of sugar potato mixture.
- Roll up like as a jelly roll.
- Put in fridge for about an hour then cut into slices.
- Store in fridge.

186. Jamaican Marshmallows Recipe

Serving: 60 | Prep: | Cook: 20mins | Ready in:

Ingredients

- 2/3 cup cold water, divided
- 2 tbsp unflavored gelatin
- 1 cup sugar
- 1/2 cup white or light corn syrup
- 1/4 teaspoon salt
- 1/2 tsp vanilla extract
- 1/2 tsp coconut extract
- 1/2 tsp rum extract

Direction

- Line a 13 x 9" baking pan with well-greased plastic wrap. Dust with some powdered sugar.
- In a stand mixer bowl fitted with the whip attachment, add gelatine to 1/3 cup cold water. Set aside.
- In a heavy saucepan, add sugar, corn syrup, salt, and remaining water.
- Stir to dissolve sugar.
- Cover and place over moderately low heat, and cook for 5 minutes.
- Remove the cover and increase the heat to high.
- Boil the syrup, without stirring, until it reaches 240F on a candy thermometer.
- Immediately remove from the heat.
- Start the mixer at medium speed, and slowly pour the hot syrup into the bowl.
- Increase the speed to high and whip for 10 minutes until the mixture is lukewarm.
- Add the extracts and beat 1 minute more.
- Pour the marshmallow mixture into the prepared pan and smooth the top (add some shredded coconut on top if desired!).
- Let the pan stand, uncovered, at room temperature to dry (this can take up to 10 hours). Generally, the longer you let it set up, the easier it will be to cut.
- Invert the pan of marshmallow onto a cornstarch-dusted board.
- Remove the plastic wrap and dust the top with cornstarch or powdered sugar.
- Cut into squares or desired shapes.
- Store in an airtight container.

187. Just Like A Payday Bar Recipe

Serving: 8 | Prep: | Cook: 45mins |Ready in:

Ingredients

- Centers:
- 1/4 C whole milk
- 5 Unwrapped caramels
- 1 T light corn syrup
- 1 tsp peanut butter
- 1/4 tsp vanilla
- 1/4 tsp salt
- 1 1/4 C confectioners sugar
- <
- <
- Coating
- 20 unwrapped caramels
- 1 1/2 tsp water
- 2 C dry roasted peanuts

Direction

- Combine all ingredients for centers except sugar over low heat, stirring as caramel melts.
- When caramels are melted and mixture is smooth, add 3/4 C sugar, and stir into mix. (Reserve remaining sugar).
- Using a candy thermometer, bring mixture to EXACTLY 230 degrees, stirring constantly, then turn off heat.
- When the temperature drops, stir in remaining sugar and use a hand mixer set on high to combine.
- Mix continually until the mixture is cooled and can no longer be worked. (1-2 minutes)
- Let cool in the pan 10-15 minutes or until you can safely touch it.
- Take a small chunk and roll it between your palms until it forms a rope shape about the diameter of your index finger and 4 1/2" long.
- (About a tablespoon)
- Repeat until all mixture is used. Place on waxed paper and leave for 1-2 hours to firm up.
- Meanwhile combine 20 unwrapped caramels wit 1 1/2 tsp. water in a saucepan over low heat.
- Stir often.
- Now working quickly, pour peanuts onto a baking sheet,
- Quickly paint the caramel mixture on the bars with a pastry brush on one side of bar, then roll it over into peanuts, and repeat for the other half of the bar.
- Press the peanuts firmly into the bar to set.

- If needed brush on more caramel and roll into peanuts until fully covered.

188. Kahlua Truffles Recipe

Serving: 24 | Prep: | Cook: 15mins | Ready in:

Ingredients

- 1/4 cup heavy cream
- 2 tablespoons Kahlua
- 6 ounces sweet chocolate
- 4 tablespoons sweet butter softened
- Powdered unsweetened cocoa

Direction

- Boil cream in a small heavy pan until reduced to 2 tablespoons.
- Remove from heat then stir in Kahlua and chocolate.
- Return to low heat and stir until chocolate melts.
- Whisk in softened butter.
- When mixture is smooth pour into a shallow bowl and refrigerate about 40 minutes.
- Scoop chocolate up with a teaspoon and shape into 1" balls.
- Roll balls in unsweetened cocoa.
- Store truffles covered in the refrigerator.
- Let truffles stand at room temperature for 30 minutes before serving.

189. Key Lime "truffles" Recipe

Serving: 20 | Prep: | Cook: 2hours | Ready in:

Ingredients

- 2 tbsp cream cheese (regular or low fat – NI is for full fat), softened
- 3 tbsp salted butter, softened (add a pinch of salt if using unsalted)
- ¼ cup sugar
- Zest of 1 lime
- juice of ½ lime
- ¼ cup whole wheat flour
- ½ cup graham cracker crumbs
- Dark or white chocolate, melted, for coating

Direction

- In a bowl, beat together the cream cheese, butter, sugar, lime zest and lime juice until well combined.
- Mix together the flour and graham cracker crumbs and beat into the cheese mixture to form a scoopable "batter-dough".
- Roll small balls of the mixture and refrigerate at least 1 hour to firm up (or freeze at this point).
- Dip in melted chocolate and allow to set. When coated, truffles can be kept at room temperature for 1 week or 3 weeks in the fridge.

190. Krafts Chocolate Peanut Butter Snowballs Recipe

Serving: 13 | Prep: | Cook: 80mins | Ready in:

Ingredients

- 1 pkg. (8 squares) BAKER'S Semi-sweet chocolate
- 1/2 cup KRAFT smooth peanut butter
- 2 cups thawed Cool Whip whipped topping
- 1/4 cup icing sugar

Direction

- MICROWAVE chocolate in large microwaveable bowl on MEDIUM 2 min. or until chocolate is almost melted, stirring after 1 min. Stir until chocolate is completely melted.

- STIR in peanut butter until well blended. Cool to room temperature. Gently stir in whipped topping. Refrigerate 1 hour.
- SCOOP peanut butter mixture with melon baller or teaspoon, then shape into 1-inch balls. Roll balls in icing sugar. Store in refrigerator.

191. Lemon Fudge Recipe

Serving: 35 | Prep: | Cook: 15mins | Ready in:

Ingredients

- 1 1/2 tsp. plus 6 Tbs. butter, divided
- 2 packages (10 to 12 oz. each) vanilla or white chips
- 2/3 c. sweetened condensed milk
- 2/3 c. marshmallow creme
- 1 1/2-3 tsp. lemon extract (depending on your taste) :)
- A few drops of yellow food coloring

Direction

- Line a 9-in. square pan with foil.
- Grease foil with 1 1/2 tsp. butter; set aside.
- In a large saucepan, melt remaining butter over low heat.
- Add chips and milk; cook and stir for 10-12 minutes or until chips are melted.
- Stir in marshmallow crème and extract; cook and stir 3-4 minutes longer or until smooth.
- Pour into prepared pan.
- Chill until set.
- Using foil, lift fudge out of pan.
- Discard foil; cut fudge into squares.
- Store in the refrigerator.
- Yield: about 2 lbs.

192. Lemonade Jellies Recipe

Serving: 12 | Prep: | Cook: 20mins | Ready in:

Ingredients

- vegetable oil for coating pan
- 3 envelopes unflavored gelatin
- 1 cup water
- 2 cups granulated sugar
- 3/4 cup fresh lemon juice
- 1 teaspoon grated fresh lemon rind
- Superfine sugar for coating candy

Direction

- Oil a square pan then set aside.
- In small bowl sprinkle gelatine over 1/2 cup water.
- Let gelatine soften at room temperature for five minutes.
- Meanwhile combine remaining water and granulated sugar in heavy medium saucepan.
- Place pan over medium heat then stir until sugar dissolves and mixture comes to a boil.
- Clip candy thermometer to inside of pan and cook without stirring until syrup reaches 260.
- Remove pan from heat then add gelatine to hot syrup and stir until completely dissolved.
- Stir in lemon juice and rind then pour syrup into prepared pan.
- Cool at room temperature until candy is set at least three hours.
- Cover top of candy with superfine sugar.
- Invert pan and gently remove candy in one piece placing sugared side down on a cutting board.
- Using a wet knife cut candy into 1" squares and coat each square with additional superfine sugar.
- Store in airtight container in layers separated by wax paper at room temperature up to one week.

193. Light Cranberry Fudge Recipe

Serving: 81 | Prep: | Cook: 5mins | Ready in:

Ingredients

- 2 cups (12 ounces) semisweet chocolate chips
- 1/4 cup light corn syrup
- 1/2 cup confectioners' sugar
- 1/4 cup reduced-fat evaporated milk
- 1 teaspoon vanilla extract
- 1 package (6 ounces) dried cranberries
- 1/3 cup chopped walnuts

Direction

- Line a 9-in. square pan with foil. Coat the foil with cooking spray; set aside.
- In a heavy saucepan, combine chocolate chips and corn syrup. Cook and stir over low heat until melted. Remove from the heat. Stir in the confectioners' sugar, milk and vanilla. Beat with a wooden spoon until thickened and glossy, about 5 minutes. Stir in cranberries and walnuts.
- Spread into prepared pan; refrigerate until firm.
- Using foil, lift fudge out of pan; discard foil. Cut fudge into 1-in. squares. Store in an airtight container in the refrigerator.
- Yield: 1-1/3 pounds (81 pieces).
- Nutrition Facts
- One serving: 1 piece Calories: 36 Fat: 2 g Saturated Fat: 1 g
- Cholesterol: 0 mg Sodium: 3 mg Carbohydrate: 6 g Fiber: 0 g Protein: 0 g

194. Low Sugar Nutty Fudge Recipe

Serving: 24 | Prep: | Cook: 15mins | Ready in:

Ingredients

- 1/2 cup sugar
- 1 cup Splenda granular
- 2/3 cup evaporated skim milk
- 2 tbsp butter or hard margarine (not low-fat)
- 1/4 tsp salt
- 2 cups miniature marshmallows
- 3 1/2 oz chopped bittersweet chocolate
- 3/4 cup peanut butter chips
- 1 tbsp vanilla

Direction

- Line an 8" square pan with greased foil.
- Combine sugar, Splenda, evaporated milk, butter and salt in a large saucepan.
- Bring to a full rolling boil over medium-high heat, stirring.
- Cook, stirring, 7 minutes. Remove from heat.
- Stir in marshmallows, chips and vanilla until completely melted and smooth.
- Pour mixture into pan.
- Refrigerate at least 3 hours before removing foil and cutting into squares.
- Refrigerate any remaining fudge.

195. Low Carb Fudge Toffee Recipe

Serving: 36 | Prep: | Cook: 30mins | Ready in:

Ingredients

- 2 cups Splenda
- 1 cup whole milk powder (available in health food stores)
- 1 cup natural whey protein powder
- 1/2 cup unsalted butter, melted
- 1/4 cup whipping cream
- 2 Tbs water
- 2 oz unsweetened baking chocolate, melted

Direction

- In a large bowl, combine the Splenda, milk powder, and protein powder.
- In a small bowl, combine the butter, cream, and water. Stir this into the dry ingredients. Stir in the melted chocolate until well combined.

Press the mixture into a 9 x 9-inch baking dish. Freeze for approximately 30 minutes, then refrigerate. Cut into squares and serve.

196. MARSHMALLOW FLOWERS Recipe

Serving: 21 | Prep: | Cook: 280mins | Ready in:

Ingredients

- Ingredients:
- 2 envelopes of unflavored gelatin
- ½ cup cold water
- 2 cups sugar
- ¾ cup hot water
- 1 cup light corn syrup, divided
- 1 tsp. vanilla extract
- confectioners' sugar
- 1 ½ pounds white candy coating, melted
- Red and Yellow paste food coloring
- ½ cup miniature semisweet chocolate chips
- Non-stick cooking spray

Direction

- Coat a 13-inch x 9-inch pan and a 9-inch square pan with cooking spray; set aside. In a bowl, combine gelatine and cold water; let stand for 5 minutes. Meanwhile, in a saucepan, combine the sugar, hot water and ½ cup corn syrup. Bring to a boil over medium heat, stirring constantly. Cook, without stirring, until a candy thermometer reads 238F. (Soft-ball stage). Remove from the heat; stir in the remaining corn syrup.
- Pour into a large bowl. Beat on high speed; gradually add gelatine mixture by tablespoonfuls until well blended. Continue beating until fluffy and thickened, about 10 minutes. Stir in vanilla; mix well. Pour into prepared pans. Let stand, uncovered, overnight.
- Cut with a flower-shaped cookie cutter coated with cooking spray. Dip flowers in confectioners' sugar, brush off excess. In a microwave or heavy saucepan, melt candy coating; cool for 5 minutes. Divide candy coating in half; tint one portion pink and the other yellow. Using an icing knife, cover the flowers with candy coating. Place on waxed paper-lined pans. Sprinkle chocolate chips in center of flowers. Yield: 21 (3-inch) flowers.

197. MICROWAVE PEANUT BUTTER FUDGE Recipe

Serving: 10 | Prep: | Cook: 5mins | Ready in:

Ingredients

- 12 oz. semi-sweet chocolate chips
- 1 can sweetened condensed milk
- 2 heaping Tbs peanut butter

Direction

- Place chocolate chips and milk in microwave safe bowl.
- Cook on high for 5 minutes.
- Remove from microwave, stir in 2 heaping tablespoons of peanut butter.
- Spread in pan.
- Cool and cut.

198. MICROWAVE RAINBOW PRETZELS Recipe

Serving: 20 | Prep: | Cook: 5mins | Ready in:

Ingredients

- 1/2 lb. white chocolate or almond bark
- 2 Tbs. light corn syrup
- 2 Tbs. butter
- 1 Tbs. water
- food color

- 50 mini pretzels

Direction

- Place chocolate, syrup, butter and water in microwave casserole.
- Cover; cook on Medium 4 to 5 minutes or until melted.
- Stir.
- Divide and tint as desired.
- Dip pretzels in tinted chocolate; remove excess.
- Place on waxed paper covered rack to dry.

199. MILKY WAY FUDGE Microwave Recipe Recipe

Serving: 12 | Prep: | Cook: 3mins | Ready in:

Ingredients

- milkY WAY FUDGE
- 1 can sweetened condensed milk
- 12 oz. semi-sweet chocolate chips
- 1 tsp. vanilla
- 3 milky Way candy bars, cut into chunks
- Microwave together and pour into 9x9 buttered dish.

Direction

- Microwave chocolate and milk on high for two minutes.
- After one minute stir to keep from burning.

200. Macadamia Cashew Crunch Recipe

Serving: 6 | Prep: | Cook: 20mins | Ready in:

Ingredients

- 2 cups bittersweet or semi-sweet chocolate (The orig. recipe used milk chocolate chips.)
- 1 cup chopped salted macadamia nuts
- 1 cup chopped salted cashews
- 1/2 cup sugar
- 1/2 stick softened butter - do not substitute margarine
- 2 TB corn syrup
- *Options:
- This can be made with walnuts, pecans or even peanuts. You can use nuts that are not salted in this recipe.

Direction

- Line a 9 inch pan with "release" aluminum, making sure that the foil goes over the edge of the pan so that you can pick the candy out of the pan with ease. You can butter regular foil and use that instead.
- Sprinkle the bottom of the pan with the chocolate chips.
- Place your butter, sugar, corn syrup and nuts in a large and heavy skillet and cook over low heat.
- Stir constantly until the butter melts and the sugar dissolves. (10-12 minutes on my stovetop)
- Increase the heat to medium and stir constantly until the candy turns into a light golden brown color.
- Watch the candy carefully and stir when the candy starts to stick together. It will get harder to stir at this point.
- Pour the mixture over the chocolate in the pan.
- Spread the candy evenly over the chips. Do not mash the chips and allow them to melt on their own.
- Let this all cool for at least one hour and then refrigerate until firm.
- Remove from pan, peel off the foil and break into pieces or cut into squares.
- ***** I have to add this. I over-cooked this once because I could not get a golden "brown" color out of the sugar mass. It came out like a thick brittle after I refrigerated it and tried to cut it.

So watch your candy while it cooks. It was still good but be careful!

201. Mackinac Island Fudge Recipe

Serving: 10 | Prep: | Cook: 40mins | Ready in:

Ingredients

- 1/2 cup milk
- 1/2 cup butter
- 1/2 cup firmly packed brown sugar
- 1/2 cup granulated sugar
- 1/8 teaspoon salt
- 1 teaspoon vanilla extract
- 2 cups confectioners' sugar
- 1/2 Cup cocoa
- 1/2 cup nuts (optional)

Direction

- Mix milk, butter, brown sugar, granulated sugar and salt in heavy pan. Cook at medium heat until boiling. Boil exactly 6 minutes, stirring constantly. Remove from heat and add vanilla extract, cocoa and confectioners' sugar. Beat with mixer until smooth and thick. Add nuts, if desired. Pour into a buttered pan and freeze 20 minutes. Cut into pieces.
- Makes approximately 1 pound of fudge.
- Peanut Butter Mackinac Island Fudge
- Reduce butter to 1/4 cup and add 1/2 cup peanut butter.
- Great Hint: If you want to make "authentic" Michigan fudge, when the fudge has cooled somewhat, (find that marble cheese server your sister in law gave you years back and never used) and spoon the mixture on it and make a log! Then chill of course.

202. Maine Potato Candy

Serving: 22 | Prep: | Cook: 20mins | Ready in:

Ingredients

- 4 cups confectioners' sugar
- 4 cups sweetened shredded coconut
- 3/4 cup cold mashed potatoes (without added milk and butter)
- 1-1/2 teaspoons vanilla extract
- 1/2 teaspoon salt
- 1 pound dark chocolate candy coating, coarsely chopped

Direction

- In a large bowl, combine the first five ingredients. Line a 9-in. square pan with foil; butter the foil. Spread coconut mixture into pan. Cover and chill overnight. Cut into 2x1-in. rectangles. Cover and freeze.
- In a microwave, melt candy coating; stir until smooth. Dip bars in coating; allow excess to drip off. Place on waxed paper to set. Store in an airtight container.
- Nutrition Facts
- 1 piece: 155 calories, 7g fat (6g saturated fat), 0 cholesterol, 55mg sodium, 25g carbohydrate (23g sugars, 1g fiber), 1g protein.

203. Make Your Own Gummi Bears Recipe

Serving: 6 | Prep: | Cook: 20mins | Ready in:

Ingredients

- 1 small box Jello with sugar (any flavor)
- 7 envelopes unflavored gelatin
- 1/2 cup water

Direction

- Place all ingredients in a saucepan and hand mix until the mixture looks like dough

- Place pan over low heat and stir until melted.
- Once completely melted, pour into plastic candy molds or any molds you prefer.
- Put it in the freezer for 5 min.
- Put them in the fridge for 5 min.
- Take them out.
- When very firm remove from the mold and munch! For sour gummies spritz lightly with water and sprinkle with kosher sour salt (also known as ascorbic acid or vitamin c powder)

204. Mamas Peanut Butter Fudge Recipe

Serving: 24 | Prep: | Cook: 30mins | Ready in:

Ingredients

- 12 oz. peanut butter(can use crunchy, but it's better with creamy)
- 3 1/2 cups sugar
- 1 1/2 cups of whole milk
- 1/4 tsp. salt
- 1 tsp. vanilla
- 1 tb. butter

Direction

- Mix sugar, salt and milk
- Cook until it makes a soft ball in a cup of water.
- Remove from heat.
- Add butter and stir until completely mixed.
- Pour into a buttered pan.
- Cool completely and cut into squares.

205. Marbled Orange Fudge Recipe

Serving: 117 | Prep: | Cook: 20mins | Ready in:

Ingredients

- 1 1/2 teaspoons plus 3/4 cup butter, divided
- 3 cups sugar
- 3/4 cup heavy whipping cream
- 1 package (10 to 12 ounces) vanilla or white chips
- 1 jar (7 ounces) marshmallow creme
- 3 teaspoons orange extract
- 12 drops yellow food coloring
- 5 drops red food coloring

Direction

- Grease a 13"x9"x2" pan with 1 1/2 teaspoons butter; set aside.
- In a heavy saucepan, combine the sugar, cream and remaining butter. Cook and stir over low heat until sugar is dissolved. Bring to a boil; cook and stir for 4 minutes.
- Remove from the heat; stir in chips and marshmallow crème until smooth.
- Remove 1 cup and set aside.
- Add orange extract and food coloring to the remaining mixture; stir until blended.
- Pour into prepared pan.
- Drop reserved marshmallow mixture by tablespoonfuls over the top; cut through with a knife to swirl.
- Cover and refrigerate until set. Cut into squares.
- Makes about 2 1/2 pounds.

206. Marbled Peanut Clusters Recipe

Serving: 24 | Prep: | Cook: 10mins | Ready in:

Ingredients

- 1 12-ounce package (2 cups) semisweet chocolate pieces
- 1-1/2 cups peanuts
- 1-ounce vanilla-flavor candy coating
- 1-ounce green candy coating (optional)

Direction

- Heat semisweet chocolate pieces in a heavy medium saucepan over low heat, stirring constantly just until melted.
- Stir in peanuts.
- Spoon by rounded teaspoons onto a waxed-paper-lined baking sheet.
- Heat vanilla-flavor candy coating in a heavy small saucepan over low heat, stirring constantly just until melted.
- If using, heat green candy coating in a similar manner.
- Drizzle a small amount of each candy coating atop each cluster, swirl gently with a toothpick to create a marbled effect.
- Chill candy about 30 minutes or until firm.
- Store tightly covered in the refrigerator for up to 3 weeks.

207. Marshmallow Goodies Recipe

Serving: 20 | Prep: | Cook: 5mins | Ready in:

Ingredients

- 12 ounces Spanish peanuts
- 10 ounces miniature marshmallows
- 12 ounces semi-sweet chocolate morsels
- 12 ounces butterscotch flavored morsels
- 1 cup smooth peanut butter

Direction

- Combine marshmallows and peanuts in large bowl; set aside. Combine semi-sweet chocolate chips, butterscotch chips and peanut butter in a large sauce pan. Cook over medium heat, stirring constantly until completely melted. Pour hot mixture over peanuts and marshmallows and stir to thoroughly mix.
- Pour into a flat pan (10' x 6') and spread mixture evenly. The mixture should be about one inch in thickness. Cool candy until firm (place in refrigerator for faster cooling). Cut into 2 X 2-inch squares and place on serving tray.
- This makes about 20 squares.

208. Marshmallow Peanut Butter Fudge Recipe

Serving: 1 | Prep: | Cook: 10mins | Ready in:

Ingredients

- peanut butter Fudge
- INGREDIENTS:
- * 5 cups sugar
- * 1 large can evaporated milk
- * 1/2 cup butter
- * 1-1/2 cup crunchy peanut butter
- * 1 pint marshmallow creme
- * 1 teaspoon vanilla

Direction

- Put sugar, butter and milk in a heavy saucepan. Bring to a boil and boil for 10 minutes, stirring often. Remove from heat and add the rest of the ingredients. Stir until thick. Pour into buttered 9x13 inch pan.
- Let stand for several hours before cutting.

209. Marshmallows Recipe

Serving: 6 | Prep: | Cook: 15mins | Ready in:

Ingredients

- 4 (1/4 -ounce) envelopes unflavored gelatin
- 1 1/2 cups cool water
- 1 1/4 cups light corn syrup
- 1/4 teaspoon salt
- 3 cups granulated sugar
- 1 tablespoon vanilla extract
- 1 1/2 cups confectioner's sugar for dusting

Direction

- Line a 9 x 13 inch pan with waxed paper and spray paper with cooking spray; set aside. Sprinkle gelatine over 3/4 cups water in the bowl of a stand mixer. Set aside while the gelatine dissolves. It will be semi-firm.
- In a heavy saucepan on high heat, bring remaining 3/4 cups water, corn syrup, salt, and sugar to 240° F., about 10 minutes.
- Pour the hot sugar mixture over the gelatine and beat until it's fluffy and pure white, about 10 to 15 minutes. Beat in the vanilla. Spread the marshmallow in the prepared pan, smoothing the top well. Top with a cookie sheet, and set aside to solidify at room temperature for 12 hours.
- When the marshmallows are tacky to the touch, but not soft, use a moistened, serrated knife to cut them into 1 1/2 inch squares. The marshmallows will be sticky and elastic; wet the knife frequently. Sieve confectioner's sugar onto a cookie sheet. Roll each square in the confectioner's sugar, shaking off any excess. Store in an airtight container. Makes about 4 dozen.
- Chocolate Marshmallows: If desired, sieve 1/2 cup unsweetened cocoa and 1 cup confectioner's sugar on a cookie sheet. Roll marshmallows in the cocoa mixture.
- Brownies: Bake your favorite brownie recipe. Remove brownies from the oven 5 minutes before they're done. Crumble on 3 - 4 sheets of graham crackers, sprinkle with 1 cup diced marshmallows and 3 to 6 ounces plain milk chocolate candy. Return to oven for 5 minutes, or until the marshmallows soften and the chocolate melts.

210. Marshmallows With Variations Recipe

Serving: 16 | Prep: | Cook: 60mins | Ready in:

Ingredients

- 1 cup potato starch OR cornstarch
- 2 tablespoons light corn syrup
- 2 1/4 ounce packets unflavored gelatin
- 3 large egg whiyes, room temperature
- 3/4 cup cold water
- 1 tablespoon pure vanilla extract
- 1 1/4 cups PLUS 1 tablespoon sugar

Direction

- Line a rimmed baking sheet with parchment paper.
- Dust parchment generously with potato/cornstarch.
- Have the candy thermometer ready for use.
- Put 1/3 cup water, 1 1/4 cups sugar and corn syrup into a medium sauce pan over medium heat.
- Bring to a boil, stirring until sugar dissolves.
- Once sugar dissolves, continue to cook, without stirring, until mixture reaches 265 degrees on the candy thermometer (about 10 minutes).
- While syrup is cooking, sprinkle the gelatine over the remaining cold water.
- Let sit for about 5 minutes, until spongy.
- Heat in microwave for 30 seconds to liquefy OR dissolve in pan over low heat.
- Fit stand mixer with whisk attachment and beat egg whites on medium-high speed until firm but still glossy.
- When syrup reaches 265 degrees, remove from heat.
- With mixer on medium speed, add the syrup, pouring it between the spinning beaters and sides of bowl.
- Add gelatine. Beat 3 minutes more.
- Beat in the vanilla extract.
- Scrape mixture onto baking sheet, spreading to corners but keeping at 1" height.
- Pan will not fill. Lift excess parchment to meet edge of batter.
- Rest bowl to keep paper in position.
- Dust marshmallows with potato/cornstarch.
- Let cool in a dry place for 3 to 12 hours.

- Once cool and set, cut marshmallows with a long, thin knife, rinsing often.
- Have big bowl with remaining potato/cornstarch handy.
- Cut marshmallows into shapes and drop into the bowl.
- Toss to coat every so often and then toss from hand to hand to remove excess starch.
- Transfer to a serving bowl.
- Cut and coat the rest of the batch.
- STORE marshmallows in a cool, dry place. Don't cover them tightly. They last about a week.
- FRUIT: Reduce vanilla to 1/4 teaspoon. Fold in generous 1/3 cup pureed fruit to batter.
- PUMPKIN-SPICE: Whisk together 1/2 cup unsweetened canned pumpkin puree, 1 teaspoon ground cinnamon, 1/2 teaspoon ground ginger, a pinch freshly grated nutmeg and a pinch of ground allspice. Fold into batter.

211. Marzipan Caramel Apples With Sesame N Almonds Recipe

Serving: 8 | Prep: | Cook: 20mins | Ready in:

Ingredients

- For the apples:
- ------------
- 8 slightly sour apples, such as Granny Smith, at room temperature
- marzipan
- 8 craft sticks or chopsticks
- For the coating:
- ------------
- 3/4 cup sliced almonds, toasted
- 3/4 cup sesame seeds, toasted
- 1 3/4 cups heavy cream
- 2 cups packed light brown sugar
- 3/4 cup dark corn syrup
- 2 tablespoons unsalted butter (1/4 stick)
- 2 teaspoons kosher salt

Direction

- For the apples:

212. Mayan Truffles Recipe

Serving: 12 | Prep: | Cook: 10mins | Ready in:

Ingredients

- 1 cup whipping cream
- 12 ounces semisweet chocolate chips
- 1 teaspoon instant coffee
- 1/8 cup coffee liqueur
- 6 ounces semisweet chocolate pieces
- 1/4 cup cocoa

Direction

- Bring cream to the boiling point in a medium saucepan.
- Remove from heat and add 12 ounces chocolate chips and instant coffee then cover.
- Allow to sit 10 minutes then remove lid and stir.
- Add coffee liqueur then allow mixture to cool 2 hours in the refrigerator.
- Shape into small balls on wax paper lined trays and place in freezer.
- Melt remaining chocolate and cool slightly.
- Dip balls in chocolate and roll in the cocoa then store in refrigerator.

213. Microwave Peanut Brittle Recipe

Serving: 8 | Prep: | Cook: 7mins | Ready in:

Ingredients

- 1 cup sugar
- 1/2 cup white corn syrup
- 1/8 teaspoon salt

- 1 cup raw peanuts
- 1 teaspoon vanilla
- 1 teaspoon butter
- 1 teaspoon baking soda

Direction

- Put sugar in a medium glass bowl.
- Add white corn syrup and stir.
- Add salt and stir.
- Add peanuts and stir well.
- Microwave for 3 minutes.
- Take out and stir.
- Microwave again for 3 minutes.
- Take out and add vanilla and butter and stir.
- Microwave for 1 minute.
- Take out and sprinkle the soda over mixture and gently stir.
- Quickly pour onto a cookie sheet that has been sprayed with Pam.
- Let harden, then break into pieces.

214. Microwave Pralines Recipe

Serving: 18 | Prep: | Cook: 12mins | Ready in:

Ingredients

- 2 1/2 cups of brown sugar
- 1 cup of heavy whipping cream
- 2 cups of pecan halves
- 2 TB of regular, salted butter
- 1 tsp. of pure vanilla extract

Direction

- Using a large microwave-proof glass bowl, add the cream and the brown sugar together.
- Microwave on high for 12 minutes.
- Remove the bowl from microwave and add the butter, vanilla and pecans.
- Stir well.
- Using a large tablespoon, drop the candy on to "Release" aluminum foil, a silicone matt or waxed paper.
- Let cool and eat!

215. Microwave Toffee Recipe

Serving: 4 | Prep: | Cook: 8mins | Ready in:

Ingredients

- 1 cup chopped pecans or toasted almonds
- 1 cup sugar
- 1/4 cup water
- 1 stick of regular salted butter
- 1/2 cup semi-sweet chocolate morsels

Direction

- Sprinkle your chopped nuts over either a silicone pad or a 12 inch piece of Release aluminum foil. (This foil is great to use!)
- Sprinkle the nuts in a circle about 10 inches length, keeping the nut pieces close together. You can also use a 9 inch pan, well-buttered!
- In a microwave-proof glass bowl, add the water, butter and sugar.
- Cook on high for seven minutes.
- Do not stop and stir your mixture. Just let it cook!
- If the mixture in the bowl is not a caramel-ish, lightly brown color, cook for one minute more.
- Remove bowl from microwave and pour the sugar mixture directly over the nuts.
- Using a rubber spatula, push the nuts on the sides into the edges of the mixture before it cools so that you don't waste nuts that are not attached to the candy.
- Quickly sprinkle your chocolate chips over the top of the candy and let it melt there for about 2 minutes.
- Spread the melting chips over the top of your toffee.
- I like to sprinkle this with extra nuts.
- Let the toffee cool completely.

- Break into pieces and serve!

216. Mint Cookie Candies

Serving: 0 | Prep: | Cook: | Ready in:

Ingredients

- 12 ounces white candy coating, coarsely chopped
- 6 teaspoons shortening, divided
- 1/4 teaspoon green food coloring
- 4 mint creme Oreo cookies, crushed
- 2 packages (4.67 ounces each) mint Andes candies

Direction

- In a microwave-safe bowl, melt candy coating and 4 teaspoons shortening; stir until smooth. Stir in food coloring. Pour evenly into miniature muffin cup liners. Sprinkle with cookie crumbs.
- In a microwave, melt mint candies and remaining shortening; stir until smooth. Pour over cookie crumbs. Let stand until set.
- Nutrition Facts
- 1 each: 58 calories, 3g fat (2g saturated fat), 0 cholesterol, 5mg sodium, 8g carbohydrate (7g sugars, 0 fiber), 0 protein.

217. Mint Meltaways Recipe

Serving: 64 | Prep: | Cook: 100mins | Ready in:

Ingredients

- 16 squares (16 oz.) semisweet chocolate, chopped or 2 2/3 c. semisweet chocolate chips
- 2 TBSP. vegetable shortening
- 1/2 c. heavy whipping cream
- 1 TBSP. peppermint extract
- 2 TBSP. unsweetened cocoa
- mint baking chips, for decorating, optional

Direction

- ***Cook time includes chilling time.***
- Line bottom of 8-inch square baking pan with waxed paper.
- In heavy 3-quart saucepan, melt chocolate and shortening over low heat, stirring frequently, until smooth. Remove from heat.
- Meanwhile, in small saucepan, heat cream to simmering over medium heat. Immediately add hot cream and peppermint extract to chocolate mixture; with wire whisk, mix until blended and smooth.
- Pour mixture into prepared pan, tilting pan to spread mixture evenly. Refrigerate until firm, about 1 1/2 hours.
- With small metal spatula, loosen chocolate mixture from sides of pan. Lightly dust cutting board with cocoa; invert pan onto board. Remove pan and discard waxed paper. Let candy stand 10 minutes at room temperature to soften slightly. With sharp knife, cut chocolate mixture into 8 strips, then cut each strip crosswise into 8 pieces.
- If using, place a mint baking chip on top of each piece for decoration, pressing the chip lightly onto each piece to adhere.
- To store, layer between waxed paper in airtight container. Refrigerate up to two weeks.

218. Missouri Colonels Recipe

Serving: 8 | Prep: | Cook: | Ready in:

Ingredients

- 4 cups sifted confectioners' sugar, divided
- 1 cup finely chopped pecans
- 1/2 cup butter, softened
- 1/4 cup green creme de menthe
- 1 (6 ounce) package semisweet chocolate pieces (1 cup)

- 1 teaspoon shortening

Direction

- In large mixing bowl, beat together 2 cups of the confectioners' sugar, the pecans, butter and crème de menthe. Beat or stir in remaining confectioners' sugar. Cover and chill mixture for 1 hour or until firm.
- Shape into 1-inch balls. Place balls on a foil- or wax paper-lined baking sheet. Chill for 15 minutes.
- In a small, heavy saucepan, heat chocolate pieces and shortening over very low heat, stirring constantly, until chocolate melts. Dip one side of each of the chilled balls into melted chocolate. Return to baking sheet. Chill until set.
- Makes about 60 candies.
- NOTE: For a non-alcoholic candy, use 1/4 cup corn syrup, 1/4 teaspoon peppermint extract and a few drops green food coloring for crème de menthe.
- Make-Ahead Tip: Prepare candies as above. Cover and store in refrigerator for up to 1 week. Or freeze candies in a freezer container for up to 3 months.

219. Mocha Macadamia Candy Recipe

Serving: 40 | Prep: | Cook: | Ready in:

Ingredients

- 1 tsp cornstarch
- 2 tbsp hot water
- 2 cups chopped macadamia nuts
- 2/3 cup pure icing sugar
- 1/2 cup sugar
- 1 tsp vanilla
- 1 tablespoon instant coffee
- 1 tbsp unsweetened cocoa powder

Direction

- Whisk together the cornstarch and water, set aside.
- Blend the chopped macadamias, sugars and vanilla in a food processor until well combined. Add cornstarch mixture and grind to a coarse paste.
- Remove half of the mixture and press into a lightly greased 8" square tin.
- Add coffee and cocoa to remaining mixture, and process until smooth.
- Pat on top of bottom layer, pressing down gently with hands.
- Cover with plastic and refrigerate at least 1 hour before cutting.

220. Mochi With Nutella Strawberry Filling Recipe

Serving: 6 | Prep: | Cook: 1hours | Ready in:

Ingredients

- Filling
- 120 g nutella or other chocolate hazelnut spread
- 1/2 tsp sea salt
- 2 1/2 tbsp cocoa powder
- 20 g sweetened hot cocoa drink mix
- 6 strawberries
- Mochi Dough
- 1 cup sweet rice flour
- 1 cup water
- 2-3 drops red food colouring (optional)
- 1/3 cup sugar
- 1/2 cup cornstarch or potato starch, for rolling

Direction

- In a small bowl, beat together Nutella, salt, cocoa powder, and hot cocoa mix until thick and doughy.
- Form paste around each strawberry, rolling the berries between your palms to smooth.
- Place on a parchment or wax paper lined sheet and freeze until solid, about 1 1/2 hours.

- Mix sweet rice flour, water, food colouring and sugar in a large bowl until smooth.
- Cover with plastic wrap and microwave 3 1/2 minutes.
- Stir mixture and heat for another 30 seconds.
- Place cornstarch in an 8" square pan, evenly coating the bottom.
- Remove the rice dough from the microwave and scrape into the cornstarch. Dust with a little extra cornstarch and divide into 6 pieces.
- Roll balls from the dough and flatten each to a thin layer.
- Place 1 frozen Nutella-strawberry ball in the center of each, then pinch the mochi over top until the filling is completely covered.
- Place seam side down in paper muffin liners to prevent sticking.
- These are best served within 2 days of making but can be frozen in an airtight container up to 4 months.

221. Molasses Taffy A Family Affair Recipe

Serving: 150 | Prep: | Cook: 40mins | Ready in:

Ingredients

- 1 1/2 cup molasses
- 3/4 cup sugar
- 1 tbsp butter
- 1/8 tsp salt
- 1 tbsp vinegar
- 1/8 tsp soda

Direction

- Combine Molasses, sugar and vinegar in sauce pan
- Cook to soft crack stage or 270*
- Stir once and awhile to keep from burning
- Remove from heat stir in Butter, soda and salt
- Stir to blend
- Pour into a buttered pan and wait. I said WAIT…until cool enough to handle.
- Grab a Family Member. Butter those hands, gather the taffy into a ball and pull between the two of you until satiny and light. Keep hands buttered to keep from sticking. It will become too firm to pull.
- Divide into your own ball roll out or twist into a rope and cut into pieces with buttered scissors wrap each piece in plastic or waxed paper.
- Make a date to do again.

222. Moms Remarkable Fudge Recipe

Serving: 96 | Prep: | Cook: 25mins | Ready in:

Ingredients

- 4 cups sugar
- 2 5-ounce cans (1 1/3 cups total) evaporated milk
- 1 cup margarine or butter
- 1 12-ounce package (2 cups) semisweet chocolate pieces
- 1 7-ounce jar marshmallow creme
- 1 teaspoon vanilla
- 2 heaping spoonfuls of creamy peanut butter (or chunky if that's your thing)

Direction

- Line a 13x9x2-inch baking pan with foil; extend foil over edges.
- Butter foil, set aside.
- Butter sides of a heavy 3-quart saucepan. Combine sugar, milk, and margarine in saucepan.
- Cook and stir over medium-high heat to boiling. Clip candy thermometer to side of pan.
- Cook and stir over medium heat to 236 degrees, soft-ball stage (about 12 minutes).
- Remove saucepan from heat, remove thermometer.

- Add chocolate pieces, marshmallow crème, vanilla and peanut butter; stir 'till chocolate melts.
- Spread into pan.
- Score into squares while warm. When firm, cut into squares.
- Store in refrigerator. Makes about 3 1/2 pounds.

223. Moms Secret Fudge Recipe Recipe

Serving: 15 | Prep: | Cook: 20mins | Ready in:

Ingredients

- 1 king size Hershey chocolate Bar.... (7 - 8 oz.)
- 12 oz. bag of Nestle's chocolate Dots --- mini semi sweet chocolate chips
- 1 1/2 cups walnuts -chopped
- 1/2 cup pecans - chopped
- 1/4 cup almonds - chopped
- 1 jar (7-8 oz.) Marshmellow Fluff
- ....
- 1/3 cup butter
- 1 cup evaporated milk
- 4 1/2 cups superfine sugar
- extra butter

Direction

- In a large heavy bowl that can stand heat.
- Break up Hershey Bar into pieces.
- Add chocolate dots on top.
- Then add the nuts.
- And top with marshmallow fluff.
- Put in a warm spot so the chocolate starts to soften.
- ....
- In a heavy pan, butter the sides and bottom of the pan heavily.
- Put in 1/3 cup of butter and the evaporated milk.

- Heat until warm.
- Slowly add the sugar. Stir after each addition.
- Make sure the dry sugar does not touch the sides of the pan.
- Don't stir too hard, you don't want the sugar mixture all over the sides of the pan.
- Heat slowly until the sugar is dissolved keep stirring.
- DON'T scrap the sides of the pan.
- The turn the heat up to medium.
- Using a candy thermometer bring temperature to 225-228' F.
- Stir mixture to keep from burning.
- Pour hot sugar mixture over chocolate mixture in the bowl.
- DO NOT scrape the pot out.
- Use a new spoon and blend the together as quickly as possible.
- DON"T over mix. There will be some streaks of the fluff that's ok.
- Spread mixture on a well-buttered jelly roll pan. (Large spatula works).
- Work quickly. This fudge sets up very fast.
- Cover tightly with plastic wrap and then foil.
- Put in a cold spot for 4 hours. Cut into pieces.
- ....
- Keep wrapped tightly. This fudge dries out very fast.

224. My Grandmas Peanut Butter Fudge Recipe

Serving: 48 | Prep: | Cook: | Ready in:

Ingredients

- 3/4 cup peanut butter (creamy or chunky)
- 1/3 cup butter, softened
- 1/2 cup white corn syrup
- 1 teaspoon vanilla
- 1/2 teaspoon salt
- 1 pound confectioner's sugar

Direction

- In large mixing bowl, cream together the peanut butter, butter, white corn syrup, vanilla, and salt until smooth.
- Gradually add sifted powdered sugar.
- Knead well until completely blended together.
- Press into ungreased 9 x 13-inch pan.
- Refrigerate until firm.
- Cut into small squares.

225. Never Fail Fudge Recipe

Serving: 6 | Prep: | Cook: 6mins | Ready in:

Ingredients

- 6 1/2 ounces of evaporated milk
- 2 cups of sugar
- 12 marshmallows (cut up)
- 1 large bag of semi-sweet chocolate chips
- 4 ounces of margarine or butter
- 1 cup of chopped nuts (optional)

Direction

- Mix the evaporated milk with the sugar in a saucepan.
- Bring to a boil.
- After the mixture has come to a boil, reduce heat to medium and time for 6 minutes.
- Stir constantly or it will stick.
- Remove from heat and stir in the cut up marshmallows, the chocolate, butter and nuts.
- Spread the mixture in a greased 8x8x2 pan.
- Refrigerate and when firm, cut.

226. No Bake Cashew Brittle Bars Recipe

Serving: 4 | Prep: | Cook: 30mins | Ready in:

Ingredients

- 11/4c old fashioned oats
- 1c(about 5oz) salted cashews
- 11/2oz(3Tbs)unsalted butter
- 1/2c packed dark brown sugar
- 3/4tsp ground cinnamon
- 3Tbs light corn syrup
- 1Tbs molasses
- 1/2tsp coarse salt

Direction

- Line a 41/2x9" loaf pan with plastic wrap, leaving a 1" overhang on each long side. Toast oats and cashews in a large skillet over med-high heat, stirring often, until aromatic and just starting to turn golden brown, 5-6 mins. Transfer to med. bowl.
- Add butter, sugar, cinnamon, corn syrup, molasses and salt in skillet, and cook over med. heat, stirring, until butter melts and mixture bubbles, 2-3 mins. Pour hot mixture over oats and cashews, and stir to combine.
- Transfer mixture to loaf pan. Using a spatula, press mixture into an even layer. Refrigerate till set, about 30 mins Remove chilled mixture from pan using plastic, discard plastic wrap and cut into 1" thick bars.

227. No Cook Fudge Recipe

Serving: 8 | Prep: | Cook: 10mins | Ready in:

Ingredients

- 4 (1 ounce) squares unsweetened chocolate
- 1/2 cup butter or margarine
- 1 box confectioners' sugar
- 1 egg
- 1/3 cup sweetened condensed milk
- 1 teaspoon vanilla extract
- 1 cup chopped nuts

Direction

- Melt chocolate and butter in a large sauce pan.

- Sift sugar and mix with egg and milk.
- Stir in chocolate and butter mixture.
- Add vanilla extract and nuts.
- Pour into buttered 8-inch square pan.
- Chill in refrigerator at least 2 hours, and make sure you hide it until it's ready.

228. Nut Goodie Candy Bars Recipe

Serving: 30 | Prep: | Cook: | Ready in:

Ingredients

- --------FOR ONE 13x9-INCH PAN OF CANDY, ABOUT 5 LBS. -----------
- 1 package (12oz) semi-sweet chocolate chips
- 2 cups creamy or chunky peanut butter
- 1 cup (2 sticks) butter or margarine
- 2 tablespoons cornstarch
- 1/2 cup milk
- 1/2 cup nonfat dry milk
- 1 teaspoon vanilla
- 1 package (1 lb.) powdered sugar
- 2 cups flaked coconut
- 1 lb. (3 1/2 cups) dry roasted, salted mixed nuts or salted peanuts

Direction

- Melt chocolate chips in a bowl placed over hot water. Stir in peanut butter. Spread half the mixture in a 13 x 9-inch pan. Chill until firm.
- In a saucepan, combine butter, cornstarch, mil and non-fat dry milk.
- Bring to a boil, stirring. Boil 1 minute until thickened. Remove from heat and add vanilla.
- Stir in powdered sugar until smooth and creamy, use an electric mixer, if you wish. Add coconut.
- Spread over chilled chocolate layer in pan.
- Add nuts to remaining melted chocolate. Spread nut-chocolate mixture over the creamy layer.
- Chill 1 hour until firm. Cut into 1-inch squares for cookie-candy holiday tray, or into 1-by-2-inch pieces for snacks

229. Nut Goody Candy Bars Recipe

Serving: 24 | Prep: | Cook: | Ready in:

Ingredients

- Candy Bar Topping:
- 1½ pounds sweet chocolate (I use three 8 ounce Hershey Bars) - divided
- ¾ pound Spanish peanuts (not cocktail peanuts)
- Fondant Filling:
- 2½ cups powdered sugar
- ½ cup sweetened condensed milk
- ½ teaspoon maple extract

Direction

- For the topping, melt 16 ounces of chocolate in the microwave. If you've never melted chocolate in the microwave, you must be very careful. Overheating it will turn it into a grainy mess. In a glass microwavable bowl, break up chocolate into small pieces; microwave on High for 45 seconds to start; stir, and then keep heating for 20 to 30 seconds at a time, stirring after each time. When it gets to the point where it only has a few lumps of chocolate left, heat for 10 seconds at a time.
- Once chocolate is completely melted, stir in the Spanish peanuts.
- For fondant, mix together the ingredients. It will be thick and stiff.
- Spray a large piece of waxed paper with cooking spray and use a paper towel to wipe off any excess.
- Roll the fondant into little balls, about 1" in diameter.
- Place the balls about 3" apart on the waxed paper, then flatten each ball with the heel of

your hand. The flattened balls should be a circle about the size of a silver dollar, and NOT paper thin.
- Cover the flattened balls with the melted chocolate/nut mixture, letting it cover the top of the fondant and flow slightly over the edges.
- Let the candies cool completely, allowing the chocolate to harden again, then flip each one over (use a spatula for best results - they should come away from the waxed paper easily once the chocolate has cooled and hardened).
- To cover the bottom of the fondant with melted chocolate, melt the remaining 8 ounce chocolate bar in a separate bowl and use a spoon to spread the melted chocolate over the exposed fondant.
- Let the chocolate set and harden completely before storing the candies in a container with waxed paper between the layers. If it's hot outside, I would suggest you keep them in the refrigerator until serving.

230. Nutty Buddies Recipe

Serving: 4 | Prep: | Cook: 3mins | Ready in:

Ingredients

- buttery crackers, I use Ritz
- creamy peanut butter
- almond Bark chocolate
- wax paper
- Variation, White almond Bark plus 1 Tbsp. peanut butter for every 3 chunks of bark

Direction

- Spread half the crackers with peanut butter.
- Place the other half of the crackers on top to make a sandwich.
- Melt the almond bark in the microwave in a shallow bowl.
- If you're using the white bark, stir in the peanut butter after you've melted the white bark.
- Set one cracker sandwich in the bowl and using a fork, turn it over to coat the other side.
- Slide the fork under the cracker and lift up and let the chocolate drip back into the bowl before setting it on the wax paper.
- Let the cookies cool completely before eating.
- Store in airtight container.

231. Old Fashioned Date Confection Recipe

Serving: 12 | Prep: | Cook: 20mins | Ready in:

Ingredients

- 2 cups sugar
- 1 cup whole milk
- 2 tablespoons butter
- 1-1/2 cups chopped dates
- 1 cup chopped pecans

Direction

- Combine the sugar, milk and butter in a heavy saucepan.
- Stirring occasionally, cook over medium heat to soft ball stage (238°F on candy thermometer).
- Stir the dates and pecans into the syrup and continue cooking until dates are dissolved and mixture reaches firm ball stage (248°F on candy thermometer).
- Remove from heat and allow to cool.
- Pour mixture out onto clean, damp dishtowels or tea towels and shape into 2-inch diameter rolls.
- Chill until firm.
- Slice in half-inch slices.

232. Old Fashioned Sponge Toffee Recipe

Serving: 5 | Prep: | Cook: 20mins | Ready in:

Ingredients

- 1c sugar
- 1 c corn syrup
- 1 tbsp vinegar
- 1tbsp baking soda

Direction

- Combine sugar, syrup and vinegar in large sauce pan.
- Stir over med. heat until sugar is dissolved.
- Continue to cook to 300F (hard crack stage).
- Remove from heat, stir in baking soda quickly (will become frothy)
- Pour into a buttered pan.
- Cool and break into pieces.

233. Orange Creamsicle Fudge Recipe

Serving: 20 | Prep: | Cook: 12mins | Ready in:

Ingredients

- 6 -ounces (1.5 sticks) butter
- 2- cups granulated sugar
- 3/4- cup heavy cream
- 1- package (12 oz) white chocolate chips
- 1- jar (7 oz) marshmallow cream (or fluff)
- 1- tablespoon orange extract
- orange (or a combination of red and yellow) food coloring

Direction

- Prepare a 13x9 pan by lining it with aluminum foil and spraying the foil with non-stick cooking spray.
- In a large heavy saucepan, combine the sugar, cream, and butter over medium heat.
- Continually stir the mixture until the butter melts and the sugar dissolves.
- Brush down the sides with a wet pastry brush.
- Bring the mixture to a boil, and once it starts boiling, stir continuously for four minutes.
- After four minutes of boiling, remove the pan from the heat and immediately stir in the marshmallow cream and white chocolate chips.
- Stir until the white chocolate has melted and the fudge is completely smooth.
- Working quickly, pour about a third of the white fudge into a bowl and set aside.
- To the remaining fudge, add the orange extract and orange food coloring, stirring until it is a smooth, even color. It is important to perform these steps quickly, because the fudge will start to set if you take too long, and the end result will not be smooth
- Pour the orange fudge into the prepared pan and spread it into an even layer.
- Drop the white fudge over the top by the spoonful, then drag a table knife or toothpick through the fudge to create orange-white swirls. You can spray your hands with non-stick cooking spray and gently press them into the top to smooth out the swirls, if desired.
- Allow the fudge to set at room temperature for 2 hours, or in the refrigerator for 1 hour.
- To cut, pull the fudge out of the pan using the foil as handles.
- Use a large sharp knife to cut the fudge into small 1-inch squares. Store Orange Creamsicle Fudge in an airtight container in the refrigerator for up to a week, and bring it to room temperature to serve.

234. Pa & Ma's Peanut Butter Fudge Recipe

Serving: 20 | Prep: | Cook: 25mins | Ready in:

Ingredients

- 2-3/4 cups smooth peanut butter.
- 3/4 cup evaporated milk.
- 3/4 stick butter, (6 tablespoons).
- Add after cooking
- 1 7 oz jar Kraft marshmallow creme.
- 1-3/4 cups Jif creamy peanut butter.
- 1-1/2 cups broken English walnuts.

Direction

- 1. Prepare marshmallow crème, peanut butter, and walnuts, set aside.
- 2. Set a good digital timer to 6 minutes, set aside
- 3. Butter a 9 X 13 inch glass baking dish, set aside.
- 4. In 10 inch Dutch oven over medium heat, cook first 3 ingredients, blending well.
- 5. When mixture begins to boil, (just a few bubbles appear).
- 6. Start timer and cook covered 6 minutes.
- 7. Do not remove cover until cooking time is over.
- 8. Remove from heat immediately; add marshmallow crème, and peanut butter.
- 9. Stir until well blended, add nuts and mix well.
- 10. Pour into buttered dish, cover, cool, cut, and enjoy.

235. Pa & Ma's Wonderful Holiday Fudge Recipe

Serving: 30 | Prep: | Cook: 1hours | Ready in:

Ingredients

- 1 stick butter.
- 4-1/2 cups sugar.
- 1 12 oz. can evaporated milk.
- 1 12 oz. package milk chocolate.
- 1 12 oz. package chocolate chips.
- 2 oz. unsweetened chocolate squares, broken apart.
- 1 tablespoon vanilla.
- 1/2 pound Kraft miniature marshmallows.
- 2 cups broken walnuts, or pecans.

Direction

- 1. Prepare the Kraft marshmallows, nuts of choice, vanilla, and chocolates, set aside.
- 2. Set a good digital timer to 6-1/2 minutes, set aside.
- 3. Butter a 10 X 15 inch jelly roll pan, set aside.
- 4. In a 10 inch Dutch oven, over medium heat, cook the first three ingredients, stirring well.
- 5. When the mixture begins to boil, start the timer and cook 6-1/2 minutes.
- 6. Do not remove cover until cooking time is over. Immediately remove from heat.
- 7. Add Kraft marshmallows, and stir well. Add chocolates, 1 at a time stirring well.
- 8. Add vanilla, stirring well, then add nuts, and mix until well blended.
- 9. Pour into buttered Jelly roll pan and spread out evenly. Cover, cool, cut, and enjoy.

236. Pasteli Greek Sesame Seed Candy Recipe

Serving: 45 | Prep: | Cook: 30mins | Ready in:

Ingredients

- vegetable oil for oiling pan
- 1 cup mild honey
- 1 cup sesame seeds, toasted in oven
- 1/2 teaspoon salt
- ~~~~
- Needed: a nonstick bakeware liner such as Silpat; an 8- to 9-inch springform pan; a candy thermometer

Direction

- Put bakeware liner in a large shallow baking pan (1 inch deep). Remove bottom of springform pan and set aside. Oil inside of springform ring with vegetable oil and put ring, upside down, in center of bakeware liner.
- Bring honey, sesame seeds, and salt to a boil in a 2-quart heavy saucepan over moderate heat, stirring, then boil undisturbed until mixture registers 280 to 290°F on thermometer, about 15 minutes.
- Holding ring in place, quickly pour mixture into ring, then cool on a rack until candy is set but still warm, about 40 minutes.
- Unmold by peeling ring with candy off bakeware liner. Transfer candy to a cutting board, then run a paring knife around edge of springform ring and lift ring off candy.
- Cut candy into 1-inch diamond-shaped or rectangular pieces with an oiled large knife.
- ** Candy keeps, layered between sheets of parchment or wax paper, in an airtight container in a cool dry place 1 week.

237. Pasteli Recipe

Serving: 0 | Prep: | Cook: 20mins | Ready in:

Ingredients

- 1 cup mild honey
- 1 cup sesame seeds, toasted
- 1/2 tsp. salt

Direction

- Preheat oven to 350
- Toast sesame seeds on baking sheet for 5-10 minutes or until just slightly darker
- Put Silpat on sheet pan
- Oil inside of spring form ring (put bottom of pan aside)
- Place upside down in center of Silpat
- In a saucepan, bring honey, sesame seeds, and salt to a boil over medium heat, stirring until it starts to boil

- Boil undisturbed until mixture read 285 on thermometer (about 15 minutes)
- Pour mixture into ring
- Cool until candy sets, about 1/2 hour
- Unmold, and slice into bite size pieces with an oiled knife

238. Pates De Fruits Fruit Jewels Recipe

Serving: 24 | Prep: | Cook: 65mins | Ready in:

Ingredients

- 1.1/2 cups mango pulp/pureed mango
- -or-
- 1 1/2 cups pureed strawberries
- 2 1/2 cups sugar
- 1 Tbsp butter
- 6 fl oz liquid pectin

Direction

- Prepare an 8x8-inch square pan by lining it with aluminum foil or parchment paper and spraying the bottom with non-stick cooking spray.
- Cook mango or strawberry pulp and sugar together in a medium saucepan over low heat until they form a very thick syrup. Depending on the thickness of your pulp, it will take between 30 minutes to 1 hour. The syrup should thickly coat the back of a spoon or spatula.
- Once the syrup has thickened enough, add the butter and cook for 3 minutes more, stirring constantly.
- Remove from the heat and stir in the pectin while hot. Pour immediately into prepared pan.
- Allow to cool to room temperature.
- Cover pan with foil and refrigerate overnight until set.

- Once the candies are completely set, cut them into small squares with a knife dipped in water.
- Roll in granulated sugar or leave plain. (The sugar makes them easier to store and stack, as it prevents them from sticking together.)
- Candies can be stored in the refrigerator in an airtight container for 2-3 days.

239. Payday Candy Bar Squares Recipe

Serving: 1 | Prep: | Cook: 3mins | Ready in:

Ingredients

- 3 cups salted peanuts (no skins)
- 3 teaspoons butter
- 2 cups peanut butter chips
- 1 can sweetened condensed milk
- 2 cups miniature marshmallows

Direction

- Put half the peanuts in lightly greased 11x7 pan.
- Melt butter and chips on low. Remove from heat.
- Add milk and marshmallows. Stir well. Pour over peanuts.
- Sprinkle with remaining peanuts. Chill and cut into bars.

240. Peach Jelly Chews Recipe

Serving: 20 | Prep: | Cook: 20mins | Ready in:

Ingredients

- salad oil
- 2 pounds frozen unsweetened sliced peaches
- 3-3/4 cups granulated sugar divided use
- 2 tablespoons unflavored gelatin
- 2 teaspoons grated lemon peel
- 1 tablespoon lemon juice
- Oil a square metal pan.

Direction

- In a large pan combine peaches with 1/3 cup water then bring to boil over high heat.
- Stir constantly then reduce heat and simmer covered stirring occasionally for 12 minutes.
- Whirl fruit mixture in blender a portion at a time until smoothly pureed then return to pan.
- In bowl mix 3-1/2 cups of the sugar with gelatine then add to fruit puree.
- Bring to boil over high heat stirring often then stir and boil 5 minutes then reduce to medium.
- Stir often until thick enough to leave trail when spoon is drawn across pan about 30 minutes.
- At once remove from heat then stir lemon peel and lemon juice into peach mixture.
- Scrape mixture into oiled pan then let candy dry uncovered for 24 hours.
- On a board coat a 10" square area with remaining 1/4 cup sugar then invert pan to release candy.
- With a long sharp knife dipped in sugar to prevent sticking cut candy into equal pieces.
- Coat each piece with sugar then arrange in container with plastic wrap between layers.
- Seal airtight then store up to 1 month at room temperature.

241. Peanut Brittle From Microwave Recipe

Serving: 8 | Prep: | Cook: 5mins | Ready in:

Ingredients

- * 1-1/2 cup dry roasted or salted peanuts, coarsely chopped or cashews
- * 1 cup sugar
- * 1/2 cup light corn syrup
- * dash salt

- * 1 tablespoon butter
- * 1 tablesppon vanilla
- * 1 teaspoon baking soda

Direction

- PREPARATION:
- Lightly grease microwavable glass bowl with butter, metal baking sheet and utensil used for stirring.
- Mix nuts, sugar, syrup and salt in glass bowl. Cook for 4 minutes in microwave on high. Stir. Cook for 3-1/2 more minutes. It will be hot and bubbly, light gold.
- Stir in butter and vanilla. Cook for 3 more minutes. Golden color, Add baking soda. (It will foam.) Pour onto cookie sheet. Slightly shake sheet so that it'll spread out a little.
- Once cool, break into small pieces. Keep in an airtight container.

242. Peanut Butter Balls 1 Recipe

Serving: 10 | Prep: | Cook: 5mins | Ready in:

Ingredients

- peanut butter Balls
- 12 ounces peanut butter (smooth or crunchy)
- 1 cup butter (real)
- 1 box confectioners' sugar
- 1 teaspoon vanilla
- 1 package chocolate chips or Chocolate brick (for dipping balls)

Direction

- Mix peanut butter, butter, sugar and vanilla. Roll into balls and place on cookie sheet, place in freezer for an hour. Melt chocolate in a double boiler. Dip balls into mixture. Cool.

243. Peanut Butter Bonbons Recipe

Serving: 0 | Prep: | Cook: 30mins | Ready in:

Ingredients

- 1 cup icing sugar
- 1/2 cup smooth peanut butter (I prefer Kraft)
- 3 tbsp. margarine
- 1/2 cup flaked sweetened coconut
- 5 squares Semi-sweet Baker's chocolate

Direction

- Combine the icing sugar, peanut butter, margarine and coconut with a fork and roll into balls a bit smaller than a ping pong ball. Chill 'til hard. In the meantime, melt chocolate squares in a double boiler.
- Dip cold peanut butter balls in melted chocolate and transfer to a waxed paper lined cookie sheet. I sometimes use a combination of a teaspoon and a wooden skewer to roll the balls around in the melted chocolate. If you have any bare spots on the bonbons once you're done you can just paint them with any extra melted chocolate from the pan.
- Return chocolate covered bonbons to the freezer so the chocolate can set. If you can resist eating them straight away, they do keep nicely in the freezer. Store in little gift boxes. I prefer to serve mine straight from the freezer.

244. Peanut Butter Chocolate Balls Recipe

Serving: 12 | Prep: | Cook: 10mins | Ready in:

Ingredients

- 8 ounces of cream cheese
- 1 1/2 pounds of smooth peanut butter

- 3 pounds of chocolate wafers for melting, either dark or milk chocolate OR 3 pounds of Wilbur's chocolate wafers
- 2 1/2 pounds of powdered sugar
- 2 tsp of vanilla extract
- 1 1/4 pounds of margarine

Direction

- Margarine and cream cheese need to be at room temperature.
- Mix together and add peanut butter, then add vanilla.
- Add sugar in small amounts.
- Chill mixture then form into egg shape.
- Rechill.
- Melt chocolate over low heat or on low setting in microwave.
- Dip chilled eggs or balls in melted chocolate and cool on wax paper. Suggestion: Melt 1 lb. Chocolate at a time - use fork for dipping

245. Peanut Butter Easter Eggs Recipe

Serving: 16 | Prep: | Cook: 35mins | Ready in:

Ingredients

- 1/2c butter, softened
- 2 1/3c confectioners sugar
- 1c graham cracker crumbs
- 1/2c creamy peanut butter
- 1/2 tsp. vanilla
- 1 1/2c dark chocolate chips
- 2 Tbs. shortening
- Pastel sprinkles

Direction

- In large bowl, cream butter; gradually add confectioners' sugar, cracker crumbs, peanut butter and vanilla. Shape into 16 eggs; place on waxed paper-lined baking sheets. Refrigerate for 30 mins or till firm.
- In microwave, melt chocolate chips and shortening; stir till smooth. Dip eggs in chocolate; allow excess to drip off. Decorate with sprinkles; return eggs to waxed paper. Chill till set. Store in airtight container in refrigerator.

246. Peanut Butter Fudge Recipe

Serving: 20 | Prep: | Cook: 3mins | Ready in:

Ingredients

- 2 C. sugar
- 1/2 C. milk
- 1-1/3 C. peanut butter
- 1 jar (7 oz) marshmallow creme

Direction

- In a saucepan, bring sugar and milk to a boil; boil for 3 minutes.
- Add peanut butter and marshmallow crème; mix well.
- Quickly pour into a buttered 8-inch square pan; chill until set.
- Cut into squares.

247. Peanut Butter Meltaways Recipe

Serving: 72 | Prep: | Cook: | Ready in:

Ingredients

- 1 pound milk chocolate (you can either use a premium chocolate or a confectionery coating)
- 1 pound white confectionery coating
- 1 cup smooth peanut butter

Direction

- Melt the milk chocolate and white confectionery coating either on top of a double boiler over barely simmering water or very carefully in the microwave (stopping and stirring every 20-30 seconds) until completely melted and smooth; mix very well to combine together.
- Add the peanut butter and mix until fully incorporated.
- Spoon into small candy cups and allow to dry.
- Enjoy!
- NOTE: Prep time does not include drying time.

248. Peanut Chew Ee Recipe

Serving: 24 | Prep: | Cook: 10mins |Ready in:

Ingredients

- 1c   creamed honey
- 2c   semisweet chocolate chips
- 1c   smooth peanut butter
- 2c   salted peanuts

Direction

- You will need a 10x15" jelly roll pan and foil.
- Dampen pan with water, center the foil over pan. Press it into place, pressing into the corners as well. The damp pan makes the foil cling so it doesn't move around when you spread the candy bar mixture on it.
- Combine the honey and chocolate chips in a heavy bottomed saucepan. Cook over low heat until chocolate starts to melt, stirring often. Turn up heat to med-high and cook to a boil stirring often.
- Remove from heat.
- Add peanut butter; stir until smooth; stir in peanuts.
- Moving quickly pour the mixture down the center of prepared pan, spreading evenly to edges. Let the pan sit on the counter several hours to set.

- Place in refrigerator for about 15 mins. before cutting. Invert pan onto cutting board and cut into bars with a sharp knife.

249. Peanut Crunchies Recipe

Serving: 12 | Prep: | Cook: 10mins |Ready in:

Ingredients

- 2 cups Rice Krispies cereal (any brand will do!)
- 2 cups mini puffed marshmallows
- 2 cups salted cocktail-style peanuts
- 1/2 stick regular salted butter
- 30 unwrapped caramels (This takes the longest amount of time.. the unwrapping of those caramels!)(Get the kids to help!)

Direction

- Using an ungreased 13x9 inch aluminum pan or a pan covered in Release Aluminum foil, pour the rice krispies into the bottom of the pan.
- In a glass microwave-proof bowl, add the caramels and butter.
- Heat on high for 2 minutes and stir.
- Add 2 cups of marshmallows.
- Heat on high for one minutes and stir.
- Pour this mixture directly over the rice krispies and spread quickly and evenly.
- Pour the peanuts over the caramel mixture and press FIRMLY into the caramel.
- Cool and cut into small squares and serve!
- I have to add this. Men love these!

250. Peanut Sesame Candy Recipe

Serving: 12 | Prep: | Cook: 15mins |Ready in:

Ingredients

- 2 pounds of roasted and shelled peanuts
- 2 pounds brown sugar
- 1/4 cup vinegar
- 1/4 cup water
- 1/2 cup sesame seeds, toasted

Direction

- In a saucepan, dissolve sugar in vinegar and water and boil until quite thick. (The thicker the sugar solution, the more brittle the candy.)
- Pour peanuts into saucepan and mix well.
- Sprinkle the bottom of a pan or a smooth, clean cutting board with three-quarters of the toasted sesame seeds. (I use a large baking pan covered in "Release Aluminum foil or a silicone mat.)
- Pour the peanut mixture into the pan or on a board, flattening it out by rolling over it a bottle or jar smeared with enough peanut oil to keep the candy from sticking to the bottle.
- Sprinkle the top with remaining sesame seeds.
- Allow to cool; cut into squares or diamonds.

251. Pecan Caramel Candies

Serving: 24 | Prep: | Cook: | Ready in:

Ingredients

- 54 pretzels
- 54 Rolo candies (about 11 ounces)
- 54 pecan halves

Direction

- Preheat oven to 250°. Place pretzels 1 in. apart on foil-lined baking sheets. Top each with a Rolo candy.
- Bake 3-4 minutes or until candies are softened. (Rolos will still retain their shape.) Immediately top with pecans, pressing to spread candy into pretzel. Let stand until set.
- Nutrition Facts

- 1 piece: 44 calories, 2g fat (1g saturated fat), 1mg cholesterol, 24mg sodium, 6g carbohydrate (4g sugars, 0 fiber), 1g protein.

252. Pecan Roll Recipe

Serving: 10 | Prep: | Cook: 10mins | Ready in:

Ingredients

- 1 cup cream
- 2 cups sugar
- 1/2 cup white corn syrup
- 1-1/2 cups pecans
- 1 cup light brown sugar

Direction

- Boil cream, sugar, syrup, to soft-ball stage. (234-238 F).
- Cool to room temperature then beat till creamy.
- Turn out onto board dusted with powdered sugar and knead until firm.
- Shape into a roll and cover the outside with pecans.
- Put in cool place to harden.
- Slice when firm with a sharp knife.

253. Peppermint Balls Recipe

Serving: 12 | Prep: | Cook: 15mins | Ready in:

Ingredients

- 5 cups rice crispy cereal
- 4 cups mini marshmellows
- 4 Tbls. butter
- 2 1/2 tsp. milk + 1 tsp. mint extract
- 6 oz. semi sweet chocolate chips
- 6 oz. white chocolate chips
- 2 regular sized peppermint candy canes-crushed

- 36-40 mini muffin papers

Direction

- Make a basic Rice Crispy Treat by melting the butter over medium heat in a very large saucepan. Add the marshmallows and stir till melted, then add in milk with mint extract. Stir again. Then add in cereal and stir till well coated. Remove from heat and work quickly with damp hands, break off a small amount of the coated cereal and form into a small ball. Place the ball on a waxed paper covered cookie sheet. Continue doing this till all the balls are formed. You should have about 36 - 40 balls. Set aside.
- Melt semi-sweet chocolate in microwave according to directions on bag. Dip each ball in the chocolate and smear the chocolate all over the ball with your hands making sure to evenly but thinly coat the ball. Place back on waxed paper covered cookie sheet. Repeat this for half the balls. Sprinkle the crushed candy canes over top of the balls before they dry. Repeat this method with the white chocolate.
- When all the peppermint balls are dry, place each one in the mini paper cups.
- Serve and enjoy!

254. Peppermint Patties Recipe

Serving: 28 | Prep: | Cook: | Ready in:

Ingredients

- 3/4 cup sweetened condensed milk
- 1 1/2 teaspoons peppermint extract
- 1 teaspoon vanilla extract
- 3-4 cups confectioners' sugar
- 3 cups semisweet chocolate chips
- 2 tablespoons shortening

Direction

- In a large mixing bowl, combine condensed milk and extracts. Stir well.
- Stir in enough confectioners' sugar to form a stiff dough.
- Knead until no longer sticky.
- Form dough into 1 inch balls and flatten to form patties.
- Chill for 1 hour or until firm.
- In medium saucepan over low heat, melt chocolate with shortening, stirring constantly.
- Remove from heat.
- Dip patties one at a time into chocolate using a fork.
- Place chocolate dipped patties on wax paper and chill until set.
- Keep refrigerated.

255. Peppermint Taffy Recipe

Serving: 1 | Prep: | Cook: 30mins | Ready in:

Ingredients

- *Time varies from one stove top to another - best to gauge with the candy thermometer as it yields best results.
- 2 cups light corn syrup
- 1 tablespoon butter or margarine
- 1 tablespoon vinegar
- peppermint extract

Direction

- Put all ingredients except flavoring in large heavy saucepan.
- Bring to boil, and cook until a small amount of mixture forms a hard ball when dropped in very cold water (254 degrees F. on a candy thermometer).
- Pour onto a large buttered platter.
- As edges cool, turn mixture toward center with a spatula. When just cool enough to handle make a hollow in center of taffy and add a few drops of flavoring.

- Gather up taffy and pull until light, using a little butter to grease hands while pulling. Twist into a long rope and cut into pieces with scissors. Wrap each piece in wax paper and store in a cool dry place. Makes about 1 1/4 pounds.

256. Pink Popcorn Candy Recipe

Serving: 20 | Prep: | Cook: |Ready in:

Ingredients

- 12 cups (3.6 oz) popped popcorn
- 1 ½ cups sugar
- ½ cup vanilla sugar
- ⅔ cup whole milk
- 2 tbsp golden corn syrup
- ¼ tsp kosher salt
- 1 tbsp vanilla
- ½ dram concentrated cherry flavour
- 3 drops liquid red food colouring

Direction

- Place popcorn in a food processor and pulse until broken up into small "pebbles". Pour into a large bowl and set aside.
- In a saucepan combine sugars, milk, corn syrup and salt. Place over medium heat and cook until sugar dissolves.
- Raise heat and bring mixture to a slow boil. Cook until the temperature reaches 230F, stirring occasionally.
- Remove from heat, stir in vanilla, cherry flavour and food coloring.
- Pour over the popcorn "pebbles" and stir well to coat.
- Pour onto a parchment-lined baking sheet and let stand overnight.
- Heat the oven to 300F. Bake the sheet of popcorn for 15 minutes, until lightly golden and no longer super sticky on top.
- Flip the piece of candy (it should be essentially a solid mass) and return to the oven for 5 minutes.
- Turn off the oven and let cool completely inside.

257. Pistachio Fudge Recipe

Serving: 25 | Prep: | Cook: |Ready in:

Ingredients

- 1 pound white baking chocolate
- 1 package (8 ounces) cream cheese, softened
- 3 cups confectioners' sugar
- 1/2 teaspoon McCormick® pure vanilla extract
- 1/4 teaspoon McCormick® Pure almond extract
- 1/8 teaspoon McCormick® green food color
- 1/2 cup chopped pistachios
- Additional pistachios for garnish, if desired

Direction

- Line an 8-inch square pan with foil, allowing foil to extend over sides of pan.
- Spray with no stick cooking spray.
- Melt chocolate as directed on package.
- Beat cream cheese in large bowl with electric mixer until smooth. Gradually beat in sugar on low speed until well blended.
- Add melted chocolate, extracts and food color; mix well.
- Stir in chopped pistachios.
- Spread evenly in prepared pan.
- Garnish with additional pistachios, if desired.
- Refrigerate at least 1 hour or until firm.
- Use foil to lift out of pan onto cutting board.
- Cut into 25 (1 1/2-inch) squares.
- Store in refrigerator.
- Substitute: One bag (12 ounces) white chocolate chips can be substituted for the white chocolate squares.

258. Polka Dot Fudge Recipe

Serving: 6 | Prep: | Cook: 2mins | Ready in:

Ingredients

- 3 cups of semi-sweet chocolate chips
- 1 can of regular Eagle Brand sweetened condensed milk
- 2 tsp. of vanilla extract
- 1/2 cup of chopped glace cherries (maraschino cherries will not work as they'll "bleed" into the fudge."
- 1/2 cup of fresh mini marshmallows
- *You can skip the cherries and add other dried fruits to the fudge, such as cranberries or apricots.

Direction

- Using a microwave-proof glass bowl, melt the chips and Eagle Brand together in your microwave for 1 minute.
- Stir and return to microwave for one more minute.
- Stir until milk and chocolate are well-combined.
- Stir in vanilla, cherries and marshmallows.
- Spread out into a lined 8 inch square pan.
- Chill for 4 hours in your refrigerator.
- Remove from pan, peel off paper.
- Cut into squares.
- Easy, isn't it?

259. Popcorn Balls Recipe

Serving: 16 | Prep: | Cook: 25mins | Ready in:

Ingredients

- 1/2 lb uncooked popcorn
- 2/3 cup light Karo corn syrup
- 2 cups sugar
- 2/3 cup boiling water
- 2 tsp cream of tartar
- 2 tbs vinegar
- 2 tbs butter, melted
- 2 tsp vanilla
- 1/8 tsp baking soda

Direction

- Popcorn and place in large pan. Combine syrup, sugar, water and vinegar. Heat to boil add cream of tartar. Continue boiling to soft crack stage 275-280 degrees. Remove from heat. Add butter and baking soda and vanilla. Pour over popcorn. Butter hands and form immediately into balls. Yield will depend on size of balls, but baseball size is great.

260. Positively Yummy Pumpkin Fudge Recipe

Serving: 36 | Prep: | Cook: 35mins | Ready in:

Ingredients

- 3 cups white sugar
- 1 cup milk
- 3 Tablespoons light corn syrup
- 1/2 cup pumpkin puree
- 1/4 teaspoon salt
- 1 teaspoon pumpkin pie spice
- 1-1/2 teaspoons vanilla extract
- 1/2 cup butter
- 1/2 cup chopped walnuts/pecans (optional)

Direction

- Butter or grease one 8 x 8 inch pan.
- In a 3 quart saucepan, mix together sugar, milk, corn syrup, pumpkin and salt.
- Bring to a boil over high heat, stirring constantly.
- Reduce heat to medium and continue boiling.
- Do not stir.

- When mixture registers 232 degrees F (110 degrees C) on candy thermometer, or forms a soft ball when dropped into cold water, remove pan from heat.
- Stir in pumpkin pie spice, vanilla, butter and nuts.
- Cool to lukewarm (110 degrees F or 43 degrees C on candy thermometer).
- Beat mixture until it is very thick and loses some of its gloss.
- Quickly pour into a greased eight-inch pan.
- When firm cut into 36 squares.

261. Potato Candies Or Bonbons Recipe

Serving: 10 | Prep: | Cook: | Ready in:

Ingredients

- 1 potato (peeled, boiled, mashed, cold)
- 1 tbsp powdered sugar (confectioner's sugar)
- 2 tbsps peanut butter

Direction

- Cook potato as usual (or use a mashed leftover potato).
- Cool and mash it well. Add the powdered sugar to the mashed, cold potato and mix well until all the sugar is absorbed.
- Roll out the potato mixture with a rolling pin on top of a long, rectangular piece of wax paper (like it was pastry crust) until it is very thin, in a rectangle. Spread the peanut butter evenly on top. Roll the dough into a jelly or pinwheel roll. Wrap the wax paper around the roll and refrigerate for 1 hour. Take out of the fridge, unwrap and slice into 1/4 inch slices. Fan out the candies (bonbons) on a plate.

262. Potato Candy Recipe

Serving: 0 | Prep: | Cook: 20mins | Ready in:

Ingredients

- 1 medium white potato
- 1 cup peanut butter Creamy or Chunky
- 1 tsp. vanilla extract
- 3 cups powdered sugar

Direction

- Peel and cube potato
- Boil until soft
- Mash potato making sure there are no lumps
- In medium sized bowl combine potato and vanilla extract
- Add powdered sugar about 1 cup at a time stirring well after each cup
- Continue adding powdered sugar until mixture is firm dough consistency
- Roll your potato "dough" out on a flat surface until it is about 1/4 inch thick
- Spread a thin layer of peanut butter over entire surface.
- Begin rolling into a log
- Slice log into 1/2 inch to 3/4 inch slices
- Store in air tight container.

263. Pumpkin Caramels Recipe

Serving: 24 | Prep: | Cook: 45mins | Ready in:

Ingredients

- 1/2 cup toasted pumpkin seeds or sunflower seeds
- 1 cup maple syrup
- 3/4 cup light brown sugar
- 1/2 cup heavy cream
- 1/4 cup dark corn syrup
- 1 teaspoon pumpkin or apple pie spice
- 1 teaspoon fresh lemon juice

- 1/2 teaspoon fine salt
- 2/3 cup canned pumpkin puree, room temperature
- 1 tablespoon unsalted butter, room temperature
- 1 teaspoon pure vanilla extract
- Special equipment: Candy thermometer

Direction

- Line an 8 by 4 inch loaf pan with waxed paper or aluminum foil. Brush the sides, but not the bottom lightly with butter and sprinkle the pumpkin seeds in the bottom.
- Whisk the maple syrup, brown sugar, cream, corn syrup, pie spice, lemon juice, and salt together in a heavy bottomed medium saucepan. Brush down the sides on the saucepan with water to remove every grain of sugar. Set the candy thermometer into the sugar. Cook the mixture over medium heat, without stirring, until the mixture reaches the firm ball stage, 248 degrees F, about 18 to 20 minutes.
- Carefully stir in the pumpkin puree. Return to the heat and cook, stirring occasionally, until the caramel reaches the soft ball stage, 240 degrees F, about 15 minutes more. Remove from the heat and stir in butter and vanilla.
- Pour the caramel over the pumpkin seeds in the prepared pan. Smooth to an even layer. Cool to room temperature.
- When fully cooled peel from the waxed paper or foil and cut into 24 (1-inch) squares. Wrap individually in parchment or waxed paper and store in an airtight container for up to a week.

264. Pumpkin Flan With Chile Spiced Brittle Recipe

Serving: 8 | Prep: | Cook: 410mins | Ready in:

Ingredients

- For the pumpkin flan
- 1 cup sugar
- 1/3 cup water
- 2 cups whole milk
- 1 cup heavy cream
- 1 cup pumpkin purée
- ¾ cup sugar
- 4 whole eggs
- 2 egg yolks
- 1 stick Mexican cinnamon (canela), about 5 grams or 1/8 ounce in weight (mexican cinnamon is a soft cinnamon rather than a hard bark cinnamon and is used a lot in drinks since it blends so well and can be ground with a mortar and pestle)
- ½ vanilla bean, split lengthwise and seeds scraped
- 2 inches sliced fresh ginger
- ½ teaspoon Ancho chile powder
- 2 whole cloves
- ¼ tsp salt
- ¼ tspallspice
- 1/8 tsp nutmeg
- For the spiced brittle
- 1 cup sugar
- 1/8 teaspoon cream of tartar
- ¼ cup room temp butter not melted
- ½ tsp vanilla extract (pure)
- ½ teaspoon Ancho chile powder
- pinch salt (don;t use kosher here)
- ¾ cup toasted pumpkin seeds
- 8 1 cup ramekins
- Silpat (optional) but worth it even if used once.

Direction

- Prepare the pumpkin flan.
- Preheat the oven to 325° F.
- Butter ramekins and line them up on a flat baking sheet.
- Combine 1 cup sugar and 1/3 cup water in a small saucepan and stir with your hand to make a wet, sandy sugar.
- Bring the sugar to a boil over medium heat and continue boiling until it turns deep amber, without stirring, but swirling the pan

- occasionally to evenly distribute the color, about 10 minutes.
- Immediately remove from heat and carefully pour the caramel into the bottom of the ramekins, evenly distributing between all eight. Watch the caramel it can go from yummy to burnt in seconds and you have to start again. And caramel is melted sugar and burns you!
- Combine the milk, heavy cream, ginger, cinnamon, vanilla bean and spices in a medium saucepan; bring to a simmer and steep for 15 minutes.
- In a large bowl, beat the eggs lightly.
- Add the sugar, salt and pumpkin purée and whisk to blend.
- Slowly temper the hot milk mixture into the egg mixture. Tempering is where you take small amounts of the hot milk and add to the eggs and whisk to bring the eggs up in temperature without cooking them. Do this in small steps until the eggs are really warm
- Whisk to fully combine, and strain the entire mixture through a fine meshed sieve twice, discarding solids.
- Evenly pour this mixture into the ramekins over the hardened caramel.
- Carefully move the baking sheet (with filled ramekins) into the preheated oven.
- Pour warm water into the baking sheet to come halfway up the sides of the ramekins, to bake in a water bath.
- Cover with another baking sheet or loosely with foil and bake for about 45 minutes, until the custard is set and a knife inserted near center comes out clean.
- Remove from the oven and let cool completely in water bath.
- Remove from water bath and refrigerate until very cold, at least 4-6 hours.
- The longer you allow the custard to remain chilled in the refrigerator, the better chance that you will have a nice liquid caramel sauce once you unmold the flans. Sugar will absorb liquid, but needs time; if served before the flans have time to set, the finished product may have a solid disc at the top of the flan. If you can leave them to rest overnight, you will not have to worry about this
- Prepare the spiced brittle
- Prepare a flat baking sheet with parchment, wax paper or a non-stick Silpat. About $25 in any restaurant supply store.
- Mix together the sugar and the cream of tartar and place in a saucepan.
- Bring to a boil over medium heat, and continue, occasionally swirling the pan, until it turns a deep amber.
- Once it has reached a dark caramel color, add the butter, vanilla, salt and Ancho chili powder, whisking continuously to completely emulsified.
- Mix in the toasted pumpkin seeds and spread out evenly onto the prepared baking sheet (try to get the brittle to be an even ¼ - ½ inch layer).
- Allow to cool and harden for at least 1 hour. Break into pieces and set aside.
- If the caramel hardens too quickly and becomes difficult to spread, just place the baking sheet in a 400 F heated oven for 30 seconds to 1 minute and it will become pliable again. Again caramel is melted sugar and will burn you very easily
- To serve
- To unmold the flans, run a knife around the edge of the custard to loosen.
- Dip the outer edge of the ramekins in hot water for a few seconds for easier release.
- Place a dish on top of the custard, invert the custard onto the dish and shake gently to release the flan.
- Carefully remove the ramekin, allowing the caramel to run over the flan and onto the plate.
- Repeat with each flan to unmold.
- Garnish with pieces of the spiced brittle.
- That's it! Wasn't that easy??!! Your taste buds will love you for it.
- And as an end note, have your sweetie clean up the kitchen since you put so much time in this.

265. Pumpkin Fudge Recipe

Serving: 16 | Prep: | Cook: 25mins | Ready in:

Ingredients

- 3 cups sugar
- 3/4 cup melted butter
- 2/3 cup evaporated milk
- 1/2 cup canned pumpkin
- 2 tablespoons corn syrup
- 1 teaspoon pumpkin pie spice
- 1 (12-ounce) package white chocolate morsels
- 1 (7-ounce) jar marshmallow crème
- 1 cup chopped pecans, toasted
- 1 teaspoon vanilla extract

Direction

- Line a 9x9 inch pan with aluminum foil, and set aside.
- Stir together first 6 ingredients in a 3 1/2-quart saucepan over medium-high heat, and cook, stirring constantly, until mixture comes to a boil. Cook, stirring constantly, until a candy thermometer registers 234° (soft-ball stage) or for about 12 minutes.
- Remove pan from heat; stir in remaining ingredients until well blended. Pour into a greased aluminum foil-lined 9-inch square pan. Let stand 2 hours or until completely cool; cut fudge into squares

266. Pumpkin Pie Fudge Recipe

Serving: 40 | Prep: | Cook: 12mins | Ready in:

Ingredients

- 1 1/2 cups granulated sugar
- 1/2 cup canned solid-pack pumpkin
- 2/3 cup evaporated milk
- 2 tablespoons butter
- 1/4 teaspoon salt
- 1 1/2 teaspoons pumpkin pie spice
- 1 package vanilla flavored baking chips (12 ounces)
- 2 cups miniature marshmallows
- 1/3 cup chopped nuts (optional)
- 1 1/4 teaspoons vanilla extract

Direction

- Using butter or margarine, lightly grease the sides and bottom of a medium saucepan.
- Place the sugar, evaporated milk, pumpkin, butter, salt, and pumpkin pie spice in the saucepan.
- Stirring constantly over medium heat, bring the mixture to a boil and boil for 12 minutes.
- Remove from the heat and stir in the baking chips and marshmallows until melted. Stir in the nuts and vanilla.
- Pour into an 8-inch square pan that has been lined with foil and greased.
- Chill mixture until set.
- Cut into small squares to serve.
- Cover and store in refrigerator.

267. Punkin Pie Fudge Recipe

Serving: 50 | Prep: | Cook: 12mins | Ready in:

Ingredients

- 1 ½ cups granulated sugar
- 2/3 cup evaporated milk
- ½ cup mashed pumpkin
- 2 tablespoons butter or margarine
- ¼ teaspoon salt
- 1 ½ teaspoons pumpkin pie spice
- 12 oz package white chocolate chips
- 2 cups miniature marshmallows
- 1 teaspoon vanilla extract

Direction

- Lightly grease the sides and bottom of a medium saucepan.

- Place the sugar, evaporated milk, pumpkin, butter, salt, and pumpkin pie spice in the saucepan.
- Stir constantly over medium heat until dissolved.
- Bring the mixture to a boil, cook 12 minutes.
- Remove from the heat, stir in the chocolate chips and marshmallows until melted.
- Stir in the vanilla.
- Pour into an 8-inch square pan that has been lined with foil and greased.
- Chill mixture until set.
- Cover and store in refrigerator

268. Queen Anne Salted Peanut Caramel Nougat Rolls Recipe

Serving: 36 | Prep: | Cook: 10mins | Ready in:

Ingredients

- 2½ cups sugar
- 2/3 cup white Karo syrup
- ½ cup hot water (not boiling)
- 2 egg whites, beaten just until foamy peaks begin to form
- 2 teaspoons vanilla extract
- 1 (14 ounce) bag Kraft caramels
- 2 tablespoons milk
- 1 to 2 pounds salted peanuts or salted cashews (I usually make a few of each so I have both varieties)

Direction

- I know this looks LONG, but it's only because I am being anal about explaining how to best coat the logs and store them!
- In a large heavy saucepan, mix together sugar, syrup and hot water. Cook mixture over medium to medium-high heat, until it reaches 275 degrees on a candy thermometer ("hard thread" stage).
- While the syrup is cooking, whip egg whites in a large mixing bowl, just until foamy peaks (not stiff peaks!) begin to form.
- With the mixer set on Medium High, gradually beat the hot syrup into the egg whites – you want to keep drizzling the hot syrup over the whites as you keep turning the bowl and beating.
- Once all the syrup is added, add the extract and continue to beat until mixture is firm enough to shape into "logs". Mixture will be quite hot, so BE CAREFEUL not to burn your hands! NOTE – be sure hands are clean and no fragrances or lotions are on them! Grab a handful and roll it into a 5" long log, with a diameter about the size of a quarter (do this on a piece of waxed paper). Set logs on a piece of waxed paper to cool completely.
- Melt the caramels with the milk – let it cool off considerably before proceeding to the "frosting" step.
- Place the nuts in a shallow dish or rimmed plate.
- Here comes the messy part! While keeping the logs on waxed paper, use a knife or spoon to frost each log with caramel, and then dip it in nuts. I have found the easiest way to do this is to frost one side of a log, dip in nuts, and then lay the nut coated side in your palm, frost the other side and dip it. Do the two ends lastly. You'll get the hang of it after the first couple logs!
- Work with the coated log for a bit, rolling it gently in your hands to be sure the nuts are firmly imbedded in the caramel coating. As the logs cool – if the caramel was too warm to "set" as you frosted the logs and it wants to "run off "the logs – you will need to pick up the log and firmly "press" the nuts and caramels into it until the caramel sets up enough to stay put.
- When logs are coated and completely cooled, wrap each one individually in saran wrap and keep tightly covered until ready to serve (no need to refrigerate unless you are storing them in a warm climate or warm room).

- To serve, slice logs into bite-size rounds and put on platter. They're very pretty when cut - you see the nut layer, then the caramel layer, and then the white fondant center (fondant is like divinity).
- Wrap logs in foil to freeze if you will not be using them within a few days.

269. Quick And Easy Fudge Recipe

Serving: 64 | Prep: | Cook: 20mins | Ready in:

Ingredients

- 3 1/3 cups sugar
- 1 1/3 cups evaporated milk
- 1 package (12 ounces_ semisweet chocolate pieces)
- 3 cups miniature marshmallows
- 1 cup chopped walnuts (or nut of choice)
- 1 cup candied red cherries quartered

Direction

- Line 8x8x2 inch pan with foil; butter foil.
- Combine sugar and milk in medium size saucepan. Cook over medium heat, stirring constantly until sugar is dissolved and mixture comes to boiling. Boil, stirring constantly, 5 minutes.
- Remove from heat; beat in chocolate and marshmallows with wooden spoon, Stir until mixture thickens; stir in nuts and cherries. Pour into prepared pan; let stand until cool and firm.
- Turn out onto a cutting board; remove foil cut fudge into 1 inch squares. Store in tightly covered container.

270. ROCK CANDY Recipe

Serving: 0 | Prep: | Cook: 30mins | Ready in:

Ingredients

- 2 1/2 cups sugar
- 1 cup water
- 1 1/2 cup white corn syrup
- 1 teaspoon of oil flavoring of your choice.. she adds extra
- 1 teaspoon food coloring. If you use paste, you can use less.

Direction

- Combine the first 3 ingredients in a saucepan.
- Bring to a boil.
- Cook to 300 for hard crack stage.
- Remove from heat add flavor and color.
- Pour in a cookie sheet that has been dusted quite heavy with powdered sugar.
- After it is hard sprinkle more powdered sugar on again.
- Break into pieces and store in an air tight container.
- Enjoy and make memories

271. Rachael Rays Fabulous Five Minute Fudge Wreath Recipe

Serving: 32 | Prep: | Cook: 5mins | Ready in:

Ingredients

- 1 bag semisweet chocolate morsels (12 ounces)
- 9 ounces butterscotch morsels (3/4 of a 12-ounce bag)
- 1 can sweetened condensed milk (14 ounces)
- 1 teaspoon vanilla extract
- 1 can or package of walnut halves (8 ounces)
- 1/2 cup currants (a couple handfuls)
- 8-inch cake pan, lightly greased with softened butter

- candied red and green cherries, for garnish (optional)

Direction

- Place a heavy pot on the stove and preheat it over low heat.
- Add chocolate and butterscotch morsels and milk and stir until morsels are melted and milk is combined.
- Save the empty condensed milk can.
- Stir in the vanilla and remove the fudge from heat.
- Add the nuts and currants and stir in immediately.
- Cover the empty condensed milk can with plastic wrap and center it in the greased cake pan.
- Spoon fudge into pan around can, making sure to center the can if it drifts.
- The fudge will set up almost immediately.
- Garnish can only be added in the first minute or two that the fudge is in the pan, so work quickly.
- Decorate your wreath with "holly" made from cut candied red and green cherries.
- A wreath left plain can be garnished with a pretty fabric bow when serving.
- Chill covered in the refrigerator.
- Slice the fudge very thin when ready to serve — a little goes a long way!

272. Raspberry Fudge Truffles Recipe

Serving: 36 | Prep: | Cook: 10mins | Ready in:

Ingredients

- 2 cups semisweet chocolate morsels
- 16 ounces cream cheese softened
- 1 cup seedless raspberry preserves
- 2 tablespoons raspberry liqueur
- 1-1/2 cups vanilla wafer crumbs
- 10 chocolate candy coating squares
- 3 white chocolate squares
- 1 tablespoon shortening

Direction

- Microwave chocolate morsels in a 4 cup glass measuring cup on high for 2 minutes stirring every 30 seconds.
- Beat cream cheese at medium speed with an electric mixer until smooth.
- Add melted chocolate preserves and liqueur beating until blended.
- Stir in crumbs then cover and chill 2 hours.
- Shape mixture into 1" balls then cover and freeze 1 hour.
- Microwave chocolate coating in a 4 cup glass measuring cup on high for 2-1/2 minutes stirring every 30 seconds.
- Dip balls in coating then place on wax paper.
- Place white chocolate and shortening in small heavy duty zip top plastic bag.
- Seal then submerge in hot water until chocolate melts kneading until smooth.
- Snip a tiny hole in 1 corner of bag and drizzle mixture over truffles.
- Let stand until firm.
- Store in refrigerator.

273. Raspberry Mousse Tartelettes Recipe Recipe

Serving: 3 | Prep: | Cook: 15mins | Ready in:

Ingredients

- For the sable crust:
- 1 stick butter (113 grams) butter, at room temperature
- ¼ cup (50 grams) sugar
- 2 egg yolks
- 1 ½ cups (190 grams) all purpose flour
- Pinch of salt
- 1 to 2 tablespoons (15 to 30gr)of cream, optional
- 1/2 cup raspberry jam

- For the raspberry Diplomat cream mousse:
- 1 1/2 teaspoons (3 sheets) gelatin
- 1 tablespoon (15ml) cold water
- 1 cup (250ml) whole milk
- 1/2 vanilla bean, split lengthwise and scraped (throw the seeds in the pot with the milk)
- 1 egg + 1 egg yolk
- 1/4 cup (50gr)sugar
- 2 tablespoons (25gr)cornstarch
- 1/3 cup raspberry jam
- 1 cup (250ml) heavy cream

Direction

- For the sable crust:
- In a stand mixer fitted with the paddle attachment, whip the butter and sugar until light and creamy. Add the egg yolks, one at a time, scraping the bottom and side of the bowl in between each addition. Add the flour and salt and beat until the dough just starts to come together. If the dough seems too crumbly, add some cream, one tablespoon at a time. Gather the dough into a ball, flatten it a little to a small disk and wrap it well in plastic wrap. Refrigerate one hour before using.
- Preheat oven to 350F. Flour your work area well and start rolling the dough from the center out, lifting it from the work area every 2-3 times you roll over it. Do not be afraid to flour the work area well as you feel the dough getting warmer and softer.
- Cut out six 4 inch rounds and fit them inside six 3 inch tartlet molds pastry dough inside them, patting the dough in with your fingertips if needed. Place a small piece of parchment paper inside the tart shells, fill with beans or pie weights and blind bake for 12-15 minutes. Let cool to room temperature and remove the shells from the rings. Divide the raspberry jam evenly among the tart shells.
- For the raspberry Diplomat cream mousse:
- In a ramekin, sprinkle the gelatine over the water and let stand until you prepare the cream. In a medium bowl, whisk the sugar, egg and egg yolk together, add the cornstarch mixing until you get a smooth paste. Set aside.
- Meanwhile in a saucepan combine the milk and vanilla bean on medium heat until boiling. Remove from heat and add slowly to egg mixture, whisking constantly to prevent curdling, (pour through a strainer if this happens). Remove vanilla bean. Place the egg mixture back into a medium saucepan and cook over medium heat until thick, stirring constantly. Add the jam, cook another 30 seconds and remove from the heat. Immediately add in the gelatine and stir until completely dissolved. Place a piece of plastic wrap on the surface of the cream so that it does not develop a skin as it cools to room temperature.
- Whip the heavy cream until stiff peaks form and gently fold it into the pastry cream. Pipe or spoon the mousse immediately in the cake rings. If you have any leftover, spoon into dessert dishes or glasses for quick snack.
- Decorate with a macaron and some chopped pistachios

274. Red Pepper Fudge Recipe

Serving: 10 | Prep: | Cook: 30mins | Ready in:

Ingredients

- 1C chopped pecans
- 1/2 stick salted butter
- 1/2 t ground red pepper
- 1+T natural sugar
- 1C Hersey's cocoa
- 2C natural sugar
- 2 C 2% All Natural milk
- 2t vanilla
- 4T melted sweet butter

Direction

- Ok this is the way we did it, in a small pot I start the pecans.
- 1C chopped pecans

- ½ stick sated butter
- Cook these until they start getting a slight roasted taste then add
- 1/2t ground red pepper (New Mexico red/pizza pepper)
- 1T heaping Florida Crystals all natural sugar
- Cook this until the sugar starts to caramelize.
- Add this to the fudge when it (fudge) gets to around 200 deg and cook according to fudge recipe. I had to redo mine because we didn't take it to 240 deg. First time, the thermometer was touching the bottom of the pot.
- This is the recipe used.
- 2C natural sugar
- 1C Hershey's cocoa
- 2C 2% promise land milk
- 2t real vanilla
- 4T melted sweet butter
- Combine these ingredients in a 3-4qt pot and cook for a bit and when around 200 add the pecan mix. Continue until the thermometer goes to the "soft ball" stage then cool it stirring like a mad man until thickening begins. Pour on/in a greased pan let it rest (I let mine set till next day)
- Watch it. It wants to stick while going for 230-240.

275. Red Velvet Fudge Recipe

Serving: 27 | Prep: | Cook: 8hours | Ready in:

Ingredients

- 1 cup sugar
- 1 cup brown sugar
- 1 cup low fat buttermilk
- 1/3 cup cocoa
- 1 1/2 tsp gel red food colouring
- 1 tbsp vanilla
- 3 tbsp salted butter

Direction

- Mix sugars, buttermilk, cocoa and food colouring in a heavy saucepan.
- Whisk until well blended and place on medium high heat. Bring to a boil, stirring almost constantly.
- Cook until the mixture hits 243-244F.
- Stop stirring and remove from heat. Add butter and vanilla at this time but do not stir in.
- Cool until mixture reaches less than 150F.
- With an electric mixer (I recommend a stand mixer with the paddle attachment) beat for 10 minutes, until fudge loses it sheen.
- Pour into a well-greased, foil lined 9x5" loaf pan.
- Chill 2-3 hours, until firm.

276. Rice Krispies Treats Recipe

Serving: 12 | Prep: | Cook: 30mins | Ready in:

Ingredients

- 3 tablespoons butter or margarine
- 1 package (10 oz., about 40) regular marshmallows
- - or -
- 4 cups miniature marshmallows
- 6 cups Rice Krispies

Direction

- 1. In large saucepan melt butter over low heat. Add marshmallows and stir until completely melted. Remove from heat.
- 2. Add KELLOGG'S RICE KRISPIES cereal. Stir until well coated.
- 3. Using buttered spatula or wax paper, evenly press mixture into 13 x 9 x 2-inch pan coated with cooking spray. Cool. Cut into 2-inch squares. Best if served the same day.

277. Rocky Road Recipe

Serving: 6 | Prep: | Cook: 5mins | Ready in:

Ingredients

- 2 cups semi-sweet chocolate pieces
- 1 cup peanut butter, creamy or chunky
- 4 cups miniature marshmallows
- chopped peanuts, salted peanuts, chopped walnuts (optional)

Direction

- Grease a 9x9 inch pan. (I use a small cookie sheet lined with parchment paper)
- Melt chocolate chips and peanut butter together in microwave. Make sure all chips are melted.
- Stir in marshmallows and nuts
- Pour into your prepared pan. Cool.
- This can be put into the refrigerator to cool.
- Either cut or break into pieces

278. Rolo Pretzel Turtles Recipe

Serving: 48 | Prep: | Cook: 3mins | Ready in:

Ingredients

- 48 Rolo candies, unwrapped (Rolos are small round caramels dipped in chocolate)
- 48 pretzel rings
- 48 whole pecans

Direction

- No need to grease the cookie sheet – just lay the pretzel rings out on it, and place a Rolo candy on top of each ring.
- Bake at 350 degrees for 3 minutes (no more or you will have a melted mess!).
- Remove pan from oven and immediately place a whole pecan on each Rolo and gently push it down just a bit.
- Allow the candies to cool on the cookie sheet, letting the chocolate harden back up again before removing them to a storage container.

279. Rum Balls Recipe

Serving: 36 | Prep: | Cook: 54mins | Ready in:

Ingredients

- 2 c. finely-crushed vanilla wafers
- 1 1/2 c. confectioner's sugar, divided
- 1/2 c. walnuts, toasted and chopped fine
- 1 TBSP. cocoa powder
- 1/4 tsp. allspice
- 1/4 c. plus 1 TBSP. dark rum
- 1/4 c. dark corn syrup
- 2 TBSP. butter, melted

Direction

- ***Cook time is standing time.***
- Reserve 1/2 c. confectioner's sugar for rolling shaped candies.
- Combine remaining sugar and remaining ingredients in a large bowl and knead together.
- Roll into 1 inch balls and roll in remaining confectioner's sugar. Arrange rum balls on a baking sheet and cover with plastic wrap. Let sit for 48 hours before serving/storing.

280. SWEET BHOR Recipe

Serving: 8 | Prep: | Cook: 20mins | Ready in:

Ingredients

- 500 grams BHOR (available at indian spice shops)
- 750 ml vinegar
- 750 ml water
- 1 tsp salt

- 3 cups brown / white sugar
- 1or2 TBS crushed red chillies (DRIED)

Direction

- Wash bor thoroughly.
- Place in pot cover with water and boil until done.
- Rinse and drain.
- Make a slightly thick syrup by dissolving the sugar in the water and vinegar add the salt and crushed red chillies (dried).
- Add the drained bor and simmer on low heat until nice and thick.
- ENJOY!!! ESPECIALLY FOR MY FRIEND TINA FROM PRETORIA!!!

281. Salt Caramel Recipe

Serving: 0 | Prep: | Cook: | Ready in:

Ingredients

- salt caramel
- 1/2 cup corn syrup
- 1/2 cup unsweetend condensed milk
- 2/3 cup sugar
- 3 tablespoons butter
- 2 teaspoons salt

Direction

- Step 1: Place a silicone backing sheet in the baking pan
- Step 2: Put all the ingredients in a pot and heat at a medium-low heat. Once all the sugar melts, reduce heat to low. Try not to stir the mixture too often.
- Step 3: After 20 minutes the mixture will turn light brown. Stir the mixture slowly and continue to reduce the liquid. Be careful not to burn yourself I did the first time.
- Step 4: When the mixture gets darker turn the stove of the mixture into a cup of cold water. If the mixture hardens in the water and you can break it with your hands, then it's ready. If the mixture hardens in the water and you can break it with your hands, then it's ready. If the mixture stays soft, turn the stove back on and reduce the liquid some more.
- Step 5: When the mixture is the right consistency, quickly pour it into the baking pan.
- Step 6: When the mixture starts to harden, make cut marks with a knife in 1 " squares. You can also make different shapes like rectangles and triangles. Place that baking pan in the refrigerator to finish hardening.
- Step 7: Take the caramel out of the baking pan and break it along the cut marks. If you warp each piece in a cooking sheet, it'll be easier to eat, also give as a gift.

282. Salted Chocolate Caramels Recipe

Serving: 64 | Prep: | Cook: 30mins | Ready in:

Ingredients

- 2 c. heavy cream
- 10 1/2 oz fine-quality bittersweet chocolate (no more than 60% cacao if marked), finely chopped
- 1 3/4 c. sugar
- 1/2 c. light corn syrup
- 1/4 c. water
- 1/4 tsp. salt
- 3 TBSP. unsalted butter, cut into tablespoon pieces
- 2 tsp. flaky sea salt such as Maldon (this is what the original recipe called for, but I found it to be a bit much, 1 tsp. would probably be plenty)
- vegetable oil for greasing

Direction

- Line bottom and sides of an 8-inch straight-sided square metal baking pan with 2 long sheets of crisscrossed parchment. Lightly oil.
- Bring cream just to a boil in a 1- to 1 1/2-quart heavy saucepan over moderately high heat, then reduce heat to low and add chocolate. Let stand 1 minute, then stir until chocolate is completely melted. Remove from heat.
- Bring sugar, corn syrup, water, and salt to a boil in a 5- to 6-quart heavy pot over moderate heat, stirring until sugar is dissolved. Boil, uncovered, without stirring but gently swirling pan occasionally, until sugar is deep golden, about 10 minutes. Tilt pan and carefully pour in chocolate mixture (mixture will bubble and steam vigorously). Continue to boil over moderate heat, stirring frequently, until mixture registers 243°F on thermometer, about 15 minutes (original recipe said 255, but I find that's a bit high for caramel). Add butter, stirring until completely melted, then immediately pour into lined baking pan (do not scrape any caramel clinging to bottom or side of saucepan). Let caramel stand 10 minutes, then sprinkle evenly with sea salt. Cool completely in pan on a rack, about 2 hours.
- Carefully invert caramel onto a clean, dry cutting board, then peel off parchment. Turn caramel salt side up. Lightly oil blade of a large heavy knife and cut into 1-inch squares.

283. Saltine Candy Recipe

Serving: 8 | Prep: | Cook: 10mins | Ready in:

Ingredients

- 1 sleeve of saltine crackers(approximately)
- 2sticks unsalted butter
- 1 8oz. bag semi-sweet chocolate morsels(more if you want thicker chocolate topping)
- 1c. chopped walnuts(or less)
- 1c. sugar

Direction

- Heat oven to 350. Line cookie sheet with foil and place saltines down in single layer. Melt butter, add sugar to melted butter and cook butter and sugar combo in microwave for a total of 3 mins; stirring every 30 seconds so sugar and butter mixture doesn't burn. Pour butter/sugar over the crackers so all are covered and bake for 5 mins.
- Sprinkle chocolate morsels over the crackers and spread as they melt to cover crackers. Sprinkle with walnuts and freeze for 2 hours.
- Break into pieces (big or small). Enjoy!

284. Salty Sweet Treat Recipe

Serving: 10 | Prep: | Cook: 2mins | Ready in:

Ingredients

- 20 mini pretzels
- 20 rolo candy pieces (I could not find the regular size ones so bought a bag of Minis and used 2 per pretzel)
- assorted "deluxe" nut mix, salted (cashews, pecans, brazil nuts and almonds are great)

Direction

- Lay pretzels on cookie sheet.
- Place rolos on top.
- Put in oven at 350 for only a few minutes - so rolos are very soft but still have their shape.
- Take them out of oven and quickly smoosh a nut down on each pretzel.
- Cool the tray in the fridge for about 15 minutes.
- Carefully remove them from the tray (may need a spatula).
- Serve cold or at room temperature.

285. Scottish Whisky Tablet Recipe

Serving: 100 | Prep: | Cook: 32mins | Ready in:

Ingredients

- 2 lbs caster sugar
- 2 tablespoons golden syrup
- 4 ounces butter
- 2 cups milk (whole milk tastes better but semi-skimmed and skimmed milk work)
- 4 tablespoons Scotch whisky

Direction

- On a low heat slowly heat the sugar, syrup, butter and milk in a large heavy bottomed pan until all the sugar is dissolved.
- It is quite important to make sure the sugar is dissolved before turning up the heat as it will not set properly. Hints to make sure all the sugar dissolved. Clean round the side of the pan with a pastry brush and boiling water. Dip a desert spoon in to the sugar liquid and if it comes out with no grains of sugar then the sugar is dissolved. Another test is to listen when stirring with wooden spoon to hear if the sound is grainy if it no longer sounds grainy then the sugar is dissolved.
- When the sugar has dissolved add the whisky.
- Bring to boil until the temperature reaches soft-ball stage (240° F or 115° C). Soft Ball Stage is when a spoonful of hot syrup is dropped into a bowl of very cold water. Then using your fingers in the water, take the cooled syrup and form it into a ball. If it has reached soft-ball stage, the syrup can be easily rolled in the cold water into a soft ball that doesn't hold its shape.
- When the mixture has reached the correct temperature take the pan off the heat.
- Beat the mixture until it is grainy. This is a faint sound that is made from the mixture against the pan when it has been beaten and slightly cooler.
- Pour into a Swiss roll tray.
- Leave to cool.
- When part set mark into bite size portions.
- Continue to leave the mixture until it is cold and set completely.
- Can store in an airtight container for up to 1 month

286. Seeds And Nuts Brittle Recipe

Serving: 8 | Prep: | Cook: 15mins | Ready in:

Ingredients

- 1 stick butter, if salted, omit salt
- 1 cup brown sugar, packed firmly
- 1/4 cup light corn syrup
- 1 3/4 tsp. cayenne
- 1/2 tsp. salt
- 2 1/2 cups peanuts, dry roasted
- 2 1/2 cups cashews, dry roasted
- 1/2 cup sunflower seeds, roasted
- 3 tbls. sesame seeds

Direction

- Put foil on baking sheet.
- Spray foil with cooking spray.
- Put butter, brown sugar, corn syrup, cayenne, and salt in large pan and over medium heat stir until melted and smooth, about 5 minutes.
- Add nuts and seeds.
- Turn heat to high and stir until mixture is very thick and nuts begin to brown, 4 to 6 minutes.
- Pour mixture onto, spreading as thinly as possible with a spatula. Cool about 15 minutes.
- Release brittle from foil, then break it into bite-size pieces.
- Store in an airtight container (sugar absorbs moisture and will become sticky).

287. Sees Candy Recipe

Serving: 15 | Prep: | Cook: 6mins | Ready in:

Ingredients

- 1 12oz can evaporated milk
- 4 1/2 cups sugar
- 3 12 oz packages of semi-sweet chocolate chips
- 2 sticks butter
- 1 7 oz jar marshmellow creme
- 3 cups nuts, chopped
- 5 teaspoons vanilla

Direction

- Bring evaporated milk and sugar to a full boil and cook 6 minutes.
- Pour over other ingredients in another bowl.
- Mix well and pour into a greased 13 x 9 x 2 dish.
- Allow to chill before cutting into squares.
- Yield: 3 dozen squares.

288. Sees Fudge The Best Recipe

Serving: 20 | Prep: | Cook: 8mins | Ready in:

Ingredients

- 18 ounces of semi-sweet or bittersweet chocolate chips (1 1/2 bags)
- 3 cups chopped walnuts or pecans
- (I have used "cocktail-style" peanuts and its good if you want a peanut flavor.)
- 1 cup of regular butter (2 sticks) Do not use margarine!
- 1 can (13 ounces) evaporated milk
- 4 cups of mini marshmallows or 20 large marshmallows, cut up
- 4 cups granulated sugar (no substitutes!)
- 2 teas. vanilla extract
- **All of your ingredients should be a room temperature!

Direction

- Put your marshmallows, chips, butter and vanilla in a large bowl.
- In a heavy pot, add the sugar and milk and bring to a boil over a medium flame.
- Bring this to a rolling boil and cook for exactly eight (8) minutes
- Pour the milk and sugar over the marshmallows, chips, butter and vanilla and let it all sit for a minute.
- Start stirring with a wooden spoon until the marshmallows have melted and add the nuts and stir until the fudge is smooth.
- Pour into a 9x13 pan or a 15x13 sheet pan. (I use a 9x13 disposable aluminium pan.)
- Cover your pan with aluminum foil. (You do not have to butter your pan before pouring your fudge into it.)
- Let fudge rest and cure overnight or for at least several hours until firm to the touch.
- *You can add more or less nuts as per your preference.
- *I have added items like M&M's during the holidays, pretzel pieces, used cashews (which was interesting!), toasted coconut, and even bits of vanilla wafers. The fudge without the nuts is excellent as well! You can even roll it into small balls and then roll it in chopped nuts for Fudge Truffles. You can add more mini-marshmallows AFTER you've mixed the fudge together for a Rocky Road Fudge.
- *This fudge is very soft before it sets as is MOST fudge. After you mix it that you can use a character cake pan and fill that with the fudge but if you do, spray the pan first with an anti-stick spray of some kind. (Bunny-shaped fudge for Easter, Santa-shaped or Xmas tree-shaped fudge)
- ___*You can always put the fudge in the fridge if you find that it hasn't set firmly enough to slice.
- *You can pour this into several small aluminum loaf pans for gift baskets or in round decorated tins for the holidays.
- **See's Candy is now $15.00 a pound!

- Serving suggestion: This fudge is best when served at room temperature.

289. Sees Fudge Candy The Quote Original Recipe Recipe

Serving: 25 | Prep: | Cook: 8mins | Ready in:

Ingredients

- 4 1/2   c   sugar
- 3   pk   chocolate chips (12 oz ea)
- 1/2   lb   margarine
- 1   t   vanilla
- 1   cn   evaporated milk
- 7   oz   marshmallow cream
- 2   c   nuts

Direction

- Mix 4 1/2 cups sugar with one (1) can evaporated milk. Boil 7 to 8 minutes, stirring often. (Rolling boil)
- Cream margarine and marshmallow cream together and add chocolate chips.
- Pour hot mixture over chocolate mixture.
- After chocolate has melted, add 2 cups of nuts and 1 tsp. of vanilla, blend well, pour into buttered pans and chill in refrigerator. Cut into squares before firm.
- This recipe makes about 5 lbs. of fudge. No one has attempted a calorie count, but it's estimated that each piece contains about 47 gazillion calories. Dieters, beware!

290. Semi Sweet And White Chocolate Peanut Butter Cups Recipe

Serving: 24 | Prep: | Cook: 30mins | Ready in:

Ingredients

- 3/4 cup of smooth peanut butter
- 1 - 6oz pkg Bakers white chocolate squares, chopped
- 3/4 cup of smooth peanut butter
- 1 - 6 oz pkg Bakers semi-sweet chocolate squares, chopped
- 3/4 cup of smooth peanut butter
- 1/4 cup crushed peanuts
- candy foil
- mini muffin or candy pan
- 1 small sandwich bag

Direction

- Line foil in mini muffin or candy pans
- Melt 3/4 c peanut butter and white chocolate squares over low heat.
- Fill foil 1/3 full and refrigerate.
- Put 3/4 cup of peanut butter in a small sandwich bag. Cut tip and pipe on top of each foil cup. Chill.
- Melt 3/4 c peanut butter and semi-sweet chocolates over low heat.
- Spoon on top of each candy cup.
- Top of crushed peanuts and chill again for 20 minutes.

291. Semolina Halva Recipe

Serving: 12 | Prep: | Cook: 15mins | Ready in:

Ingredients

- 3 tablespoon scoops of coconut oil
- 3 - 4 tablespoons of sesame seeds
- 1 Cup of semolina
- 2 Cups of Soya milk
- 1/2 Cup of coconut palm sugar
- nutmeg

Direction

- 1. Add Coconut Oil to pot on low heat till it melts

- 2. Add Sesame Seeds and roast till golden brown and sprinkle some nutmeg
- 3. Add Soya Milk and bring to boil (be careful, there's quite a reaction when you first add the milk)
- 4. Pour in Coconut Palm Sugar and stir till melted
- 5. Pour in Semolina slowly and keep stirring while doing this. Now you have to act fast. Keep stirring vigorously while on low heat. The mixture will harden fast.
- 6. Put into container and smooth over with back of spoon while spreading it out.
- 7. Allow to cool.
- Keep in fridge and cut into squares when serving. You don't have to use Sesame seeds if you prefer to use nuts. And you don't have to use nutmeg if you prefer other spices such as Cinnamon or if you prefer you can add chocolate. Adjust to taste.
- Enjoy!

292. Simple Hard Candy Recipe

Serving: 0 | Prep: | Cook: | Ready in:

Ingredients

- powdered sugar
- 3 3/4 c. water
- 1 1/2 c. Karo white corn syrup
- 1 c. water
- 1 tsp. flavoring oil (peppermint, lemon, butter rum or choice)

Direction

- Sprinkle 18 x 24 inch strip of heavy duty foil with powdered sugar.
- Mix first three ingredients in large heavy sauce pan.
- Stir over medium heat until sugar dissolves.
- Boil without stirring until temperature reaches 310 on candy thermometer or forms hard brittle threads in cold water.
- Remove from heat, and stir in flavoring oil and coloring.
- Pour onto foil.
- I let it cool just a minute, and then score it with a knife, thus making it break into uniform pieces when entirely cooled.
- Store in air tight container.
- ===
- Notes: From writer
- This is so simple, it is something that children can do. You can also pour the candy uncolored and put several drops of food coloring on poured candy when hot and swirl it through with a tooth pick.
- Note: Techdeb54 wrote:
- Techdeb54 15 hours, 17 minutes ago said:
- Hi, I'm new. My name is Debbie. I started making hard candy many years ago. When I first started I couldn't figure out why my hard candy would only have flavor on the outside and not on the inside. It turned out I wasn't letting it cool to 240 degrees before adding the candy oil. The only exception I found was peppermint oil. You can add that at any temp and it will not cook out.

293. Simple Strawberry Pte De Fruit Real Fruit Jelly Candy Recipe

Serving: 85 | Prep: | Cook: 15mins | Ready in:

Ingredients

- parchment paper
- 2 cups frozen strawberries, defrosted
- 1 3/4 tablespoons apple pectin powder (found at health food stores)
- 2 cups plus 2 tablespoons sugar, divided
- 3 1/2 tablespoons light corn syrup

- 2 teaspoons lemon juice

Direction

- Line a rimmed 9" x 12" baking sheet (with at least a 1/4-inch rim) with parchment paper. Puree strawberries in a blender until smooth. Mix pectin and 3 tablespoons sugar in a bowl. Transfer puree to a 2-quart saucepan and bring to a boil over medium-high heat. Sprinkle pectin-sugar mixture onto puree and stir until pectin dissolves. Continue to boil for 2 minutes. Add 1 3/4 cups sugar in 3 parts, stirring after each addition and waiting 15 seconds between additions. Add corn syrup; cook mixture until it thickens slightly, about 3 minutes. Remove from heat; stir in juice. Pour mixture into baking sheet, spread evenly and let set 2 hours. Cut jelly into 1-inch squares or other shapes using a sharp knife. Toss squares, a few at a time, in remaining 3 tablespoons sugar. Store at room temperature in an airtight container for up to 1 month.

294. Snicker Bar Candy Recipe

Serving: 24 | Prep: | Cook: 2mins | Ready in:

Ingredients

- 1 cup milk chocolate chips
- 1/4 cup butterscotch chips
- 1/2 cup creamy peanut butter, divided
- 1/4 cup butter
- 1 cup sugar
- 1/4 cup evaporated milk
- 1 1/2 cups marshmallow creme
- 1 teaspoon vanilla extract
- 1 1/2 cups chopped salted peanuts
- 1 (14 ounce) package caramels
- 1/4 cup heavy cream
- TOPPING:
- 1 cup milk chocolate chips
- 1/4 cup butterscotch chips
- 1/4 cup creamy peanut butter

Direction

- Combine 1 cup chocolate chips, 1/4 cu butterscotch chips and 1/4 cup peanut butter in a small saucepan. Cook over low heat until melted and smooth, stirring constantly. Spread onto the bottom of a greased 9 X 13 baking pan. Chill until set.
- Melt the butter in a saucepan over medium high heat. Add the sugar and evaporated milk. Bring to a boil. Boil for 5 minutes, stirring constantly. Remove from heat. Add the marshmallow crème, 1/4 cup peanut butter and vanilla and mix well. Stir in the peanuts and spread over the chocolate mixture. Chill until set.
- Combine the caramels and cream in a saucepan. Cook over low heat until the caramels melt and the mixture is smooth, stirring constantly. Spread over the peanut layer. Chill until set.
- Combine 1 cup chocolate chips, 1/4 cup butterscotch chips and 1/4 cup peanut butter in a saucepan. Cook over low heat until melted and smooth, stirring constantly. Pour over the caramel layer. Chill for at least 1 hour. Cut into 1 inch squares.
- Store, covered, in the refrigerator. Bet you can't eat just one!

295. Snickers Candy Recipe

Serving: 96 | Prep: | Cook: 20mins | Ready in:

Ingredients

- Icing:
- 1 cup milk chocolate chips
- 1/4 cup butterscotch chips
- 1/4 cup creamy peanut butter
- Combine in a small saucepan; stir over low heat until melted &
- smooth.
- Spread onto the bottom of a lightly greased 13 x 9-inch pan.

- Refrigerate until set.
- Filling
- 1/4 cup butter or margarine
- 1 cup granulated sugar
- 1/4 cup evaporated milk
- 1 1/2 cups marshmallow Crème
- 1/4 cup creamy peanut butter
- 1 teaspoon vanilla extract
- 1 1/2 cups chopped salted peanuts
- Melt butter in a heavy saucepan over medium-high heat;
- stir in the marshmallow Crème, peanut butter & vanilla extract. Add peanuts.
- Spread over first layer. Refrigerate until set.
- caramel Layer
- 1 (14 ounce) package caramels
- 1/4 cup whipping cream
- Combine caramels & cream in a saucepan;
- stir over low heat until melted & smooth. Spread over the filling. Refrigerate until set.
- icing
- 1 cup milk chocolate chips
- 1/4 cup butterscotch chips
- 1/4 cup creamy peanut butter
- Combine chips & peanut butter; stir over low heat until melted &
- smooth.
- Pour over the caramel layer.
- Refrigerate for at least 1 hour.
- Cut into 1-inch squares. Store in the refrigerator. Yields about 8 dozen.

Direction

- Icing ingredients:
- Combine in a small saucepan; stir over low heat until melted & smooth.
- Spread onto the bottom of a lightly greased 13 x 9-inch pan.
- Refrigerate until set.
- Filling ingredients:
- Melt butter in a heavy saucepan over medium-high heat; stir in the Marshmallow Crème, peanut butter & vanilla extract. Add peanuts.
- Spread over first layer. Refrigerate until set.
- Carmel Layer ingredients:

- Combine caramels & cream in a saucepan; stir over low heat until melted & smooth. Spread over the filling. Refrigerate until set.
- Icing ingredients:
- Combine chips & peanut butter; stir over low heat until melted & smooth.
- Pour over the caramel layer.
- Refrigerate for at least 1 hour.
- Cut into 1-inch squares. Store in the refrigerator. Yields about 8 dozen.

296. Sour Cream Orange Fudge Recipe

Serving: 16 | Prep: | Cook: 15mins | Ready in:

Ingredients

- 3 cups brown sugar
- 1 cup sour cream
- 1/4 cup orange juice
- pinch of salt
- 1/4 cup soft butter
- grated rind of one orange (or 1 tsp vanilla)
- 1 cup nuts (optional)

Direction

- Butter an 8x8" (2 L) pan.
- Over medium heat, in a fairly heavy pan, cook the brown sugar, sour cream and orange juice, stirring until the mixture reaches the boiling point.
- Continue boiling WITHOUT STIRRING until mix reaches 240 degrees on a candy thermometer (or until it forms a soft ball when dropped in cold water). This should take 8 to 10 minutes.
- Remove from heat and add salt, butter and orange rind. If you don't want a strong orange flavor use the vanilla instead.
- Beat until it thickens and loses its shine.
- Add the chopped nuts, if desired, and pour into the buttered pan.
- Cool and cut into squares.

297. Sour Cream Walnuts Recipe

Serving: 4 | Prep: | Cook: 5mins | Ready in:

Ingredients

- 2 cups granulated sugar
- 1/2 cup sour cream
- 1 tsp pure vanilla extract
- 4 cups of whole and halved walnuts
- Optional: 1/2 cup chocolate sprinkles

Direction

- In a large saucepan, bring sugar and sour cream to a boil. Boil for 1 minute.
- Remove pan from heat and stir in vanilla extract and walnut halves and pieces; stir until coating sets.
- Spread on cooking sheet to cool.
- * Before the nuts set, you can sprinkle them with chocolate sprinkles or holiday-colored sprinkles of your choice.

298. Southern Peanut Brittle Recipe

Serving: 8 | Prep: | Cook: 15mins | Ready in:

Ingredients

- 1 cup sugar
- 1 cup light (Karo) corn syrup
- 1/2 cup water
- 2 cups raw peanuts
- 2 tbs butter
- 1 1/2 tsp baking soda

Direction

- Boil sugar, corn syrup and water to hard boil. Stir in peanuts and continue to boil until peanuts pop., (about 295 degrees). Remove from heat.
- Stir in 1 1/2 tsp. baking soda and 2 tbsp. butter.
- Pour onto greased cookie sheet.
- Break apart when cool
- Note: Other nuts such as pecans or walnuts can be used for a different flavor.

299. Spiced Almond Brittle Recipe

Serving: 8 | Prep: | Cook: 20mins | Ready in:

Ingredients

- ½ cup sugar
- 2 tablespoons corn syrup
- 1 tablespoon brandy
- 1 teaspoon salt
- ¼ cup (½ stick) unsalted butter
- ⅛ teaspoon baking powder
- ¼ teaspoon smoked paprika (pimentón)
- ¼ teaspoon chipotle powder
- ½ cup toasted slivered almonds

Direction

- Line a baking sheet with a non-stick baking liner, such as a Silpat. In a heavy, medium saucepan combine the sugar, corn syrup, brandy, and salt, and stir together with a wooden spoon. Cover the pot and bring to a boil over medium high heat. Uncover the pot and brush down any stray sugar crystals with a wet pastry brush. Turn the heat to high, insert a thermometer, and cook until the mixture is golden brown and has reached 325°F, 10 to 15 minutes. Remove from the heat and wait until the caramel stops bubbling.
- Add the butter and baking powder and stir in until incorporated. Add the spices and almonds and combine well.

- Pour the mixture out onto the prepared baking sheet and spread to ⅛-inch thick. Allow to cool thoroughly, then break into pieces. The brittle should be stored in an airtight container with wax paper separating each layer of brittle. This can be stored for up to a week at room temperature in a cool, dry place.

300. Spiced Nuts Recipe

Serving: 16 | Prep: | Cook: 45mins | Ready in:

Ingredients

- 1 lb nuts (pecans or walnuts, halves or large pieces are best)
- 2 egg whites
- 1 tbsp water
- 1 cup sugar
- 1 tsp cinnamon
- 1 tsp salt

Direction

- Preheat oven to 300oF.
- Mix together egg whites and water and whisk until foamy.
- Stir in nuts.
- Add sugar, cinnamon, and salt.
- Stir well to coat and evenly mix.
- Pour onto a baking sheet (line it with foil or a silicone) and place in oven.
- Stir nuts thoroughly every 15 minutes for a total of 45 minutes.
- Remove from oven and cool.

301. Spiced Pumpkin Fudge Recipe

Serving: 16 | Prep: | Cook: 10mins | Ready in:

Ingredients

- 3 cups sugar
- 3/4 cup butter
- 2/3 cup evaporated milk
- 1/2 cup solid pack pumpkin
- 1 teaspoon pumpkin pie spice
- 12 ounces butterscotch flavored chips
- 7 ounces marshmallow creme
- 1 cup chopped almonds toasted
- 1 teaspoon vanilla

Direction

- Combine sugar, butter, milk, pumpkin and spice then bring to a boil stirring constantly.
- Continue boiling over medium heat stirring constantly for 10 minutes.
- Remove from heat and stir in chips.
- Add crème, nuts and vanilla mixing until well blended.
- Quickly pour into a greased rectangular pan spreading evenly.
- Cool at room temperature and cut into squares.
- Store in refrigerator.

302. Spiced Pumpkin Fudge Recipe

Serving: 48 | Prep: | Cook: 15mins | Ready in:

Ingredients

- 2cups granulated sugar
- 1 cup packed light borwn sugar
- 11/2 sticks of butter
- 2/3 cup evaporated milk
- 1/2 cup pumpkin
- 2 teaspoon pumpkin pie spice
- 2 cups white morsels (12 oz)
- 1 (7oz) marshmallow creme
- 1 cup chopped pecans
- 11/2 t. vanilla

Direction

- Line an oblong cake pan with foil.
- Combine sugar, brown sugar, evaporated milk, pumpkin, butter and spice in medium, heavy duty saucepan.
- Bring to a full rolling boil over medium heat, stirring constantly for 10 to 12 minutes or until candy thermometer reaches 234 degrees to 240 degrees, the soft ball stage.
- Quickly stir in morsels, crème, nuts and vanilla.
- Stir vigorously for 1 minute or until morsels are melted.
- Immediately pour into prepared pan.
- Stand on wire rack for two hours or until completely cool.
- Refrigerate tightly covered.
- To cut, lift from pan and remove foil.
- Makes 48 2" pieces.

303. Spicy Caramel Coated Apples Recipe

Serving: 8 | Prep: | Cook: 10mins | Ready in:

Ingredients

- 8 medium green apples, washed and dried well
- 16 oz caramel squares
- 1/4 cup whole milk
- 1/8 tsp cayenne pepper

Direction

- Line baking sheets with parchment paper.
- Place a craft stick or chopstick into the base of each apple and set aside.
- In a saucepan, melt together caramels and milk until smooth.
- Stir in cayenne pepper.
- One by one, swirl in apples, coating thoroughly. Place on prepared sheets.
- Allow to set 8-12 hours before enjoying.

304. Spicy Fudge Recipe

Serving: 16 | Prep: | Cook: 25mins | Ready in:

Ingredients

- 4 cups sugar
- 1/4 cup corn syrup
- 1/4 tsp salt
- 1 1/3 cup milk or cream
- 4 oz chocolate or 2/3 cup cocoa
- 1/2 tsp cayenne pepper
- 1/2 tsp cinnamon
- 5 Tbsp butter
- 2 tsp vanilla

Direction

- Butter 8x8 brownie pan and the sides of large saucepan.
- In saucepan to medium heat, combine sugar, corn syrup, salt, milk, chocolate, cayenne pepper and cinnamon.
- Stir frequently until melted, then occasionally to 235 degrees.
- Place butter on top of mix but do not stir.
- Cool for 1-2 hours until 110 degrees.
- Using wooden spoon, lift spoonfuls of mix into air and allow to drop back into pan until mixture is slightly thicker and no longer shiny (about 5 minutes).
- Quickly scrape into buttered brownie pan, spreading to even thickness.
- Allow to cool (about 20 minutes).
- Enjoy!

305. St Patricks Day Layered Mint Chocolate Fudge Recipe

Serving: 64 | Prep: | Cook: 5mins | Ready in:

Ingredients

- 2 cups (12 oz. pkg.) semi-sweet chocolate chips
- 1 (14 oz.) can Eagle Brand sweetened condensed milk, divided
- 2- tsps. vanilla extract
- 6 -oz. white confectioners' coating* or 1 cup (6 oz.) premium white chocolate chips
- 1 -tbsp. peppermint extract
- Green or red food coloring (optional

Direction

- Line 8- or 9-inch square pan with wax paper.
- Melt chocolate chips with 1 cup sweetened condensed milk in heavy saucepan over low heat; add vanilla.
- Spread half the mixture into prepared pan; chill 10 minutes or until firm.
- Hold remaining chocolate mixture at room temperature.
- Melt white confectioners' coating with remaining sweetened condensed milk in heavy saucepan over low heat (mixture will be thick).
- Add peppermint extract and food coloring, if desired.
- Spread on chilled chocolate layer; chill an additional 10 minutes or until firm.
- Spread reserved chocolate mixture on mint layer.
- Chill 2 hours or until firm.
- Remove from pan by lifting edges of wax paper; peel off paper.
- Cut into squares.
- Yield: About 1 3/4 pounds.

306. Stained Glass Fudge Recipe

Serving: 80 | Prep: | Cook: 10mins | Ready in:

Ingredients

- 1-1/2 teaspoons plus 1/2 cup butter, divided
- 2 cups sugar
- 3/4 cup sour cream
- 12 squares (1 ounce each) white baking chocolate, chopped
- 1 jar (7 ounces) marshmallow creme
- 3/4 cup chopped dried apricots
- 3/4 cup chopped walnuts

Direction

- Line a 9-in. square pan with foil and grease with 1-1/2 teaspoons butter; set aside. In a heavy saucepan, combine sugar, sour cream and remaining butter. Bring to a boil over medium heat, stirring constantly. Cook and stir until a candy thermometer reads 234° (soft-ball stage), about 5-1/2 minutes.
- Remove from the heat. Stir in chocolate until melted. Stir in marshmallow crème until blended. Fold in apricots and walnuts. Pour into prepared pan. Cover and refrigerate overnight. Using foil, lift fudge out of pan. Discard foil; cut fudge into 1-in. squares.
- Yield: about 2 pounds.

307. Steamed Cassava Sweets Khanoom Monsompalang Recipe

Serving: 10 | Prep: | Cook: 70mins | Ready in:

Ingredients

- 17.6 oz Cassava Root
- 1.4 Cups sugar
- 3.4 Fluid oz rose water
- 1.1 Cups desiccated coconut.

Direction

- 1. Peel the cassava leaving only the white flesh.
- 2. Grate the cassava flesh until finely shredded.
- 3. Mix the water with the sugar and cassava then blend it in a food processor.

4. Divide into portions for steaming, wrap each portion in aluminium foil to form parcels. You will cut these portions into smaller cubes later.
5. Steam the parcels for 25 minutes.
6. Leave to cool in the fridge.
7. Remove the foil, cut the cassava sweets into bite sized pieces.
8. Dust with the shredded coconut.

308. Strawberry Candies Recipe

Serving: 24 | Prep: | Cook: | Ready in:

Ingredients

- 1 (14 oz) can sweetened condensed milk
- 1 lb coconut, finely ground
- 2 (3 oz.) pkgs. strawberry jello
- 1 tlb. sugar
- 1 c. finely chopped almonds
- 1 tsp, vanilla

Direction

- Combine milk, coconut, 1 pkg. Jell-O, almonds, sugar and vanilla. Mix well.
- Shape into strawberries and roll each one in remaining Jell-O coating thoroughly.

309. Strawberry Sparkling Wine And Chilli White Chocolate Truffles Recipe

Serving: 4 | Prep: | Cook: 10mins | Ready in:

Ingredients

- Ingredients:
- 80 g butter
- 80 g powder sugar
- 325 g white chocolate
- 100 ml strawberry sparkling wine (or any other)
- dried chilli flakes
- powder sugar and cocoa for coating

Direction

- Whisk butter and powder sugar with a mixer until frothy while melting chocolate over steam.
- Stir in molten chocolate with the help of the mixer. Add wine and chilli flakes and mix until it gets thick enough to inject small portions on a baking sheet. Let it cool for some hours. After form balls and coat with powder sugar and cocoa.

310. Sugar Free Coconut Balls Recipe

Serving: 6 | Prep: | Cook: | Ready in:

Ingredients

- 1 pkg (8oz) light cream cheese, softened
- 2 tsp liquid sugar substitute
- 1/2 tsp coconut extract
- 1 cup unsweetened coconut flaked or shredded
- Grated unsweetened chocolate, cocoa powder, toasted almonds, or crushed sugar free candy.

Direction

- Beat cream cheese, sugar substitute & coconut extract in medium bowl with mixer till smooth.
- Stir in coconut.
- Refrigerate until slightly firm, above 20 mins.
- Place grated chocolate in shallow bowl
- For each candy, shape scant 1 TBSP of the mixture into 1" ball.
- Rolls balls in chocolate.
- Store in refrigerator.

311. Sugar Nuts Recipe

Serving: 6 | Prep: | Cook: 20mins | Ready in:

Ingredients

- 1 cup brown sugar packed
- 1/2 cup granulated sugar
- 1/2 cup dairy sour cream
- 1 tsp vanilla
- 2 cups walnut halves

Direction

- Combine both sugars and sour cream in a medium saucepan
- Cook over medium heat, stir until sugar is dissolved.
- Continue cooking without stirring to 238 degrees on candy thermometer or soft ball stage
- Remove from heat
- Add vanilla and nuts
- Stir until coated
- Turn onto waxed paper-Separate nuts with a fork
- Let dry and cool

312. Sugar Free Chocolate Fudge Recipe

Serving: 16 | Prep: | Cook: 480mins | Ready in:

Ingredients

- Ngredients:
- 2 packages (8-oz each) 1/3 less fat cream cheese
- 2 Squares (1-oz each) unsweetened chocolate, melted and cooled
- 24 packets sugar substitute (equivalent to ½ cup sugar or using stevia (a natural herb sugar substitute), you use less than regular sugar subs ... 2 tbsp is equal in flavor for 1/2 cup .
- stevia is relatively expensive to buy, but it lasts a long time!
- 1 tsp. vanilla extract
- ½ cup chopped pecans

Direction

- In a small mixing bowl, beat the cream cheese, chocolate, sweetener and vanilla until smooth. Stir in pecans. Pour into an 8-inch square baking pan lined with foil. Cover and refrigerate overnight. Cut into 16 squares. Serve chilled.
- Serving size 1 piece
- Nutrition Values: Calories per serving: 147, Sodium: 84mg, Fat: 14gm, Cholesterol: 31mg, Carbohydrate: 5gm, Protein: 3gm
- Diabetic Exchanges: 3 fat
- Note: This recipe is Diabetic Friendly, Gastric Bypass Friendly, and anyone can eat this.

313. Sugared Nuts Delight Recipe

Serving: 1 | Prep: | Cook: 45mins | Ready in:

Ingredients

- * 1 egg white
- * 1/2 teaspoon water
- * 1/2 cup sugar
- * 1/2 teaspoon salt
- * 3/4 teaspoon cinnamon
- * 1/2 pound raw nuts such as: pecans or walnuts

Direction

- Preheat oven to 300 degrees F. Beat (with fork) egg white and water in large bowl. Combine sugar, salt, cinnamon on resealable bag. Shake. Place nuts in egg mixture. Drain back into bowl with slotted spoon.

- Shake in bag. Spread out in foil-lined pan. Bake for 30 to 45 minutes.
- If doubling, do one half at a time, but bake all at once.

314. Super Easy Homemade Marshmallow Recipe

Serving: 6 | Prep: | Cook: 120mins | Ready in:

Ingredients

- 75g unflavored gelatin
- 400g Castor sugar
- 700ml hot water
- desiccated coconut / icing sugar for final touch up

Direction

- Soften the gelatine with 200ml of hot water. (Keep the bowl warm in the double boiler if necessary.)
- Melt the sugar in the rest of the hot water.
- Pour the sugar water into the gelatine and mix them with an electric mixer for about 5 minutes.
- The mixture will start to set once it cools, so quickly pour the mixture into the container.
- Let cool and chill for 2 hours.
- Cut into squares and dip them in desiccated coconut / icing sugar to prevent them from sticking each other.

315. Superfood Peanut Butter N' Cookies Fudge Recipe

Serving: 48 | Prep: | Cook: | Ready in:

Ingredients

- 1/4 cup maca powder (raw or roasted, see note)
- 1/4 cup peanut flour (I used Protein Plus) or ground almonds
- 2 oz vegan white chocolate, coarsely chopped
- 1/2 oz vegan butter (I used Earth Balance) or refined coconut oil
- 1 1/2 cups very well-cooked cannellini beans, drained and rinsed well
- 2 tbsp amber agave nectar
- 2 (1 gram) packets vanilla flavoured stevia
- 2 (1 gram) packets caramel flavoured stevia
- 1/4 cup natural, smooth peanut butter
- 10 small chocolate crisp cookies (I used my cookies-for-creme.html">Kamut cookies For Creme, you can use Teddy Grahams too)
- fine sea salt and/or raw sugar, to sprinkle

Direction

- Note:
- If using roasted / gelatinized maca, skip the first step.
- Recipe:
- In a large, dry frying pan over medium high heat, toast the maca powder and ground almonds if using (stirring constantly) until the mixture is a "toasty" brown colour and the bitter/sour smell of the maca becomes almost butterscotchy - about 8-10 minutes.
- Immediately pour into a bowl and cool completely. Stir in the peanut flour if using this instead of the almonds.
- Combine the chocolate and butter in a small bowl and melt gently in the microwave. Set aside.
- In a food processor, puree the beans with the agave nectar and stevia until very smooth.
- Add the chocolate mixture, maca and ground almonds and puree in.
- Add the peanut butter and process in until completely smooth.
- Pulse in the cookies until combined but still chunky.
- Line an 8x5" loaf pan with cling wrap and evenly press in the fudge. Sprinkle with sea salt.

- Chill 1 hour, uncovered, then press a layer of plastic onto of the surface and keep in the fridge.
- This tastes better if you chill it overnight and let it stand at room temperature for 30 minutes before enjoying.

316. Sweet Cocoa Flax Truffles Recipe

Serving: 25 | Prep: | Cook: 145mins | Ready in:

Ingredients

- 1/3 cup diced dates
- 1 cup water
- 1 tsp honey (or agave nectar)
- 1/2 tsp toasted sesame oil
- 1/4 tsp sea salt
- 1 cup ground flax seeds
- 1/2 cup cocoa powder
- toasted sesame seeds and flax seeds, for rolling

Direction

- Combine dates and water in a small saucepan and place over medium heat.
- Bring to a simmer and cook, stirring often, for 15-20 minutes, until very soft and falling apart.
- Drain, reserving the liquid, and place into a blender with honey, oil and salt. Puree until very smooth (you are looking for a paste consistency).
- Mix together ground flax and cocoa in a small dish and add to the blender. Blend until the mixture is smooth and all one "paste" - add 1-2 tbsp. of the saved date water if necessary, but you need to be able to form the mixture into balls.
- Place sesame and flax seeds in a shallow bowl or plate and roll small balls of the paste in them to coat.
- Place balls on a parchment or foil lined baking sheet and chill 1-2 hours before enjoying.
- Store, covered, in the fridge.

317. Terrific Toffee Recipe

Serving: 36 | Prep: | Cook: 15mins | Ready in:

Ingredients

- 1 -cup unblanched whole almonds, toasted and coarsely chopped ..
- 3/4- cup semisweet chocolate pieces ....
- 3/4- cup milk chocolate pieces ....
- 1/3 - cup white baking pieces ....
- 2 - tablespoons malted milk powder ....
- 1- cup butter ....
- 1 - cup sugar ....
- 3 - tablespoons water ....

Direction

- Line a 13x9x2-inch baking pan with foil, extending foil over edges of pan. In a bowl combine chopped almonds, semisweet and milk chocolate pieces, and white baking pieces.
- Sprinkle half (about 1-1/2 cups) of the nut/chocolate piece mixture over the bottom of prepared baking pan.
- Sprinkle malted milk powder over mixture in pan.
- In a 2-quart heavy saucepan combine butter, sugar, and water.
- Cook over medium heat to boiling, stirring to dissolve sugar.
- Clip a candy thermometer to the pan. Cook, stirring frequently, until thermometer registers 290 degree F (soft-crack stage), about 15 minutes.
- Mixture should boil at a steady rate over the entire surface. (Adjust heat as necessary so that mixture does not boil over.)
- Remove from heat; remove thermometer.
- Pour mixture quickly over nuts and chocolate pieces in pan. Immediately sprinkle remaining nut/chocolate piece mixture over toffee.
- Cool about 1 hour before breaking into pieces.

- If necessary, chill 15 minutes or until chocolate is firm.
- Makes about 2 pounds (36 servings).

318. Texas Style Microwave Pralines Recipe

Serving: 12 | Prep: | Cook: 13mins | Ready in:

Ingredients

- 1 cup whip cream
- 1 box dark brown sugar
- 2 Tablespoons margarine or butter
- 2 cups pecan pieces (not broken too small)
- chocolate chips (optional)

Direction

- Stir together whip cream and dark brown sugar in very large microwave safe mixing bowl. Zap in microwave on high for 13 minutes. Open microwave about half way through cooking time and give the mixture a stir or two to make sure it is mixed well. When time is up, take bowl out of microwave, add butter and stir until butter is melted. Add nuts, stir for a couple of minutes or so until mixture starts to thicken slightly. Quickly drop by spoonfuls on a sheet of foil. Allow pralines to cool and then put them in a covered container. If mixture is removed from bowl too quickly (too hot and shiny), the pralines will be too thin and may remain sticky. If the first one spreads out too much just put it back in the bowl and stir mixture for a minute or so more. If mixture gets to cool (dull in appearance) before it is spooned out on foil, it may become too firm to make individual pralines, but it can always be broken into chunks and eaten. Less attractive, but still good. Make a couple of batches and you will be able to tell when the mixture is right for spooning. Chocolate lovers can add 1/2 cup of chocolate chips to hot mixture along with the butter. The chips will melt completely producing "chocolate pralines".

319. The Best Christmas Fudge Recipe

Serving: 70 | Prep: | Cook: 10mins | Ready in:

Ingredients

- 1 cup milk
- 2 sticks unsalted butter
- 4 cups sugar
- 25 large marshmallows
- 12 ounces semi-sweet chocolate chips
- 2 ounces unsweetened chocolate
- 13 ounces big Hershey Bars
- 1 tablespoon pure vanilla extract
- 1 cup hand chopped pecans

Direction

- In heavy Dutch oven, heat milk, butter, and sugar until melted and dissolved.
- Stir in marshmallows.
- Bring to boil, remove from heat.
- Add all chocolates.
- Stir until well blended.
- Add pecans.
- Pour into greased 9 X 13 glass dish.
- Cool, then refrigerate.
- In the cook time, I listed 10 minutes, it may take longer to boil.

320. The Best Chunky Candy Ever Recipe

Serving: 6 | Prep: | Cook: 10mins | Ready in:

Ingredients

- 4 OZ. unsweetened chocolate

- 1/2 cup pure maple syrup
- 1/3 cup of raisins (optional)
- 1/4 cup of currants "   "
- 1/2 cup hazelnuts or almonds, chopped finely
- 1 tsp. vanilla or dark rum

Direction

- In microwave or double boiler, melt chocolate.
- Add raisins and currants, rum or vanilla and nuts.
- Combine well.
- Drop onto wax paper in rounded spoonfuls, using two spoons or a cookie scoop.
- REFRIGERATE for 30 minutes, then store in a Ziploc bag in a cool place.

321. The Snow Candy Recipe

Serving: 4 | Prep: | Cook: 7mins | Ready in:

Ingredients

- 1 cup real maple syrup
- 1/4 cup salted butter
- Fresh snow, vanilla ice cream, or shaved ice
- **Optional: dill pickles and saltines** *u*!

Direction

- Heat the syrup and butter in a medium saucepan over medium-high heat, stirring to avoid a boil over. (Heating syrup is strictly a parent's job if doing this with Kids.)
- The mixture is ready 6 to 7 minutes after it boils (220 to 234 degrees on a candy thermometer). It should stiffen when dripped onto a plate.
- Remove from heat and cool for 2 minutes before pouring over the snow, ice cream, or ice. It cools so quickly that kids can taste it right away.
- Finish by nibbling some pickles or saltines — a sugarhouse tradition "for getting taste buds back to normal," because sugar on snow is so sweet. Enjoy! :)

322. Toffee Almond Crunch Recipe

Serving: 100 | Prep: | Cook: 120mins | Ready in:

Ingredients

- 1 3/4 c. sugar
- 1/3 c. light corn syrup
- 1/4 c. water
- 1 c. butter (2 sticks), cut into pieces
- 2 c. blanched slivered almonds (8 oz.), lightly toasted and finely chopped (I've used whole un-blanched almonds with success)
- 2 squares (2 oz.) unsweetened chocolate, chopped
- 2 squares (2 oz.) semisweet chocolate, chopped (or 1/3 c. semisweet chocolate chips)
- 1 tsp. vegetable shortening

Direction

- ***Cook time includes chilling time.***
- Lightly grease 15 1/2" by 10 1/2" jelly-roll pan.
- In heavy 2-quart saucepan, combine sugar, corn syrup, and water; cook over medium heat, stirring occasionally, until sugar has dissolved and syrup is bubbling. Stir in butter.
- Set candy thermometer in place and continue cooking, stirring frequently, until temperature reaches 300 to 310 degrees F (hard-crack stage), about 20 minutes. (Once temperature reaches 220 degrees F, it will rise quickly, so watch carefully.) Remove from heat.
- Reserve 1/3 c. almonds. Stir remaining 1 2/3 c. almonds into hot syrup. Immediately pour hot mixture into prepared jelly-roll pan; working quickly, with two forks, spread mixture evenly. Cool candy completely in pan on wire rack.
- Meanwhile, in heavy 1-quart saucepan, melt unsweetened and semisweet chocolates and

shortening over low heat, stirring, until smooth. Remove from heat; cool slightly.
- Lift out candy, in one piece, and place on cutting board. With narrow metal spatula, spread warm chocolate evenly over candy; sprinkle with reserved 1/3 c. almonds, gently pressing them into chocolate. Let stand until chocolate has set, about 1 hour.
- Use sharp knife to help break hardened candy into pieces. Layer between waxed paper in airtight container. Store in refrigerator up to 1 month.

323. Toffee Apples Recipe

Serving: 68 | Prep: | Cook: 5mins | Ready in:

Ingredients

- 6 -8 small to medium red apples
- 6-8 wooden butcher's skewers or chop sticks
- 1 ½ cups Castor sugar
- 2 tsp white vinegar
- ½ cup water
- ½ tsp red food colouring

Direction

- Wash the apples and dry thoroughly. Push the wooden sticks or chopsticks into the centre of each apple at the stem end.
- Place sugar, vinegar and water into a deep heavy-based saucepan and stir over a low heat until the sugar is dissolved.
- Bring to the boil and boil vigorously without stirring until the toffee is just turning golden or 150°C on a sugar thermometer. This is also known as the hard crack stage. Remove from heat and place on a wetted cloth to stop further cooking. Colour with food colouring, swirling the toffee to mix the colour evenly. Do not stir.
- Carefully dip apples in the toffee, rotating to coat completely. Allow excess toffee to drip off. Take care – the toffee is very hot. Place the stem or handle upwards onto a baking paper-lined tray.
- When the toffee has set, wrap in cling film or cellophane and tie with fancy ribbon. Leave in a cool place, not the refrigerator. These are best made on the day they are to be eaten.

324. Traditional Buttermilk Pralines Recipe

Serving: 8 | Prep: | Cook: 20mins | Ready in:

Ingredients

- 2 cups sugar
- 1 cup buttermilk
- 2 tablespoons white corn syrup
- 1 teaspoon baking soda
- Pinch of salt
- Large lump of butter
- 1 teaspoon vanilla
- 1-1/2 cups pecans

Direction

- Combine sugar, buttermilk, corn syrup, baking soda and salt in a large sauce pan and boil until candy thermometer reading is 238 stirring frequently.
- Remove from heat then add butter, vanilla and pecans.
- Beat until right consistency to drop from spoon onto wax paper.
- It thickens quickly so work fast.

325. Turkish Delight Recipe

Serving: 24 | Prep: | Cook: 45mins | Ready in:

Ingredients

- 3/4 cup granulated sugar
- 1-2/3 cups water

- 1/8 teaspoon cream of tartar
- 2¼ cups confectioners' sugar, plus additional for coating
- 1/2 cup cornstarch
- 1/2 teaspoon almond extract
- 1/2 cup slivered almonds, toasted
- vegetable oil for greasing the pan

Direction

- Line a 9 x 5-inch loaf pan with wax paper, overhanging the edges by at least 2 inches.
- Lightly oil the paper and set the pan aside.
- Combine the granulated sugar, 2/3 cup water, and cream of tartar in a heavy small saucepan, set over medium heat.
- Stir until the sugar is completely dissolved and the mixture comes to a boil.
- Clip a candy thermometer to the inside of the pan and cook without stirring until the syrup reaches 260°F (hard ball).
- Turn off the heat and cover the pan to keep the syrup warm.
- Combine the remaining 1 cup water with 2 cups confectioners' sugar and the cornstarch in a heavy medium saucepan.
- Set the pan over medium heat.
- Stir until the sugar and cornstarch completely dissolve and the mixture comes to a boil.
- It will quickly become a thick paste.
- Immediately add the warm sugar syrup and stir until the mixture is creamy white and smooth.
- Return the mixture to a boil and cook for 5 minutes, stirring constantly.
- Remove from the heat.
- Add the almond extract and the almonds all at once, and mix until thoroughly combined.
- Spread the mixture into the prepared loaf pan.
- Let the candy rest at room temperature overnight or until it is firm, at least 6 to 8 hours.
- Remove the candy from the pan by lifting the wax paper.
- Sprinkle the top of the candy with the remaining 1/4 cup confectioners' sugar.
- Cut the candy into bite-sized pieces and roll each piece in additional confectioners' sugar to keep them from sticking together.
- Store the sugared pieces in an airtight container, in layers separated by wax paper, at room temperature for up to 2 weeks.
- Makes about 1 pound.
- VARIATIONS
- Apricot Turkish delight: Substitute 1/2 teaspoon vanilla extract for the almond extract and 1/2 cup finely chopped apricots for the almonds.
- Banana Almond Turkish Delight: Substitute 1 teaspoon natural or artificial banana flavoring for the almond extract.
- Lemon Turkish delight: Substitute 1/2 teaspoon lemon extract for the almond extract.
- Mint Turkish delight: Substitute 1 teaspoon mint extract or 1/4 teaspoon peppermint oil for the almond extract. Omit the nuts.
- Pistachio Orange Turkish delight: Substitute 2 teaspoons orange-flower water for the almond extract and 1/2 cup whole shelled pistachio nuts for the almonds.
- Red Hot Turkish delight: Omit the almond extract and almonds. Instead, add 1 teaspoon crushed red chili flakes and 1/2 cup pecan pieces.
- Rose Turkish delight: Substitute 2 teaspoons rose water for the almond extract.

326. Tutti Frutti Fudge Recipe

Serving: 4 | Prep: | Cook: 10mins | Ready in:

Ingredients

- 1/4 c unsweetened cocoa
- 14 oz sweetened condensed milk
- 1 c water
- 2 T ORANGE PEEL; finely grated
- 1 T light corn syrup
- 4 c GRANULATED sugar
- 1 c BROWN SUGAR; firmly packed

- 1 c DATES; chopped
- 1 c NUTS; chopped

Direction

- In a heavy 4-quart saucepan, combine cocoa, condensed milk, water, orange peel, corn syrup, granulated sugar and brown sugar. Place over medium heat and stir with a wooden spoon until mixture comes to a boil. Clip on candy thermometer. Cook to 236 F (115 C) or soft-ball stage. Remove from heat and allow mixture to cool to lukewarm. Meanwhile, butter a 9-inch square baking pan; set aside. Add dates and nuts to fudge. Using a wooden spoon, stir until mixture thickens and begins to set up. Scrape into prepared pan. Refrigerate 3 hours or until firm. Cut into 1-inch squares. Serve immediately, or store in an airtight container in the refrigerator.

327. Vegan Caramels Recipe

Serving: 50 | Prep: | Cook: 35mins | Ready in:

Ingredients

- 1 cup margarine*
- 2 cups sugar
- 2 cups soy milk
- 1 cup light corn syrup
- 1 t vanilla
- *Optional: Add 1 tsp salt if using unsalted margarine

Direction

- Grease and line with parchment an 8 inch x 8 inch baking pan.
- Place all ingredients (except vanilla) in a large saucepan (4qt minimum capacity.)
- Bring ingredients to a boil stirring often.
- Cook over medium heat while stirring until candy reaches 245 degrees F.
- Remove from heat and stir in vanilla. Pour into lined baking pan.
- Allow to cool completely. Snip into pieces using clean kitchen shears (or slice with a knife). Wrap individually with waxed or parchment paper. Makes ~100 pieces
- Variation: Cook to 230 degrees F and add vanilla. Pour into a glass jar. Warm jar in a pan of hot water before pouring over ice cream or cake.

328. Vinegar Candy Recipe

Serving: 40 | Prep: | Cook: 25mins | Ready in:

Ingredients

- 2 Cups sugar
- 1/2 Cup cider vinegar
- 2 Tablespoons unsalted butter

Direction

- Oil a marble slab or a baking sheet.
- In a heavy, 3-quart saucepan, combine the sugar, vinegar, and butter and stir well.
- Place over medium heat and bring to a boil, stirring constantly, until the sugar is dissolved.
- Cover and boil for 2 to 3 minutes.
- Uncover and insert a candy thermometer in the pan.
- Increase the heat to medium-high and cook, stirring occasionally, until the temperature reaches 260 F.
- If sugar crystals form on the pan sided, brush them down with a pastry brush dipped in warm water.
- Turn the mixture onto the prepared work surface, and let cool until it is lukewarm and can be handled comfortably, about 5 to 10 minutes.
- Butter your hands and pull the taffy with your fingertips until it is white, light, and porous, 10 to 15 minutes.
- Stretch it into a rope about 1" in diameter, and snip into 1" pieces with oiled scissors.

- Pack the pieces between sheets of waxed paper in an airtight container.
- Store at room temperature for up to 2 weeks
- Makes about 40 pieces

329. Vinegar Taffy Dated 1932 Recipe

Serving: 8 | Prep: | Cook: 20mins | Ready in:

Ingredients

- 2 cups sugar
- 1/2 cup vinegar
- pinch of salt
- 1/8 teaspoon cream of tartar
- 2 tablespoons butter

Direction

- Combine all ingredients and boil to the hard ball state.
- Pour into a well-buttered pan and cool.
- Pull taffy until it becomes white and porous.
- Cut into 1 inch pieces.

330. Vinegar Taffy Recipe

Serving: 30 | Prep: | Cook: 15mins | Ready in:

Ingredients

- 2 cups white sugar
- 1/2 cup vinegar
- 2 tablespoons butter
- 1/8 teaspoon cream of tartar
- 1 pinch salt

Direction

- In a large saucepan over medium heat combine all ingredients.
- Heat without stirring to 250 to 265 degrees F (121 to 129 degrees C) OR until a small amount dropped in cold water forms a rigid ball.
- Remove from heat and allow to cool enough to be handled.
- Pull taffy by stretching with hands, folding the candy over and repeating until taffy is white and porous.
- Cut into 1" pieces with kitchen shears.

331. Vitafiber Tootsie Rolls No Sugar Added Recipe

Serving: 0 | Prep: | Cook: 20mins | Ready in:

Ingredients

- 1/4 cup cocoa I used Ghirardelli
- 1/4 cup unflavored whey protein
- 2 tablespoons powdered whole milk
- 1/2 cup Natvia powdered
- teaspoon pinch salt about 1/8
- 60 grams VitaFiber syrup or other Oligosaccharide syrup
- 2 tablespoons butter melted
- 1/2 teaspoon vanilla extract

Direction

- Powder Natvia granular sweetener in blender or food processor.
- Mix cocoa, whey protein powder, powdered milk, Natvia, and salt in medium bowl.
- Set aside.
- Heat VitaFiber in microwave until bubbles form (about 30 seconds).
- Add melted butter and vanilla.
- Stir dry cocoa mix into wet VitaFiber mix until crumbly.
- Using hands, knead mixture until a dough is formed.
- Shape dough into a ball, then flatten out. Cut into strips and roll out each strip into a rope about the diameter of a Tootsie roll.
- Cut dough rope into Tootsie roll size pieces.

- Wrap each roll in small rectangular pieces of wax paper if desired.
- Store rolls in refrigerator so they will be firm.
- ~ ~ ~ ~ ~ ~ ~ ~ ~
- Recipe Notes:
- Can replace vanilla extract with other flavor extract such as orange or mint.
- May be able to replace Vitafiber with maltitol syrup, but Natvia (additional sweetener used) would need to be reduced.

332. Whipped Fudge Recipe

Serving: 16 | Prep: | Cook: 15mins | Ready in:

Ingredients

- 1 Can (12 oz) evaporated milk
- 4 cups sugar
- 1.5 sticks of butter
- 1.5 bags of chocolate chips(or flavor of your choice)
- 1 tsp vanilla or (flavored extract of you choice-coconut, almond etc.)
- 1 cup of chopped nuts (your choice-walnuts, pecans, pistachios etc.)

Direction

- Bring evaporated milk, sugar and butter to a hard rolling boil on medium heat. I use a non-stick Dutch oven and a long handled wooden spoon. Boil for five minutes -stirring constantly so mixture does not BURN!
- Also, take a stick of butter around the rim of your Dutch over before cooking your milk/sugar/butter...Stops it from boiling over, plus it makes sure that all of the sugar gets incorporated...No grainy bits left in your mix!
- Now for the fun part!
- Chips, nuts, flavoring in large plastic bowl! Pour the hot mixture of milk/sugar/butter over the chips, nuts and flavoring.
- USE ELECTRIC HAND MIXER: Beat everything in the plastic bowl together on HIGH SPEED for Five Minutes. This will make the most incredibly light airy delicious decadent fudge you have ever had.
- NO MARSHMALLOW STICKY STUFF TO CLEAN UP!
- Whipping the fudge with the electric mixer eliminates the marshmallow-it's great but really is just more sugar and air. The mixer takes care of adding the air to your fudge. It's better for you as you are not adding more sugar. I also have added a large Hershey's candy bar-(broken into bits) with the chocolate chips for added richness. You can add any kind of bar you would like (white chocolate etc.
- Pour mixture into 9x13 greased pan. Spray or buttered, or wax paper lined.
- Let cool for at least 30 minutes. You can then cut it and turn it out if you want. I let this fudge cool for at least another 4 hours to set up thoroughly.
- I have prepared this recipe using many different ingredients-it is fun to experiment and try new flavors together. Crushed candy canes, orange extract, almond extract and almonds, coconut, Maraschino cherries, cranberries, peanut butter and butterscotch, be brave, explore your options! My husband loves the peanut butter and milk chocolate chips together for this fudge.
- Happy Holidays and Enjoy...........DIANA!

333. White Choc Fudge Different Recipe

Serving: 21232 | Prep: | Cook: 30mins | Ready in:

Ingredients

- 1 1/2 cups sugar
- 3/4 cup sour cream
- 1/2 cup or 1 stick butter
- 2 Pkgs {6 Squares each} Bakers white choc. coarsely chopped

- 1 Jar{Jett puffed Marshmellow cream
- 3/4 cup walnuts
- 3/4 cup dried apricots chopped

Direction

- Bring sugar sour cream and butter to full rolling boil in large heavy sauce pan on medium heat stirring constantly
- Boil 7 minutes or till candy thermometer reaches 234 degrees stirring constantly.
- Remove from heat stir in choc till melted. Add remaining ingredients; stir until well blended.
- Pour into greased 8-or 9 inch square pan.
- Cool completely, cut into 64 squares to serve.
- Calories -180-{per serving}
- Sodium 35 Mg.
- Protein 1 gram
- Total fat 9 gr.
- Sat. fat 4.5 Mg.
- Cholesterol 15 mg.
- Sugars 21 Grams
- I used cashews in place of walnuts
- Courtesy of Breakstone's sour cream

334. White Chocolate Marshmallow Drops Recipe

Serving: 48 | Prep: | Cook: 3mins | Ready in:

Ingredients

- 12 oz white chocolate
- 1 Tbsp vegetable oil
- 24 oz marshmallow cream
- 2 Tbsp vanilla sugar

Direction

- Line a baking sheet with wax paper.
- Scoop out 1 Tbsp. portions of marshmallow cream onto wax paper.
- Put in the freezer for 20 minutes.
- After the marshmallow cream has been in the freezer for 15 minutes, begin melting the white chocolate in the microwave at 30 second intervals, stirring between each. (The defrost setting works the best. white chocolate seizes easily, so be careful.)
- After the chocolate is melted, stir in the vegetable oil until completely incorporated.
- Remove marshmallow cream from the freezer and spoon on enough chocolate to the top.
- Sprinkle with vanilla sugar and return to the freezer.
- When the chocolate has set, remove from the freezer and turn each drop.
- Coat the bottom of the drop with chocolate. (You may need to heat the chocolate a little to return to the proper consistency.)
- Sprinkle with vanilla sugar and return to the freezer.
- Remove from the freezer and pull the drops away from the wax paper.
- Store in an airtight container.
- Top you favorite hot chocolate with these drops or eat them as is.
- To make the vanilla sugar, place 1 split vanilla bean in 1 cup of granulated sugar. Leave in an airtight container for at least one week before use.

335. White Garbage Snack Recipe

Serving: 10 | Prep: | Cook: 3mins | Ready in:

Ingredients

- 1 cup Cheerios cereal
- 1 cup Crispex cereal or rice Chexx cereal
- 1 cup pretzel sticks
- 1/2 cup peanuts
- 1/2 cup cashews
- note: you can also just use 1 cup of peanuts or 1 cup of cashews
- 12 ounce bag of vanilla baking chips
- 1 tablespoon vegetable oil OR peanut oil (DO NOT use olive oil!)

Direction

- In a bowl, combine cereals, pretzels and nuts.
- Set aside.
- In a microwave bowl, melt the vanilla chips being careful not to "cook" them! OR Melt them in a double boiler on the stove.
- Stir oil into the melted vanilla chips
- Pour vanilla mixture over the dry mixture and stir to coat.
- Press onto a waxed paper covered cookie sheet.
- Allow to cool overnight, about 10 hours.
- Break up into pieces and store in a tight lid container.

336. White Popcorn Balls Recipe

Serving: 6 | Prep: | Cook: 10mins | Ready in:

Ingredients

- 1 cup granulated sugar
- 1/2 cup white corn syrup
- 1/2 cup water
- 2 tablespoons butter
- 1/2 tablespoon white vinegar
- 1/2 cup popped popcorn
- 1 cup pecans chopped and toasted

Direction

- Put sugar, corn syrup, water, butter and vinegar in a heavy saucepan.
- Cook to 260 on a candy thermometer.
- Pour over popped corn and toasted pecans then stir to coat.
- Butter hands and shape into balls.

337. White Trash Candy Recipe

Serving: 12 | Prep: | Cook: 20mins | Ready in:

Ingredients

- 2 cups Crispix cereal
- 4 cups small pretzels
- 2 cups dry roasted peanuts
- 1 lb. M&M's chocolate candies
- 1 1/4 lb. white chocolate (melted)

Direction

- Melt white chocolate carefully in microwave or on top of double boiler.
- Mix all ingredients in a large mixing bowl.
- Cover with white chocolate and mix well.
- Spread on cookie sheet and cool.
- After the mix is cool, place in a large serving bowl.

338. YOU GOTTA BE KIDDING ME FUDGE Recipe

Serving: 48 | Prep: | Cook: 3mins | Ready in:

Ingredients

- 1 can vanilla frosting
- 1-12 oz. bag chocolate chips

Direction

- Put frosting in a microwavable bowl and melt for 90 seconds.
- Take out and stir well until completely melted.
- Pour in Chocolate chips, spread about and put back in microwave for another 90 seconds.
- Take and stir until well blended and then pour into a lightly buttered 8 x 8 or 9 X 9 pan.
- Refrigerate until firm then cut into squares and enjoy.

339. Yogurt Pretzels Recipe

Serving: 48 | Prep: | Cook: 180mins | Ready in:

Ingredients

- 1 bag of your favorite miniature pretzels
- 2 cups strawberry or vanilla yogurt
- 5 cups confectioners sugar

Direction

- Preheat oven to 250°F.
- In a large mixing bowl, mix the confectioners' sugar into the yogurt one cup at a time with a hand blender.
- Using tongs or chopsticks, dip the pretzels, one at a time into the frosting and place them on the wire cooling rack.
- (Place a cookie sheet under the wire rack to catch the excess frosting that will drip from the pretzels.)
- Once all pretzels are coated, turn your oven off and place the wire rack and cookie sheet in, leaving the oven door slightly open.
- The excess heat will help the frosting dry without leaving the pretzels soggy.
- Allow frosting to harden for 3-4 hours, remove from oven, and store pretzels in an airtight container for up to 3 days.
- Per Serving: (7 pretzels)
- Calories 230; Calories from Fat 10; Total Fat 1g; Cholesterol 0mg; Total Carbohydrates 52g; Protein 3g

340. Braunschweiger Recipe Recipe

Serving: 20 | Prep: | Cook: 120mins | Ready in:

Ingredients

- 2 lbs lean pork
- 1 lb pork fat yum yum
- 1 1/4 lb pork liver
- 1 med onion diced
- 2 tbl salt
- 2 tea cloves
- 1 tea blkj pepper
- 1/2 tea allspice
- 1/2 tea nutmeg
- cut into cubes- freeze for 2 hours
- saute onions in a little pork fat-sprinkle with spices- add to pork- process--till you have a smooth puree.

Direction

- Pack puree into earthenware baking dish or 2 9x5 - loaf pans- cover tight with tin foil.
- Put in a dish with 2 inches of water, boiling.
- And bake at 300 degrees until meat is cooked not browned.
- Thermometer 160 - 165 degrees about 2 hours.
- Remove the dish from the water and let the dish cool.
- Refrigerate for 1--2 days before using.

341. Coconut Fudge Recipe

Serving: 12 | Prep: | Cook: 10mins | Ready in:

Ingredients

- 1 12 oz. bag white chocolate chips
- 1 6 oz bag flaked coconut
- 1/2 cup butter
- 2 cups sugar
- 2/3 cups evaporated milk
- 1 teaspoon coconut flavoring
- 1 7 oz jar marshmallow creme

Direction

- In large pot over med heat, cook and stir butter, sugar and milk.
- Bring to boil for 5 minutes or candy temp of 230 degrees.

- Remove from heat.
- Add marshmallow crème and white choc chips stirring till well blended and chips are melted.
- Add in coconut and flavoring.
- Mix and pour into sprayed medium baking dish.
- Cool then chill till firm.

342. Coffee Walnut Recipe

Serving: 1 | Prep: | Cook: | Ready in:

Ingredients

- 1 c. brown sugar
- 1/2 c. granulated sugar
- 1/2 c. sour cream
- 1 tbsp. instant coffee
- 1 tsp. vanilla
- 2 1/2 c. walnut halves

Direction

- In saucepan combine brown sugar, granulated sugar, sour cream and coffee. Cook and stir until mixture reaches soft ball stage. Remove from heat. Add vanilla and walnuts. Gently stir until all nuts are coated. Pour mixture onto buttered large shallow pan or platter. Separate with fork. Cool until set.

343. Easy Chocolate Fudge Recipe

Serving: 30 | Prep: | Cook: 10mins | Ready in:

Ingredients

- 1 lb 2 ozs dark chocolate
- 1/3 cup sweet butter
- 14 oz can sweetened condensed milk
- 1/2 tsp vaniila essence

Direction

- Lightly grease an 8 inch square cake pan.
- Break choc into pieces and place in a large saucepan with the butter.
- And condensed milk.
- Heat gently stirring until the chocolate and butter melts and the mixture is smooth.
- Do not allow to boil.
- Remove the pan from the heat. Beat in vanilla essence.
- Beat the mixture for a few minutes until thickened.
- Pour into prepared pan level the top.
- Chill in fridge until firm.
- Tip the fudge out onto a cutting board cut into squares & serve.

344. White Chocolate Truffles Recipe

Serving: 20 | Prep: | Cook: 10mins | Ready in:

Ingredients

- 2 TABS sweet butter
- 5 TABS heavy cream
- 8 ounces good quality Swiss white chocolate
- COATING:::
- 3 1/2 ounces white chocolate
- 1 ounce =28 grams

Direction

- Line a Swiss roll pan with parchment paper.
- Place the butter and cream in a small saucepan, and bring slowly to the boil, stirring constantly, boil for 1 minute, remove from the heat.
- Break the chocolate into pieces, add to cream, and stir until melted.
- Pour into prepared pan.
- Place in fridge to chill until firm +-2 HOURS.
- Break off teaspoon size of mixture and roll them into balls.

- Chill again for about 30 minutes.
- Melt the 2nd amount of white chocolate in a double boiler.
- Dip the balls in the melted chocolate.
- Place them on waxed paper, swirl the chocolate with a fork, for an effect.
- Allow to set.
- Drizzle a little melted dark chocolate over the truffles, allow to set.
- Place in tiny gold paper cases to serve to guests, if any left by the time you finish making these.

345.   ~ Rock Candy ~ Recipe

Serving: 0 | Prep: | Cook: | Ready in:

Ingredients

- You have your choice of cool clear water...Sitting here and cracking my knuckles :o)
- OK...Here Goes!
- 1 Cup
- Shamrock
- Summit Mountain...Summit Valley
- Puritan Purified Springs
- Patriots Choice
- Misty Mountain
- Mountain Forest...Mountain Valley
- Just Squeezed
- ice Mountain...ice jam
- Great Bear
- Get-N-Go
- Deer Park
- Deep Rock
- Eureka !
- Clear Mountain
- Cold Country
- American Fare...American Star
- 3 and 3/4 Cups sugar...C&H
- 1 and 1/4 Cups light corn syrup...Karo
- A Dash of red food coloring
- 2 teaspoons cinnamon oil...Save some for cinnamon oil Tooth Picks :o)
- Confectioners sugar...Canes

Direction

- Butter your parchment paper in the pan that your candy will stand.
- In a deep sauce pan bring the water of choice, sugar, corn syrup to a hard crack stage, 300 degrees south!
- Remove from the fire and add the red food coloring, and cinnamon oil.
- Cool it!
- Then whack it with a wooden spoon, it will crack into pieces, or use a tip of a sharp knife to break the candy in bit size pieces.
- Place the confectioner sugar in a zip lock, shake to coat.
- ~ Devil's Candy-Cane ~
- 1/2 oz. Rumple Minze Peppermint Liqueur
- 1/2 oz. Bacardi 151 Rum
- 1 Splash Grenadine Syrup
- Mix ingredients together in a shot glass, carefully ignite and allow to burn, then extinguish and shoot.
- ~ Hot Damn ~
- 1 Part Schnapps Cinnamon...Hot Damn
- 1 Part Sour Watermelon Pucker
- Add both in a shot glass and drink...for added effect...Float Bacardi 151 on top and light.
- Make dang sure you blow out the flame first!

Index

A
Almond 3,4,5,6,7,9,10,11,44,45,54,96,134,143,145

Apple 3,5,6,7,13,14,25,96,136,144

Apricot 4,60,145

B
Banana 145

Beans 5,78

Blood orange 30

Blueberry 3,16

Bran 21,24,37,44,62,115,137

Butter 3,4,5,6,7,8,9,12,15,18,19,20,22,26,31,32,38,39,40,42,45,50,53,57,63,66,68,69,79,82,87,92,93,94,100,101,105,106,109,110,115,117,130,133,136,140,144,146,150,153

C
Cake 3,4,38,66

Caramel 3,4,5,6,7,8,13,25,26,27,33,68,69,80,84,96,112,116,120,126,136,146

Cashew 3,4,5,20,27,28,37,60,91,102

Cassava 6,137

Champ 3,28

Cheese 3,4,16,35,49,50,62

Cherry 3,32,33

Chilli 6,53,138

Chipotle 3,30

Chips 32,62,148

Chocolate 3,4,5,6,7,8,9,22,29,30,31,32,33,34,35,36,37,38,39,40,41,42,43,51,52,53,54,55,56,57,60,61,67,72,76,77,78,87,95,109,110,126,130,136,138,139,142,149,150,152

Cider 3,13

Cinnamon 5,81,131,153

Coconut 4,6,7,41,44,45,46,61,130,131,138,151

Coffee 4,7,67,152

Corn syrup 73

Cranberry 4,5,49,58,88

Cream 3,4,5,6,35,40,45,48,49,50,61,62,105,116,130,133,134

Crumble 39,95

Curry 4,45

D
Date 4,5,7,66,104,147

E
Egg 3,4,6,24,35,38,64,110

F
Fat 89,139,151

Flour 123

Fruit 4,5,6,66,71,72,107,131

Fudge 3,4,5,6,7,11,12,14,15,16,17,20,22,23,26,30,33,35,37,38,39,43,46,49,57,59,60,62,63,64,66,67,68,69,72,73,74,79,85,88,89,92,93,94,100,101,102,105,106,110,114,115,119,121,122,123,124,129,130,133,135,136,137,139,140,142,145,148,151,152

H
Ham 4,62

Hazelnut 5,79,80

Honey 5,54,84

I
Icing 132,133

J

Jam 5,85

Jelly 6,106,108,131

Jus 5,41,76,86,97,153

L

Lemon 5,75,88,145

Lime 5,87

Liqueur 50,153

M

Macadamia 4,5,45,91,99

Macaroon 3,34

Margarine 110

Marshmallow 3,4,5,6,7,37,65,79,82,85,94,95,133,140,149

Marzipan 5,96

Milk 12,62,79,131

Mint 3,4,5,6,15,37,38,61,98,136,145

Molasses 5,100

N

Nougat 6,120

Nut 3,4,5,6,13,22,29,45,56,57,62,63,72,79,80,84,89,92,98,99,100,103,104,112,128,135,139

O

Oil 37,82,88,107,108,130,146

Orange 3,4,5,6,30,38,66,75,76,93,105,133,145

P

Peach 6,108

Peas 4,64

Pecan 5,6,81,112

Peel 19,66,72,116,137

Pepper 3,4,6,21,37,57,64,71,75,112,113,123,153

Pie 6,78,79,119

Pistachio 5,6,84,114,145

Popcorn 6,7,114,115,150

Potato 5,6,85,92,116

Praline 3,4,5,6,7,16,63,81,97,142,144

Pulse 140

Pumpkin 4,6,50,115,116,117,119,135

R

Raspberry 3,6,39,61,122

Rice 6,9,27,29,30,43,111,113,124

Rum 4,6,43,64,75,125,153

S

Salt 6,120,126,127

Seeds 6,128,131

Semolina 6,130,131

Sesame seeds 131

Soya milk 130

Strawberry 5,6,77,99,131,138

Sugar 3,5,6,7,17,71,73,79,85,89,118,131,138,139,147,149

Sweets 3,6,33,137

Syrup 22,44,153

T

Toffee 3,4,5,6,7,31,50,56,57,65,66,89,97,105,141,143,144

Truffle 3,4,5,6,7,12,15,28,30,31,38,39,40,41,50,52,61,67,68,75,77,80,87,96,122,129,138,141,152

Turkish delight 145

V

Vegan 7,146

Vinegar 7,146,147

Vodka 58

W

Walnut 3,4,6,7,33,70,134,152

Watermelon 153

Whisky 6,128

Wine 6,138

Z

Zest 77, 87

Conclusion

Thank you again for downloading this book!

I hope you enjoyed reading about my book!

If you enjoyed this book, please take the time to share your thoughts and post a review on Amazon. It'd be greatly appreciated!

Write me an honest review about the book – I truly value your opinion and thoughts and I will incorporate them into my next book, which is already underway.

Thank you!

If you have any questions, **feel free to contact at:** author@bisquerecipes.com

Susan Perrin

bisquerecipes.com

Made in United States
Orlando, FL
06 May 2022